MENU COMMAND SHORTCUT KEYS

File

New	Ctrl+N
Open	Ctrl+O
Open in Frame	Ctrl+Shift+O
Close	Ctrl+W
Close All	Ctrl+Shift+W
Save	Ctrl+S
Save As	Ctrl+Shift+S
Print Code	Ctrl+P
Check Links	Shift+F8
Validate Markup	Shift+F6

MW00966049

Copy	Ctrl+C, Ctrl+Ins
Select All	Ctrl+A
Select Parent Tag	Ctrl+[
Select Child	Ctrl+]
Find and Replace	Ctrl+F
Go to Line	Ctrl+G
Indent Code	Ctrl+Shift+>
Outdent Code	Ctrl+Shift+<
Balance Braces	Ctrl+'
Preferences	Ctrl+U

MENU COMMAND SHORTCUT KEYS

View

Zoom In	Ctrl+=
Zoom Out	Ctrl+-
Fit Selection	Ctrl+Alt+0
Fit All	Ctrl+Shift+0
Fit Width	Ctrl+Shift+Alt+0
Switch Views	Ctrl+`
Refresh Design View	F5
Server Debug	Ctrl+Shift+G
Live Data	Ctrl+Shift+R

Head Content	Ctrl+Shift+H
Show	Ctrl+Alt+R
Show Grid	Ctrl+Alt+G
Snap To Grid	Ctrl+Alt+Shift+G
Show Guides	Ctrl+;
Snap To Guides	Ctrl+Shift+;
Play	Ctrl+Alt+P
Stop	Ctrl+Alt+X
Show Panels	F4

MENU COMMAND SHORTCUT KEYS

Insert

Tag	Ctrl+E
Image	Ctrl+Alt+I
Table	Ctrl+Alt+T
Named Anchor	Ctrl+Alt+A

Text

Indent	Ctrl+Alt+]
Outdent	Ctrl+Alt+[
Check Spelling	Shift+F7

Modify

Page Properties	Ctrl+J
CSS Styles	Shift+F11
Quick Tag Editor	Ctrl+T
Make Link	Ctrl+L
Remove Link	Ctrl+Shift+L

Commands

Start Recording	Ctrl+Shift+X
Get	Ctrl+Shift+D
Check Out	Ctrl+Alt+Shift+D
Put	Ctrl+Shift+U
Check In	Ctrl+Alt+Shift+U

MENU COMMAND SHORTCUT KEYS

File

New	⌘+N
Open	⌘+O
Open in Frame	⌘+Shift+O
Close	⌘+W
Close All	⌘+Shift+W
Save	⌘+S
Save As	⌘+Shift+S
Print Code	⌘+P
Check Links	Shift+F8
Validate Markup	Shift+F6

Edit

Undo	⌘+Z
Redo	⌘+Y, ⌘+Shift+Z
Cut	⌘+X, Shift+Del
Copy	⌘+C
Select All	⌘+A
Select Parent Tag	⌘+[
Select Child	⌘+]
Find and Replace	⌘+F
Go to Line	⌘+G
Indent Code	⌘+Shift+>
Outdent Code	⌘+Shift+<
Balance Braces	⌘+'
Preferences	⌘+U

MENU COMMAND SHORTCUT KEYS

View

Zoom In	⌘+=	Head Content	⌘+Shift+H
Zoom Out	⌘+-	Show	⌘+Opt+R
Fit Selection	⌘+Opt+0	Show Grid	⌘+Opt+G
Fit All	⌘+Shift+0	Snap To Grid	⌘+Opt+Shift+G
Fit Width	⌘+Shift+Opt+0	Show Guides	⌘+;
Switch Views	⌘+`	Snap To Guides	⌘+Shift+;
Refresh Design View	F5	Play	⌘+Opt+P
Server Debug	⌘+Shift+G	Stop	⌘+Opt+X
Live Data	⌘+Shift+R	Show Panels	F4

MENU COMMAND SHORTCUT KEYS

Insert

Tag	⌘+E
Image	⌘+Opt+I
Table	⌘+Opt+T
Named Anchor	⌘+Opt+A

Text

Indent	⌘+Opt+]
Outdent	⌘+Opt+[
Check Spelling	Shift+F7

Modify

Page Properties	⌘+J
CSS Styles	Shift+F11
Quick Tag Editor	⌘+T
Make Link	⌘+L
Remove Link	⌘+Shift+L

Commands

Start Recording	⌘+Shift+X
Get	⌘+Shift+D
Check Out	⌘+Opt+Shift+D
Put	⌘+Shift+U
Check In	⌘+Opt+Shift+U

the Unofficial Guide® to
Macromedia®
Dreamweaver® 8

Lynn Kyle

WILEY

Wiley Publishing, Inc.

The Unofficial Guide® to Macromedia® Dreamweaver® 8

Published by
Wiley Publishing, Inc.
111 River Street
Hoboken, NJ 07030-5774

Copyright © 2006 by Wiley Publishing, Inc., Indianapolis, Indiana

Published simultaneously in Canada

For general information on our other products and services or to obtain technical support please contact our Customer Care Department within the U.S. at (800) 762-2974, outside the U.S. at (317) 572-3993 or fax (317) 572-4002.

For technical support please visit www.wiley.com/techsupport.

Wiley also publishes its books in a variety of electronic formats. Some content that appears in print may not be available in electronic books. For more information about Wiley products, please visit our web site at www.wiley.com.

Library of Congress Control Number: 2005938250

ISBN-13: 978-0-471-77497-6
ISBN-10: 0-471-77497-9

Manufactured in the United States of America

10 9 8 7 6 5 4 3 2 1

Page creation by Wiley Publishing, Inc. Composition Services

For Drew

Acknowledgements

My biggest thanks goes to Lynn Haller for finding me. A big thanks also to Wiley's Jody Lefevere, Tim Borek, and Cricket Krengel. Thanks also to Jamie Henderson and Lisa Eckstein for their encouragement. Finally, I am forever indebted to Alanna Spence and Zaldy Dingle for their invaluable support and contributions.

Credits

Acquisitions Editor
Jody Lefevere

Project Editor
Cricket Krengel

Technical Editor
Yolanda Burrell

Copy Editor
Lynn R. Northrup

Editorial Manager
Robyn Siesky

Business Manager
Amy Knies

Vice President & Group Executive Publisher
Richard Swadley

Vice President & Publisher
Barry Pruett

Project Coordinator
Maridee Ennis

Graphics & Production Specialists
Elizabeth Brooks
Mary J. Gillot
Lauren Goddard
Joyce Haughey
Denny Hager
Melanee Prendergast
Amanda Spagnuolo

Quality Control Technicians
John Greenough
Joe Niesen
Brian H. Walls

Proofreading
Evelyn Still

Indexing
Sherry Massey

Book Interior Design
Lissa Auciello-Brogan
Elizabeth Brooks

About the Author

Lynn Kyle has been a Web professional since 1992. She has worked for the Naval Research Laboratory as a computer scientist, Palm, Inc. as a Webmaster, and more recently at Yahoo! Inc. as an advertising engineer. She has authored books and training videos on Adobe Photoshop, Macromedia Flash, and Macromedia Dreamweaver.

Contents

Welcome to *The Unofficial Guide to Macromedia Dreamweaver 8.* In this book, I've combined all my insight from previous versions of Dreamweaver as well as my approach to the newest release, Dreamweaver 8. This book should suit the beginning Web designer, and at the same time offer advanced information to the Web programmer who may be new to Dreamweaver, but an old hand at working on the Web.

To make this the most effective book possible, I've used my past experience and the insight of fellow Dreamweaver users, both beginning and advanced, to answer any questions you might have about Dreamweaver as you become a skilled user.

The text of the book gives you hands-on experience as well as provides you with a reference for those smaller tasks you know you can do with Dreamweaver, but need a little direction to help you accomplish.

This is a comprehensive Dreamweaver reference. I've covered topics from creating a page without typing code to using templates and libraries to interfacing with databases and hooking up forms. Dreamweaver is suited for many different levels of Web developers, and this book reflects Dreamweaver's robust nature.

In the course of the book I've made every effort to present a completely unbiased view of Dreamweaver. Dreamweaver is a really powerful product, and when used properly it can help you build pages and sites in an unbelievably short amount of time. However, being such a powerful product, it is of extreme importance that you know what you are doing. Using Dreamweaver without understanding what Web pages are and at least the basics of how they work can lead to disastrous results. A little Dreamweaver knowledge is a dangerous thing. Read my guide and you'll know how to make the most out of this extremely versatile and powerful tool. You'll be creating spectacular sites in no time!

I welcome feedback, and can be reached at lynnkyle@gmail.com. I hope you enjoy this guide and have a fantastic time learning Dreamweaver for the first time, or discovering more about it even if you have used it for years!

Special Features

Every book in the Unofficial Guide series offers the following four special sidebars that are devised to help you get things done cheaply, efficiently, and smartly.

1. **Hack:** Tips and shortcuts that increase productivity.

2. **Watch Out!:** Cautions and warnings to help you avoid common pitfalls.

3. **Bright Idea:** Smart or innovative ways to do something; in many cases, this will be a way that you can save time or hassle.

4. **Inside Scoop:** Useful knowledge gleaned by the author that can help you become more efficient.

We also recognize your need to have quick information at your fingertips, and have provided the following comprehensive sections at the back of the book:

1. **Glossary:** Definitions of compluicated terminology and jargon.

2. **Resource Guide:** List of Web sites of Dreamweaver tutorials and user groups.

3. **Index**

PART I

Planning Your Web Site

GET THE SCOOP ON...
Your Web site objective ▪ Your audience ▪
Types of planning ▪ Content considerations

Designing Your User Interface

Y ou are creating a Web page or site for one reason: to communicate something to someone. You may be trying to sell beach balls, or creating a showplace for your limericks, or building a fan site for your favorite supermodel. You must think about the visitors to your site and what you are trying to say, and realize that the Web site content and navigation are the ways you will be bridging the gap. This seems obvious, but a lot of Web designers never spend any time planning. Visit some random sites on the Web for a few minutes, and you'll see what I mean.

As important as it is to pay attention to what other Web designers do, both good and bad, there are other useful bits of information you can take away from the sites you visit. Pay attention to the different types of Web sites. Is the site you are visiting selling some product? If so, does it sell it effectively to you? Are you the target audience for this product? Begin noticing what other sites do well, and then extend that new knowledge to your own site. Even just a few minutes of planning and research can help you end up with a much more effective Web site.

Figuring out your purpose

There are four categories of Web sites you may want to build. Macromedia Dreamweaver provides special site development features that are especially useful for each particular type of Web site.

The sales site

On the Web you'll find sites selling literally everything; from toasters that imprint images of the Olsen twins on bread to sparkling new Porsches. If your site is selling online, you will want to have links to your e-commerce pages easily accessible from your main page. You may also be selling your products indirectly, by describing them and providing links to your resellers.

Dreamweaver has some page design suggestions designed to help you get a quick start creating catalog pages (see Figure 1.1).

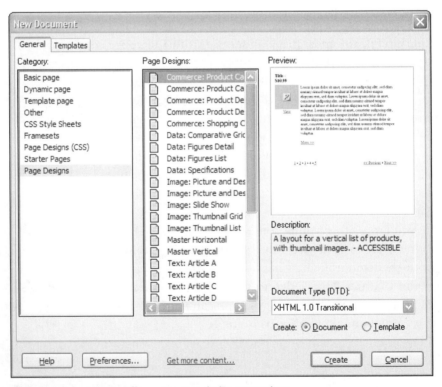

Figure 1.1. Dreamweaver offers many page design suggestions.

To access these page designs, start the Dreamweaver program and choose File ⇨ New. The dialog box shown in Figure 1.1 opens. From the Category options on the left, click Page Designs. The adjacent Page Designs list displays a number of Commerce page designs.

The company site

Most companies today have an Internet presence. Their Web sites are important for increasing business. They can also benefit the company by providing consumers information about the company's products, assistance, company history, and the location and hours of the office. A well-built, attractive Web site is like a nice storefront. A shoddy, unattractive site can be more detrimental to the company than not having a Web site at all.

Dreamweaver has included a few starter pages that can help you get some ideas for your own corporate Web presence. Figure 1.2 shows the New Document dialog box with a starter page selected.

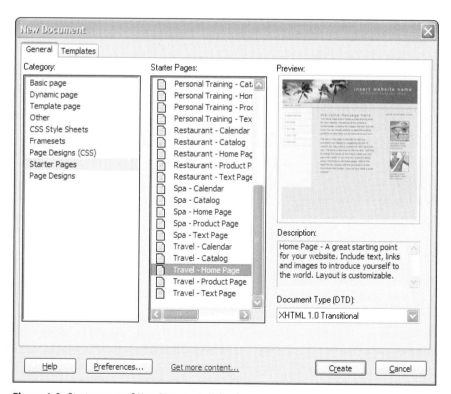

Figure 1.2. Starter page of New Document dialog box

Bright Idea

It isn't easy to tell what the starter pages actually look like without selecting one and clicking the Create button. Try creating a few and take a closer look at them. Keep in mind that fonts and colors can be easily changed to suit your taste.

To access these page designs, choose File ⇨ New. The dialog box shown in Figure 1.2 opens. From the Category options on the left, click Starter Pages. The adjacent Starter Pages list displays a number of page designs. Selecting one of these opens it in the Dreamweaver interface. These pages are easily customizable.

The dynamic information site

Dynamic information sites are listed as a separate category, but clearly sales or company sites can contain dynamic information. Any site with information that changes frequently (such as sale prices) fits in this category. Often the pages are filled with content stored in databases and are automatically generated with scripts. Dreamweaver provides templates for dynamic pages created in a number of different languages. These pages provide the basis for setting up a live database connection. Dreamweaver also provides tools to help you set up a live data connection and allows you to view the live data while you are designing the page.

To access the dynamic page designs, choose File ⇨ New. The dialog box shown in Figure 1.2 appears. From the Category options on the left, click Dynamic page. The adjacent Dynamic Pages list displays a number of different language templates. Selecting one of these opens it in the Dreamweaver interface.

While viewing the New Document dialog box, also take a look at the page designs for text pages. These are useful for article layout.

The fan or club site

The Internet is a fantastic place to meet people with common interests. Having a site devoted to your cause or passion can give you a great way to communicate your thoughts and allow others to express theirs. Some of the features a fan or club site can have to facilitate meeting and communication include a bulletin board, member directory, and live chat program. Users typically have a login on these sites if they wish to participate. Dreamweaver sample page designs include a login page and a comment form.

To access these page designs, choose File ⇨ New. The dialog box shown in Figure 1.2 opens. From the Category options on the left, click Page Designs. The adjacent Page Designs list displays a number of user interface (UI) page designs.

Understanding your visitors

From the visitor who accidentally finds your site to the customer who is looking specifically for your site, you have to decide to whom you are trying to appeal. While your site can't offer everything to everyone, knowing what your visitors will expect can help you target the most desirable ones. I have divided Web visitors into five groups:

- Random visitors
- Bored workers
- Window shoppers
- Buyers
- Information seekers

Random visitors

By random visitors, I mean those who stumble onto your site inadvertently. They may have clicked a link to your site by mistake, or incorrectly typed a URL. Chances are good that your site won't keep their attention and they will quickly leave. In your Web log you will be able to see that they visited one of your pages and then left, sometimes not even staying long enough for all of the images on your page to show up on their browser. I only mention this group to help you account for all the users you will see. When your site first goes online, these may be your most frequent visitors.

Bored workers

Every office and school has them. These are people who are taking a break from what they should be doing and trying to amuse themselves the only way they can as they sit in front of a computer in the office: Web browsing. This group is looking for entertainment. They look for jokes to e-mail friends and relatives, and Macromedia Flash animations to send around the office. Any site that provides interesting, frequently changing content is attractive to this group. Some sites that they might enjoy visiting include The Onion (theonion.com), American Greetings (americangreetings.com), and Disney (disney.com). Also extremely popular are any sites offering online Flash or Java games. There are also the temporarily popular sites. Sometimes the location of a funny Flash movie or odd Web site will be passed from one person to another until everyone in the huge company has seen Oolong the rabbit balance food on his head.

Is it worth your effort to try to capture the attention of this group? It may be, it depends on your purpose. Some sites encourage heavy traffic because their revenue comes from advertisements on the page. The more eyes that see the ads and the more clicks on the ads, the more money they make.

If you do capture the interest of bored workers, bear in mind that they are looking for variety. Your site will have to change frequently and maintain the same level of entertaining content that drew people to it in the first place.

Window shoppers

Window shoppers are looking for bargains. If you are selling something, you will be visited by window shoppers. They are thinking about purchasing, but need to be convinced. They will not give you much time to convince them before going to your competitor's site. Think about how your product looks on your Web site to the window shopper. Here are a few questions to ask yourself:

- Does the page look professional?
- Is the product presented in a clear, attractive, but quickly loading photograph?
- Are the features of the product presented accurately and concisely?
- Is the price competitive?
- Can viewers easily see how to purchase this product?
- Would you have confidence buying this product from this company?

Being able to answer "yes" to these questions will help you convert window shoppers into *buyers*.

Bright Idea

Spend some time visiting Web sites that you personally buy products from online. Notice how easy some of the best ones make product searching, researching product features, reviewing user ratings, and ultimately purchasing products.

Buyers

After researching a product, window shoppers eventually turn into buyers. Buyers coming to your site expect to be able to locate the product and purchase it as quickly and easily as possible. They don't want to be distracted by other unrelated products. Some of the best sites do try to interest buyers in other products, but they do it in an unobtrusive manner. Product listings on Amazon.com, for example, contain links to related products, but Amazon puts them after the product information. The link to purchase is always easy to find. Take a look at Figure 1.3.

I've circled the Add to Shopping Cart button, prominently located on the upper right of the page. I've also circled some other product recommendations. These are located below all the most important information on the current product.

Figure 1.3. Amazon.com product page

Inside Scoop

I find that presenting information in a number of different formats is the best approach. While it does take more time to present your matchbook collection both chronologically and geographically, for example, you will attract more visitors and your site will be more comprehensive.

Information seekers

Window shoppers are seeking information about a product, but information seekers are researching less specific things. Information seekers want to know who wrote the screenplay for *Soylent Green*, the current analysts' ratings of Google's stock, and information about Amish quilt patterns. They want to know everything. Information seekers use search engines constantly. No matter what your site is like, information seekers will visit it.

The key to attracting information seekers is providing lots of accurate information and keeping it current. For example, if you are running a site devoted to your favorite hobby, collecting matchbooks, think carefully about how your information is presented. Will it be less confusing to your visitors if your information is presented chronologically? Or geographically? Ask people who share your interest their opinions of the best approach.

If you know what groups you want to attract, you can build a Web site more likely to attract those groups. Here are some things to keep in mind while planning your site:

- Decide who you are trying to attract.
- Figure out what they are looking for and how they locate it on the Web.
- Ask your friends who are members of this group what attracts them to sites like the one you are planning to build.
- Survey existing sites and pay attention to what works and doesn't work. Incorporate the best ideas.
- Design for your audience, not for yourself. Keep your audience in mind at all times.

Creating a site structure

Now that you have considered both the purpose of your site and your audience, you need to plan your site structure. You may have a clear understanding of the type of site you are creating and who your audience is, in which case your planning may be quite simple. However, you may need to merge several types of Web sites if you seek to attract several different types of visitors. For example, you want to create a corporate identity site that offers customer support for products, provides investor information, and even sells products. Trying to satisfy the different visitors to your site can make your planning tricky. Breaking your planning up into stages can help.

Strategic planning

Knowing your audience and what your site needs to contain to appeal to that audience is the first part of strategic planning. Knowing what your competitors are offering your audience is the next. I can't stress strongly enough the importance of knowing what is already out there on the Web that is succeeding. And knowing what is failing will help you too.

Here's one more thing worth keeping in mind as you plan your strategy: If you know your audience and what you're trying to communicate to them, you will have done a good job. If you want people to visit, you have to offer them what they want. Simple, right?

Not really. Large companies spend millions of dollars a year trying to analyze what their audiences want. Throwing money at the problem and hiring firms to conduct studies certainly improves their accuracy, but sometimes it's the kooky creative idea that is wildly popular. I am not saying that you should make your site something completely new and different. I am saying that while you are sensibly addressing the obvious desires of your audience, leave a little room to play with new ideas. If they don't work, discard them and try something else.

Resource planning

Just as important as knowing your purpose and audience is knowing how much time and money you can afford to put toward the creation of your site. Unless you have free access to a Web server, your Web hosting will cost you money. Online transactions will cost you money. Large numbers of people viewing your content may also cost you money. You may also need to purchase graphics or content or hire additional help to build parts of your site. Also, think about the time involved with creating and maintaining each part of your site. It's easy to dream big, but try to be realistic. It's probably best to not include that message board if you can't spend time monitoring it, or that company news page if it will be updated only every two years.

Inside Scoop

If you don't have time to finish a Web page, think twice about putting that page on the Web. "Under Construction" gives your visitors the message that the site is dusty and defunct. If you must indicate that a page is not finished, at least include a date that it will be finished — and stick to it. Or better yet, finish the page before putting it up at all.

In planning your resources, break down the pieces of the site you are building and pencil in how long each will take and how much money each will cost. Be realistic. These numbers will change, but having them in front of you can help you prioritize the most and least important parts of your site. You will know which you should build first, and which you may want to reconsider including at all. Your Lance Armstrong Emulator program might sound wonderful, but if it takes two months to build it, you might want to put it off until version 2 of your site. Look at your Web site as an ever evolving project that can grow and change.

Site architecture

The simplest way to begin planning the architecture of your site is to sit down with a few sheets of paper and create a simple flowchart. Figure 1.4 shows a very simple diagram of a site.

The Spontaneous Combustion (SC) Prevention Web site serves as an historical reference about spontaneous combustion, an online store selling products to keep it at bay, and a community where interested visitors can talk about it on the message board. Each line simply means there is a link on the page that will take you from one page to another.

This is a good way to begin planning. Create a list of all the pages your site will have and map them out. This flowchart doesn't tell you everything, however. For example, it doesn't make clear that all the top-level navigation (History of Spontaneous Combustion, SC Prevention, Message Board, About This Site, Contact Us) have links to each other. Figure 1.4 represents only the links from the home page to the other pages. Each page should have its own flowchart, showing all the SC Prevention site links on the page as lines to those pages. You could also indicate with different colored lines or arrows things like dynamic pages, pages that access databases, or multimedia. You can find software, such as Microsoft Visio, that will help you design sophisticated flowcharts.

Bright Idea

If a page is important to your audience, don't require them to navigate to it by clicking links on three pages in a row to get to it. Make it one of the top-level pages, and make the link to it highly visible. Overall navigation of your site should be simple and hassle-free.

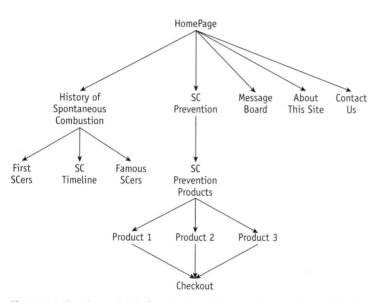

Figure 1.4. Creating a simple flowchart can help you plan your site architecture.

Technology planning

If you think you will want dynamic data, now is the time to research databases. If you will be selling your product on your site, you should be setting up a process to handle credit card transactions securely. If you think your site will be popular, don't automatically assume that your host can handle it.

There are many small but important technological aspects of your Web site that you should begin researching. Here are a few considerations:

- Which operating system would you prefer on your Web host?
- How much disk space will all your Web site files take up?

- Will your visitors need a shopping cart?

- What languages will you want? Dreamweaver offers support for a number of languages, including PHP, ASP, and Cold Fusion.

- Will you need any databases? What kind of database — MySQL? Microsoft SQL? Others?

Good content design

If I visit a Web site and I see misspelled words, I cringe. It's just too easy to check your spelling these days, and *not* doing it tells the viewer that the Web designers or programmers weren't careful. Using a lot of animated cartoons might seem cute to you, but think of the repeat visitors to your site. Do you think they want to see the same little dog running across the page again and again and again? What irritates me the most, though, is music used in Web sites. When you are in your car, stuck in traffic, and forced to listen to music coming from the car next to yours, you probably don't like it, do you? Maybe you like country, and the car next to yours is playing heavy metal. The same goes for music on Web sites. The bottom line? Don't assume everyone shares your taste. The following are a few simple rules for creating a professional site that won't drive away your audience.

Less is more

The best Web sites are often the simplest-looking ones. Look at Google (`www.google.com`), for example. Figure 1.5 shows the Google home page.

Google's main audience consists of people searching the Web. The Google search takes center stage. The other services Google offers are simple links above the search box. There are no confusing buttons with nondescript icons. It isn't particularly beautiful, but it is a simple and extremely effective site.

Watch Out!

If you are planning to include advertising on your Web site, now is the time to make some important decisions. A little advertising goes a long way. Too much will drive away visitors. Especially fight the urge to include obnoxious, intrusive pop-up type ads as well as floating, DHTML ads that obscure your content.

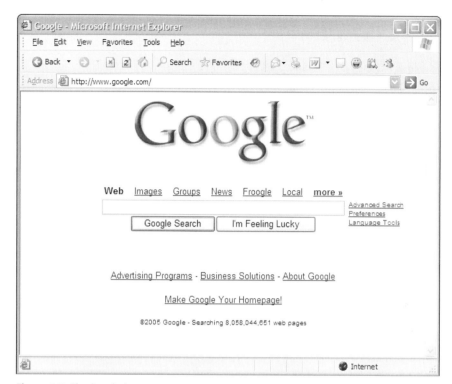

Figure 1.5. The Google home page

Simplify navigation

Always make the most important Web pages in your site accessible by the fewest clicks from your users. Take a look at the Yahoo! (www.yahoo.com) home page in Figure 1.6.

Every single page of Yahoo! contains a link back to the home page. The most popular Yahoo! sites are given large icons on either side of the logo: Finance, Music, Travel, Mail, My Yahoo!, and Messenger. Unlike the Google page shown in Figure 1.5, this page is a bit busier. The main mantle section contains 27 links to Yahoo! services and properties. This is an enormous number of sub-sites, and yet in this instance, it makes sense. The most important sites are shown next the logo, but if you frequently visit Yahoo! Maps, for example, the link is easily accessible.

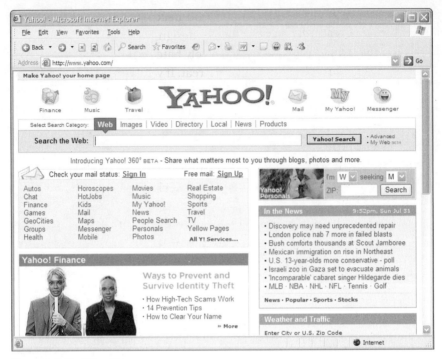

Figure 1.6. The Yahoo! home page

Keep in mind that Yahoo! is a huge site, and this is an extreme example. In spite of its size, Yahoo! keeps its navigation relatively simple. If you visit one of the sub-sites, the navigation becomes more to the point. Yahoo! Shopping is a good example. Once you click the shopping link, you no longer have those 27 links within view. Now all the links on the page are focused on shopping. Still, any time you wish to go to another Yahoo! site, you are just two clicks away. Click the upper left-hand text link that says "Yahoo!", and then from the home page click whichever of the 27 links you want.

Use images and Flash carefully

Not everyone has a fast Internet connection. You have to carefully balance the effectiveness of your images against the time it takes to download them. How long is your audience willing to wait? Secondly, while images are great for illustrating points and polishing a page, too many images distract from the text. One well-placed topical image is more powerful than five.

Flash has a few additional features you need to be cautious about. It allows you to break any rules of good design you wish. You may also embed sound, which most users absolutely hate. You have such power in Flash, and the temptation to abuse it is great. If you are going to use Flash, try to use it sparingly. Ask yourself if an image instead of a Flash movie would accomplish the same thing.

Check your spelling

Always check your spelling before you publish your page! It's very easy to do in Dreamweaver. Figure 1.7 shows the Check Spelling dialog box.

To check the spelling in your Web page, choose Text ⇨ Check Spelling. When Dreamweaver finds a word it thinks is misspelled, it opens the Check Spelling dialog box and gives you the opportunity to change the word.

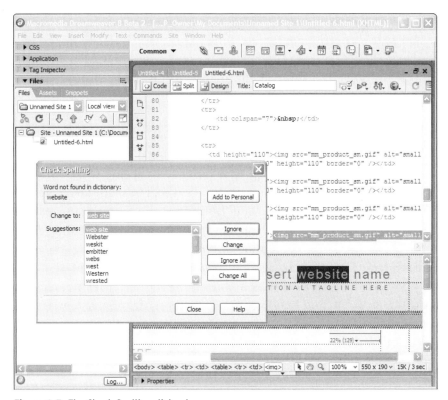

Figure 1.7. The Check Spelling dialog box

Watch Out!

The Spelling Checker won't catch misplaced apostrophes or homonyms. The most common apostrophe mistake by far is confusing *its* and *it's*. Watch out for homonym mistakes, such as using *there* instead of *their*. It's worth taking a few minutes and looking for these. You should also recruit another pair of eyes to look over your text.

Say what you mean

When you begin to write copy for your Web site, keep your writing simple. The best copy expresses ideas using common words. Not everyone will know that highly technical term for elbow that you do, so use the word *elbow.*

Avoid over explaining. By that, I mean don't explain the same thing again and again. What I'm saying is once you've explained something, you shouldn't explain it again in different words. You don't need to explain the same thing more than once if you've done it right the first time. Get it?

Unless it is appropriate for the audience of your Web site, watch out for slang, clichés, and extraneous expressions. You know what I mean? And please don't use IM-style shorthand writing and no punctuation (u know who u r lol).

Borrow (but don't steal!)

The best place for you to learn about good and bad site design is on the Web. You can get great ideas for your own site by seeing what works or doesn't work on other sites. You can also see if that brilliant idea you had exists out there and if it is successful. Don't be afraid to follow the lead of good sites. Take notes on what you like about them. Consider using similar features in your own site. But be careful. I am not suggesting you go to a Web site and steal their navigation system. Instead, figure out what you like about it. Think about it as a concept, see what other people are doing that is like it, and build your own, better navigation system, suited to your site. However tempted you may be, never copy the source code of a page and put parts of it on your own. You may be violating their copyright, and it's more fun to write your own.

Just the facts

■ Understanding the different types of Web sites can help you decide on the best type for you.

■ Different Web visitors want different things. Know what your audience wants.

■ Plan ahead. Consider your objective, audience, resources, and available technology.

■ Plan your content carefully. Inform your audience and avoid common mistakes that will leave them with a negative impression of your site.

GET THE SCOOP ON...
Image maps and rollovers ▪ Types of image files ▪
Flash use and abuse ▪ Editing images easily

Using Images and Media

Macromedia Dreamweaver is a great tool for placing images on your pages. In fact, it may be too good — it's easy to put an image anywhere, even where it doesn't belong. Image abuse on the Web is common. Images should be used to communicate your message and give your visitors a pleasant experience. They should not be used without purpose.

Not only does Dreamweaver let you place your images on your pages with ease, it also allows you to create image maps easily on those images. It is also integrated with Fireworks, Macromedia's graphics editing software. If you have both Dreamweaver and Fireworks, you can simply select your image and click a link in Dreamweaver to open Fireworks for editing. Dreamweaver also lets you designate other image editing software, such as Photoshop, to open for editing a selected image. Because of the simplicity of editing graphics in Dreamweaver's design view, it's a great program to use for page layout.

Understanding the purpose of images

Ever been to a Web site where you can't read the text because of the background? I have seen Web page text that is impossible to read because of the colors in the background image camouflaging the text.

Every image on your site should be there for a reason. In this section I list six common uses for images found on Web pages and describe each.

21

Decorative image

The majority of images on Web sites are there to decorate the page. When done well, decorative images can really help the design of a Web page. When done poorly, they can drive people away. Here are a few questions to ask yourself about your decorative images:

- Do the images make sense given the subject of the page?
- Do the images distract the viewer from the text on the page?
- Are there too many images? Do they detract from each other? Can you remove any and not miss them?
- Are there too few? Does the page seem too text-heavy?
- Do the colors and style enhance or detract from the page? You probably wouldn't wear a tuxedo with flip-flops (although I've seen it done).
- Does the placement of the images make sense? For example, does the viewer have to scroll down two screens' worth to see your image?

Dreamweaver has a few CSS page designs that show nice image placement. These page designs can be accessed through the New Document dialog box. Look at Figure 2.1.

To open this dialog box, choose File ⇨ New. Click Page Designs (CSS) from the Category list on the left. These page designs have gray image placeholders in them. Notice how the images and text balance each other. Neither dominates the page.

Product or illustrative image

If you are selling something, you will probably include images of your product. This is an important use for images on the Web. The product images you use should be attractive to the consumer. Ever seen a restaurant window with photos of the food taped to it? Sun-faded, grimy photos might be enough to make you walk away, while bright, fresh menu photos might entice you to enter. Appearance matters.

Illustrative images should be sharp and readable. They should also make sense. You may have seen diagrams on the Web that were so fuzzy they were useless. They were actually worse than useless, because they leave visitors with a poor impression of the site.

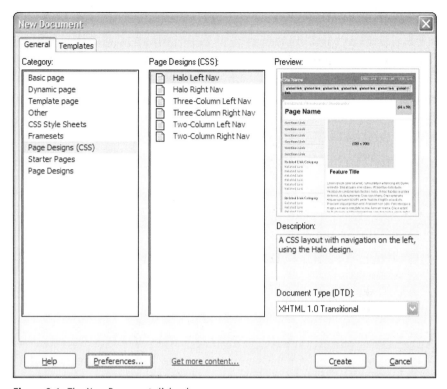

Figure 2.1. The New Document dialog box

Background image

Once extremely common, background images on Web pages are not very popular anymore. This is a good thing. It is too easy to abuse them. You don't often see them done well.

The main reason they are a bad idea is because they make the text difficult to read and the image difficult to see. If the image is important enough to be on your page, it should be presented clearly. Only a few background textures don't interfere with the text, but generally they should be avoided as well. I use background images only in table cells, and then sparingly. If you are trying to give your page more color, instead of a background image try a background color with a text color over it that contrasts well. A light gray page with medium gray text might look cool, but your visitors won't be willing to spend much time straining their eyes to read your text.

The icon

By icons, I mean small images used as links instead of words. Icons are tricky. Good icons can be wonderful. Bad ones will confuse your users. If you are determined to use icons on your pages, make sure that you test them first on people. Make sure Aunt Sally can tell that your icon is of a pencil and not of a Twinkie. Here are some tips on good icon design:

- Your audience may interpret your icon differently than you depending on their culture or background. What you recognize as a fist with a thumb sticking out may be interpreted as a rude gesture by someone else. Stick with icons your audience will recognize.

- Try to make your icons of concrete objects. The more concrete the object, the more recognizable the icon will be.

- Combine your icons with text if you can. That will clear up quite a bit of ambiguity.

- Simplify the image as much as possible. If you are depicting a mailbox, don't include the sky and lawn behind it. Use simple, cartoonish lines.

- Universal icons work better than specific ones. If you create an icon of a dog, don't make it a spotted Dalmatian. Create a silhouette of a dog shape.

- Keep in mind that your audience will be more successful at recognizing your icons if they are similar to icons they have seen in the past.

The image map

Any image with clickable links is an image map, which means that image maps are primarily used for navigation. The same rules I mentioned for icons apply here, although you can use text in your image to create your link and make the meaning clear. Here are a few considerations when working with image maps:

- If you are creating an image to be used as an image map that contains only text, you are better off simply creating regular text HTML links instead. Not only does downloading an image take longer, but search engines will not detect the graphical text.

- When creating your image map, make sure you make the clickable area large enough. Don't expect your users to have to point with extreme precision to click the link.

■ Consider breaking your image up into pieces and putting it into the cells of a table. This will help you decrease the overall download time if you optimize the pieces of the image that contain fewer colors.

Dreamweaver provides you with links to tools under the Image button to draw and link hotspots to create image maps on images in your Web page. Figure 2.2 shows these tools.

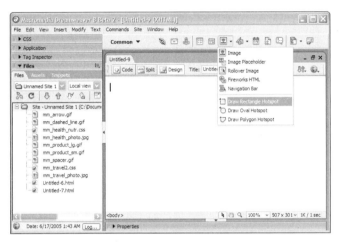

Figure 2.2. Image map hotspot tools

To access these tools, follow these steps:

1. Locate the Code, Split, and Design buttons. Just above those should be the name of the file you currently have open.

2. Above the tab with the current filename (Untitled-9 is the name shown in Figure 2.2) you will see the Common toolbar. You may have a different toolbar currently displayed. To change this, click the small black arrow and select Common.

3. The image map tools are located under the Image button on the Common toolbar. Look at Figure 2.2 to help you locate them.

Image map creation is covered in more detail in Chapter 12.

Inside Scoop

Image maps are definitely waning in popularity on the Web. They used to be everywhere, but once JavaScript and Flash became more widely used in the latest browsers, they were left behind.

The rollover image

Rollover images are images that change when your mouse cursor moves across them. When your cursor rolls over the image, a JavaScript program in your page or somewhere on your site is called and the image is replaced with a different one. This may sound complicated but Dreamweaver makes it very simple. You don't have to know JavaScript at all; you simply need two images of the same size with some difference between them. Rollovers are often used to change the color of the text in an image. Look at Figure 2.3.

This is the Insert Rollover Image dialog box. You simply give your image a name so the JavaScript in the page can distinguish it from other images. Then you locate your original image, which is the image that displays when the cursor is not over it. You select the rollover image, the image that will appear when the cursor moves over it. Finally, you can assign the rollover a URL.

Figure 2.3. The Insert Rollover Image dialog box

Types of images on your site

Different Web browsers support different image file types, but two are consistently supported: JPEG and GIF. PNG images are well supported by newer browsers and offer distinct benefits. Knowing the difference between these file types can help you create a more attractive site and decrease the download time for your visitors.

JPG or JPEG

The JPG file type is typically associated with photographs. Any image with many colors should be a JPEG, since JPEG images can display up to 16 million colors and GIF images only support 256. Figure 2.4 shows a photographic image saved as a GIF on the right and a JPEG on the left.

When saving an image as a JPEG, most image editing programs let you choose how much compression to apply. Applying more compression makes the final file size smaller, but the image quality diminishes. Finding the right amount of compression to balance image quality and file size is a skill.

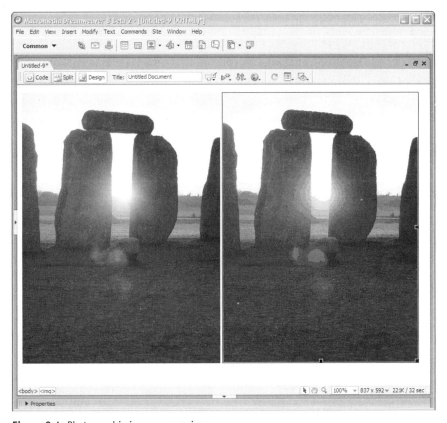

Figure 2.4. Photographic image comparison

 Hack

Graphics programs generally allow you to preview your JPG images at different compressions, so you can choose the best compromise between the file size and the quality of the image.

The JPEG file type should not be used for graphics with only a few colors and with many straight edges. An example of this is an image containing text on a solid or simple background. Saving this type of image as a JPEG will leave you with an image that appears fuzzy or ragged. The image will also have a larger file size than it would as a GIF.

GIF

GIF files are best for images with few colors and straight edges. Use this for "presentation graphics" type images: charts, graphs, or text set as graphics. The fewer colors you use, the smaller the GIF file will be. Figure 2.5 shows a vector image output as a GIF and a JPEG. It is plain to see that the GIF is on the left, because it has few colors and straight lines and looks crisp. The image on the left is an overly compressed JPEG image. Notice the artifacts surrounding it. This is an extreme example, but even a small level of compression in a JPEG image causes fuzziness and artifacts to appear.

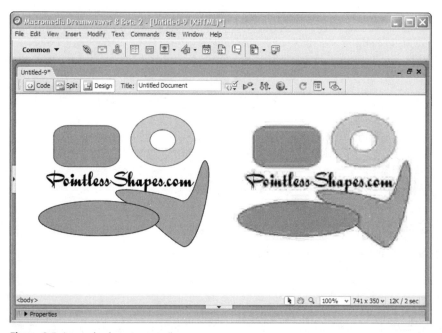

Figure 2.5. Low color image comparison

Inside Scoop

Dreamweaver has a Timeline tool that can be used to move images or objects over the page. Unlike an animated GIF with multiple frames built into the file, Dreamweaver uses DHTML and layers.

GIF files can contain up to 256 colors. You can make one of the colors in the image transparent so that your Web page's background color or image shows through the transparent part of your GIF image. You can use this transparency to make the visible part of your image seem to float on the page, rather than being constrained by a rectangular shape.

Another advantage of GIF files is that they can be animated. Animated GIFs consist of a series of individual images. Before Flash became so widely accepted, animated GIFs were all over the Web. Now you see fewer, and the once-popular cartoonish animated GIFs are relegated to amateur Web sites, such as the ubiquitous animated dog that endlessly runs across the bottom of your Uncle Fred's home page.

PNG

The newest Web graphics file format is PNG. If you're confident that your site will be viewed primarily with more recent browsers, consider using this format. You can find out which browsers support PNG by visiting the PNG-supporting Browsers page (www.libpng.org/pub/png/pngapbr.html).

PNG images combine the best features of GIF and JPEG. Like a GIF, you can assign a transparent color. Like a JPEG, your image can contain more than 256 colors. The compact and versatile PNG format is becoming more widely used as all newer browsers support it.

Good and bad uses of images

How you decide to use images on your site can make it great or destroy it. Here are a few rules to help you make decisions about your image use.

Using graphics for navigation or text

If you can avoid creating text links as graphics and still get the look you want, you should. Using graphics for text increases bandwidth, and you may have to sacrifice some image quality. If you intend to place the graphical text in an image with a photo, you will have to decide if you want to maintain the colors of the photograph or the sharp edges of the text.

Changing image height and width

When you insert an image into your Web page using Dreamweaver, the height and width of that image are calculated and automatically inserted into the code:

```
<img src="shapes.gif" width="358" height="146">
```

However, you can change the height and width either by changing these values or by resizing the image in the Design interface, as shown in Figure 2.6.

You can see from the figure that the image on the right has been resized. I recommend that you don't do this. Your results will be better if you use a graphics program to resize it.

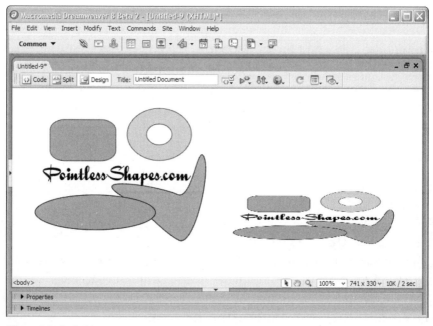

Figure 2.6. Scaled image

Bright Idea

One site that I visit is Web Pages That Suck (www.webpagesthatsuck. com). At times the judgments are a bit harsh, but it can help open your eyes to what constitutes poor Web design.

Make your image fit on the screen

Not everyone is using a monitor resolution of at least 1280x1024. It is best to design your images to work with an 800x600 display. That should be enough screen area for you to put several images without expecting your audience to scroll down to see the rest of your image. Even worse than that is making them scroll to the right.

Use colors thoughtfully

Hot pink and fluorescent lime green actually look pretty good together. But if you fill your page with them, people will leave your site quickly and never come back. Using lots of clashing colors will also annoy people. You may be thinking, "I know some really amazing sites that use clashing colors." That's great, but unless you know your audience loves wearing plaid shorts and print shirts, or painting all the walls of their house black, don't clash colors, and use glaring colors sparingly.

Using Flash effectively

A few years ago, I wrote a book about Flash. At the time, Flash was relatively new but beginning to be popular. In the intervening years Flash use has grown enormously. Flash is wonderful. It is powerful. You can do just about anything you want using Flash. And people do just that. This has led to this kind of thinking: "Who needs to follow traditional user interface rules? With Flash, I can create my own personal user interface that is unlike anyone else's!"

I have always wished that I had discussed responsible Flash use in my book. Since I know it is quite likely you will eventually create a Dreamweaver site with Flash, I will give you a few suggestions on how to use Flash effectively.

Questions to ask before using Flash

Flash is a powerful tool, but also a dangerous one. Before jumping right in, ask yourself some questions first:

Inside Scoop

Flash certainly has its share of proponents, but some very savvy usability engineers think it is dangerous. Read what Jakob Nielsen has to say about it at www.useit.com/alertbox/20001029.html.

- Why do you need to use Flash on the site? Is there a real purpose in using it on this site?

- Do you have the skill necessary to create a compelling or attractive Flash movie that adds to the value of the site?

- Are you willing to research good usability to make certain your Flash is not violating important rules?

- Will your use of Flash irritate visitors instead of attract them?

The Flash splash screen

When you first visit a site with a Flash splash screen, you are presented with an animation. It may go on for some time. These can be cute and funny, but too often they are simply annoying to users. Even including a "Skip Intro" link on the site isn't much help. Visitors to your site generally want to get right to the content, not see something flying around the screen or have to click to get rid of it. If you really want to show off your Flash skills, why not create a link to your Flash from the main page of your site?

The Flash site

Entire sites are built in Flash. If you are going to do that, you really don't need Dreamweaver, you need a good book on user interface design instead. The biggest problems with Flash-only sites are that so many of them break so many basic usability rules that they leave users confused and annoyed. The Back button on the browser doesn't work. You can't bookmark specific pages to go right to that place on the site. You can't print pages.

Accessibility

If you are going to use Flash, consider making it accessible to disabled visitors. Flash MX contains an accessibility panel. This allows you to add descriptions to objects in your Flash that can be used much like "alt" tags can be used in HTML.

More information on making Flash accessible can be found on Macromedia's Web site, www.macromedia.com/macromedia/ accessibility/features/flash/.

Flash and search engines

Although more search engines can "see" into the Flash file and extract the text content, the results are often unsatisfactory. If you are going to use Flash with important site content embedded in it, you should take some steps to make sure search engines can find that content. You can include the text in your Flash movie as hidden text on the HTML page where the Flash is called. You can also create an HTML version of your site that can then be submitted to search engines.

Dreamweaver and image editors

As you are working on your Web page in Dreamweaver, you may discover that the image you have just placed on the page needs to be edited. Dreamweaver has built-in support for Macromedia Fireworks. As Figure 2.7 shows, by right-clicking the image (⌘-clicking on the Mac), you display the Edit with Fireworks menu command. Clicking it opens the current image in the Fireworks interface. You can then make any changes you need and click the Done button on the upper left corner of the Fireworks editing window. Dreamweaver will take focus, with your edited image in place.

Figure 2.7. Edit image in Fireworks

Inside Scoop

In the last two chapters, I discuss quite a few things not to do. To show you an example of some of these abuses, I have found the self-styled World's Worst Web site. I can't vouch for it being the *worst*, but it certainly is bad. If you have the stomach for it, visit www.angelfire.com/super/badwebs/.

Obviously if you don't have Fireworks, this link will not work for you, but you can use your preferred image-editing program with Dreamweaver. Look at Figure 2.7 to locate the Edit With menu command. If you don't see your image-editing program listed, click Browse. Figure 2.8 shows the Select External Editor dialog box that appears.

In the figure, I have selected Photoshop.exe as my external editor. From now on, whenever I want to edit an image, I can choose Open With and select Photoshop. It is a little easier than having to manually open Photoshop and then choose File ⇨ Open and locate my image.

Figure 2.8. The Select External Editor dialog box

Just the Facts

- Consider the purpose of each image on your Web site.

- Know the right format to use for your image.

- Flash on your Web site should be carefully considered. It can be made usable, accessible, and visible to search engines.

- You can customize which image-editing program Dreamweaver will automatically open for you.

GET THE SCOOP ON...
What JavaScript is ▪ Creating good scripts ▪ Avoiding
bad scripts ▪ Adding scripts with Dreamweaver

Using JavaScript

While Web programming can refer to a number of different programming languages, the usefulness of JavaScript makes it the language of choice for most Web sites. It can be used in conjunction with other languages, but it is almost always present.

When you hear the word *script* as applied to the Web, people usually refer to code written in JavaScript. JavaScript is everywhere — in the images that change when your mouse pointer rolls over them, in the alert box that opens when you submit a form incorrectly, and in those loathsome pop-up windows with annoying ads.

Understanding scripts

JavaScript is a scripting language that is written into HTML files or called by HTML files. It is not a compiled language, which makes it quite simple to include in your Web pages. JavaScript can be used to validate forms, move objects on the page dynamically, change HTML characteristics of objects on the page, change images for rollovers, open pop-up windows and alert boxes, and more.

A *script* is a sequence of commands that are executed in order. A specific syntax must be used to indicate the beginning and end of the script. A script can occur anywhere on the Web page, but is typically placed in the <BODY> section

> **Inside Scoop**
>
> While putting your JavaScript functions in the <HEAD> section creates a more neatly organized Web page code, you will generally need to call those functions in the <BODY>. Your script can only interact with parts of the page that have already been processed by the Web browser. For example, you can't use a script to output text on the page unless that code is called below the <BODY> tag.

of a Web page. If the script uses functions, they can be placed in the <HEAD> portion of the page and called when needed later in the <BODY>.

Here is an example of a very basic script in a very basic Web page:

```
<HTML>
<HEAD>
</HEAD>
<BODY>
<SCRIPT LANGUAGE = "Javascript">
document.write("Page intentionally left blank")
</SCRIPT>
</BODY>
</HTML>
```

Figure 3.1 shows this Web page. The entire script consists of a command to write the line "Page intentionally left blank" into your Web page.

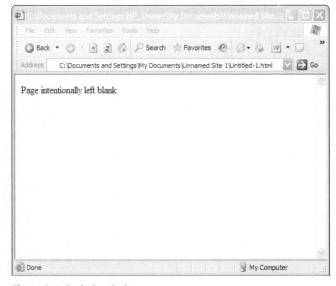

Figure 3.1. Basic JavaScript

If you create this script in the Macromedia Dreamweaver interface, you will not see it in the Design View. You will need to click the Preview in Browser button.

How to view scripts

Scripts in Web pages are freely viewable in most browsers with the View ⇨ Source menu command in the browser. Figure 3.2 shows this command in IE, as well as the text window containing the source code of the page.

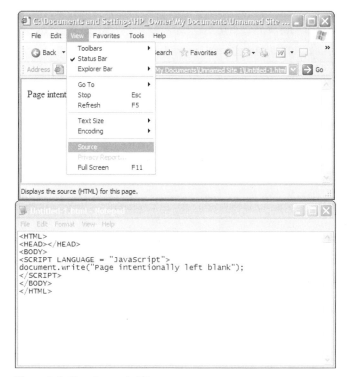

Figure 3.2. View Source in IE

Inside Scoop

IE's View ⇨ Source command can be buggy, and at times it won't work at all. The most common remedy for this is to clear your browser cache. To do this, choose Tools ⇨ Internet Options. In this dialog box, click the General Tab and then click the Delete Files button. Check the "Delete all offline content" box and then click OK.

Watch Out!
Just as you can view any JavaScript on any Web page, all of your visitors can view yours. You can add a copyright statement, but there is no real way to protect your code. The best you can do is not steal someone else's!

Sometimes the scripts are not directly visible in the source code. You might see something like this:

```
<script type="text/javascript" language="javascript"
src="rater.js"></script>
```

This bit of code tells the Web page to include everything it finds in the file rater.js. The JavaScript file rater.js contains nothing more than the code that would reside between the open script (`<script>`) and close script tags (`</script>`). You can see the source of these files by typing the filename in your browser after the URL. For example, if the Web page www.pointlessshapes.com/index.html had this sort of reference on it, you could get that source by typing in **www.pointlessshapes. com/rater.js.** Your browser will ask you if you want to open or save the file. If you save it, you can open it in any text editor and see the contents. I highly recommend taking a look at scripts you like on Web pages.

Internet Explorer and JavaScript

Microsoft has recently adopted new security standards regarding how Internet Explorer views scripts on the Web. Although your alert boxes and image rollovers will still work as expected, the current version of Microsoft IE on XP with Service Pack 2 warns users when a script attempts to download a program to the local machine or access a program on the local machine. Figure 3.3 shows the warning bar and the menu that appears when it is clicked.

This bar appears when the Web site is trying to

- Install an ActiveX control on your computer
- Open certain types of pop-up windows
- Download a file to your computer
- Run active content on your computer
- Run an ActiveX control on your computer in an unsafe manner

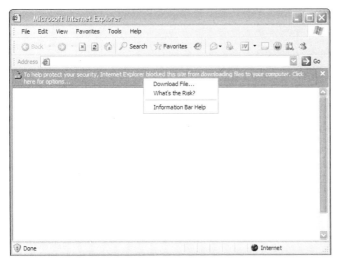

Figure 3.3. Security warning in IE

The rest of the page will open, but the code portion will not be run by the browser. Often the page is still functional, and you will not need the code to run. The security bar that opens enables you to run the code if you trust the Web site. This makes for a bad user experience because you must click at least two extra times, but it does help create a safer Web.

When you should use JavaScript

While it's relatively common to abuse JavaScript and to annoy your visitors, you can use JavaScript in many positive ways.

Add interactivity

The most obvious use of JavaScript is to make something on your Web page interact with your user or animate when the user triggers it. This can be something as simple as an alert box opening when the user does something on the page, or an image changing when the mouse cursor rolls over it. But user interactivity can be far more elaborate than this. You can see an example of an ad for Eclipse mints that ran on Yahoo! that used both Macromedia Flash and JavaScript at `http://public.yahoo.com/~wwwads/archives/wrigleys/040311/`.

In this example, the Flash movie is placed in a layer that is placed over other content on the page. The layers underneath are hidden with

JavaScript until the ad finishes. When the user clicks the Replay Ad link, JavaScript sends a message to the Flash movie and replays it, as well as hides the page content again.

For another example, visit `http://public.yahoo.com/~wwwads/archives/pepsi/050207/`. In this ad, the animated box on the right is created with JavaScript using a clipping rectangle. A Flash movie plays in the box, and when it is finished, a command is sent to a JavaScript function in the page to "close" the area with the ad. This is done by JavaScript making the area with the ad shorter and shorter until a final height is reached. Finally, the Flash movie is swapped for a static image. The Replay Ad link can then play the animation again.

Validating forms

One of the best uses for JavaScript is form validation. When you fill out a form on the Web and you don't enter one of the fields, JavaScript can check what you typed in and produce an alert box if your entry is incorrect or incomplete when you click the Submit button. JavaScript can also be used to make sure you entered only numbers in the form field for a zip code, or that you entered enough characters for your Social Security number. The data you enter on a form page that is checked by JavaScript is basically being checked by code in the page on your browser. Data isn't transmitted by the Submit button until the local JavaScript code checks it and lets the rest of the code on the page execute. It then sends the data on to be processed by the program specified in the form action.

Gathering system information

When creating a Web page, you may need to know which browser your visitor is using. You may also need to know if certain plug-ins are available. Even though JavaScript is a standard, different browsers interpret JavaScript differently, and some commands that work fine on one browser do not work on another. You must carefully test your JavaScript code on all browsers to make sure it runs correctly. You can include code that lets you detect the browser's manufacturer, version number, and operating system.

After you determine which browser your visitor is using, you can dynamically generate HTML code appropriate for that browser. JavaScript code can vary between browsers and versions. Your JavaScript code can execute JavaScript code specifically designed to work on the current browser. This is useful when developing a page with features not supported by every browser. For example, IE interprets hidden layers differently than older versions of Netscape.

Scripts that can detract

JavaScript can be used to do some really great things, but many times it is included on a Web page for no other purpose than to prove that the creator of the page can use it.

Changing background colors

Everyone likes to change things up once in a while, but with JavaScript, you can change your background color constantly while your user is on the page. This might just be worse than blinking text.

Status bar messages

With JavaScript, you can easily place text on the status bar of the browser (see Figure 3.4).

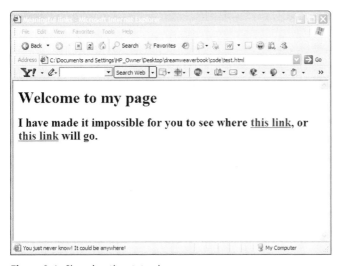

Figure 3.4. Changing the status bar

Inside Scoop

Keep in mind that when I call a JavaScript good or bad, I'm making a subjective decision. In general when scripts add no real value to a page you should avoid using them, but if you have a compelling reason to use them, feel free.

The danger in doing this is that you break the user interface. Normally, when you move your mouse over a link, you will see the URL of that link in the status bar. When you overload that information using JavaScript, your user is left without being able to see the link in the status bar. While the link itself might give a clear indication of where it goes, this is still a bad practice. Users get used to a certain interface and behavior, and any time you change that, you risk making them unhappy. And unhappy visitors don't make return visits.

Scrolling status bars

Scrolling status bars add to the crime of status bar messages. They are status bar messages that scroll across the status bar like a marquee. Just like status bar messages, they block important information from the user. But even more, they are simply annoying. If you are imparting important information, why not prominently place it on the Web page where it can easily be seen? And if it isn't important enough to go in the page, then why are you including it at all — and in such a distracting manner?

Animations following the cursor

JavaScript has a technique in which you can make an animated image follow the cursor. I have seen this done pretty well, with some really attractive, subtle animation following the cursor, but most of the time it just distracts the user from the message of the page.

Alert boxes

Alert boxes are small dialog boxes with a text message and an OK button. They can serve a valuable purpose. When you are writing JavaScript code and attempting to debug it, alert boxes can be extremely helpful. As I mentioned earlier, they are also great for alerting users to mistakes made while filling out Web forms. They let you give users the important message that something is wrong in the form without them having to fill out the entire form again.

But if you just want an alert box to open when someone first visits your page, or simply to announce something when your user clicks, you are going to annoy him. Always keep in mind that people want to click as little as possible. Just like with the scrolling status bar, if the information is important enough to include, do it on the Web page. If you are trying to tell your user that he needs a different version of Flash, for example, you can simply use that same JavaScript detection and instead of an alert, use a document.write command to place a well-formatted, prominent message on your Web page. You can even include a link to the download site — something you can't do in an alert box.

Pop-up windows

Do I even need to tell you that these are a bad idea most of the time? There are some uses for pop-up windows, however. They work well when you want to open a small browser window with no decorations to define a term on your site or provide some other type of help. But with pop-ups in such disrepute, most users have software in place that blocks your JavaScript code from being able to spawn them. Creating them in the first place becomes a waste of time. You are better off creating a Web page with your special information and simply using a `target=_blank` parameter in your link tag to make it open in another page.

Good and bad uses of scripts

I have compiled a short list of sites that use JavaScript in very effective ways and very annoying ways. First, here are a few sites with good JavaScript:

- **www.yahoo.com:** The front page of Yahoo! uses a very nice JavaScript in association with its search box. If you click one of the search types (for example, Local), the color around the search box changes, the text in it changes, and the form itself changes when appropriate. No user interface rules are being stepped on here, and it serves a clear purpose.

- **www.sony.com:** The navigation bar with drop-down menus on the Sony site is a good example of JavaScript used well. Sony didn't make the navigation bar linger once your mouse cursor moves off of it. They also didn't make the navigation bar slowly animate downward, which seems like a great effect, until you realize how quickly tired of it your users will become.

- **www.cbs.com:** On the right-hand side of the page is a section that lists which shows are on the CBS network that night. As you move your mouse over each one, JavaScript is used to show a synopsis of that show.

Here are some sites with bad JavaScript:

- **www.wrhs.net/independent_study_web_design/stacy_w/bad.html:** This may be the worst JavaScript I've ever seen. This page was written this way deliberately to demonstrate just how bad JavaScript can be. And it can be quite bad!

- **www.yuki-onna.co.uk/browserdeath.html:** This is a good page with some really bad JavaScript in it...again, on purpose. Play with it if you dare, but definitely take a look at the source code. This page will not run on some versions of IE, thankfully.

- **www.sas-hereford.bravepages.com:** Unlike the other two pages, this one doesn't seem to be purposefully bad. But take a look at the scrolling status bar; you won't find that many other places.

- **www.geocities.com:** This Web page isn't bad, but some of the pages hosted by Geocities contain some extremely irritating JavaScript. Follow the Browse link and drill down to individual pages. You'll quickly see what I mean.

Dreamweaver and JavaScript

Dreamweaver has been designed to play nicely with JavaScript. It may play too nicely. It's easy to put JavaScript in your pages. You don't have to know any code, and you don't really have to understand how it works. Dreamweaver inserts the scripts and connects them to the appropriate objects or actions in your page.

The Dreamweaver program refers to any JavaScript code it has prebuilt for adding to your page as a *behavior*. Figure 3.5 shows the Behaviors panel, which is the primary interface element for adding JavaScript to your pages with Dreamweaver.

If this panel is not visible, you can open it by checking the menu command Window ⇨ Behaviors. In Figure 3.5, the button with the plus sign on it has been clicked. This is the Add Behaviors button. I will briefly point out a few of the simpler ones here. In chapter 22 these are discussed in more depth.

Figure 3.5. Behaviors panel

- **Change Property:** This is used for changing a property of an object on your Web page. Properties are things such as colors, locations, contents, and sizes. Objects include images, text fields in forms, and divs. An example of this would be changing the source of an image, or the text inside a <DIV>div. These changes would typically be triggered by an event you specify. Examples of possible events include the user double-clicking an image or moving the mouse over an area of the screen.

- **Check Browser:** This is very useful for determining which browser your visitor is using and serving up code appropriately. A good example of this is to detect older browsers and automatically send them to an alternate page without advanced code that would break in them. Figure 3.6 shows the Check Browser dialog box that opens when you select this.

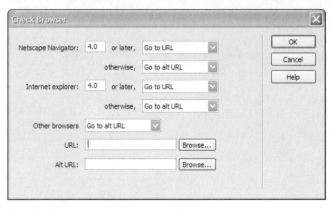

Figure 3.6. The Check Browser dialog box

■ **Check Plug-in:** With Flash used so frequently, this is a very useful
script for determining if the browser supports it, or a few other popular plug-ins. The non-Flash user can be automatically redirected to
a page with no Flash. Figure 3.7 shows the Check Plug-in dialog box
that opens when you select this.

Figure 3.7. The Check Plug-in dialog box

■ **Control Shockwave or Flash:** JavaScript can tell a Flash or Shockwave
movie in the page to quit playing, start playing, or go to a specific
frame.

■ **Go To URL:** This simply tells the browser to go to a URL when an
event you specify takes place.

Bright Idea

Whenever possible, create an alternate version of your pages that contain
JavaScript. Make this alternate version very basic and use Dreamweaver's
browser detection to serve this page to older browsers.

- **Open Browser Window:** This is the invidious pop-up window code, nicely packaged for your use.

- **Popup Message:** This is the basic alert box. Like all of these, it can be triggered by an event in the Web page.

- **Validate Form:** This is one of my favorite JavaScripts that Dreamweaver offers. It makes the tedious chore of validating data users enter in your forms much easier. It isn't terribly specific, as shown in Figure 3.8. You can't use it to make sure your phone number field is entered as (###)###-####. But you can use it to make sure a text field for area code with room for three digits contains only numbers. This behavior will save you time and give you a head start on more specific validation.

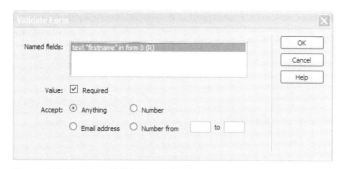

Figure 3.8. The Form Validation dialog box

- **Get More Behaviors:** This menu item will open your browser to the Macromedia Dreamweaver Exchange Web site where you can view a list of user-created script that can be added to your Dreamweaver interface for easy use. Some are free, some aren't.

To change a behavior that you have added, simply locate it in the Code View. Click it, and it appears in the list under the Add Behavior button in the Behaviors panel (see Figure 3.9).

Watch Out!

Be careful that you have selected the right behavior to delete or change. When you have multiple objects with similar behaviors, you may find it easy to get them confused.

You can change the event that triggers the behavior, or you can delete it. You can also change the order in which events occur.

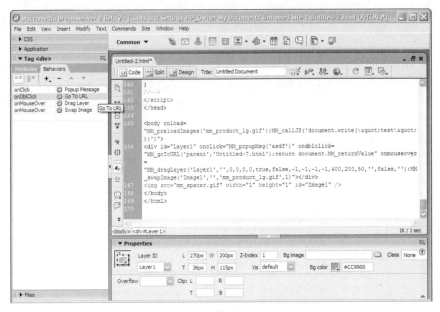

Figure 3.9. Behaviors panel with behaviors defined

Just the facts

- You can view the source of any JavaScript on the Web by using the View ⇨ Source menu command or typing in the URL of a .js file.

- JavaScript can be used to add interactivity, validate forms, and detect information about the user's browser.

- Annoying uses of JavaScript include animated cursors, scrolling status bars, and pop-up windows; these should be avoided.

- Dreamweaver has pre-written JavaScripts for inclusion in your Web page. These are known as behaviors.

GET THE SCOOP ON...
Dreamweaver technologies ■ Programming languages ■
Adding new languages

Choosing Your Technology

With Macromedia Dreamweaver you could create an entire Web site visually with the Design view and never see the code behind it. But even if you can't see it, the code is there. It may be HTML, or you may have added some image rollovers that are created by Dreamweaver as JavaScript. At least one type of language is back there, behind your page.

Dreamweaver has gotten a bad rap from some Web programmers. They feel that it gives anyone an easy way to build Web pages without having to go through the trouble of understanding how things work. But given the chance to play with the Dreamweaver interface, some programmers have become converts. Dreamweaver really does offer the programmer a customizable user interface.

Languages supported by Dreamweaver

Dreamweaver supports the following languages:

- HTML
- XHTML
- CSS
- JavaScript
- ColdFusion Markup Language (CFML)
- Visual Basic
- C#
- JSP
- PHP

51

Inside Scoop

Dreamweaver supports these languages through the use of code coloring, tag completion, and built-in language references.

HTML

HTML is not a programming language but a markup language, and so important to the functioning of the Web that I am mentioning it here. If you know HTML, you might want to skip to the section "How Dreamweaver supports HTML." Otherwise, keep reading.

HTML is the backbone of the Web. The basic job of every Web browser, from the old text-based Lynx to the modern IE, is to interpret and display HTML files. Without HTML, you can't create a Web page. Even if your site consists of one big Macromedia Flash movie, that movie must be placed in an HTML page.

HTML is made up of tags used to define the appearance of your page content. Unlike a programming language, HTML has no logic structures or mathematical operators.

You can use HTML to

- Lay out text and images on a Web page
- Define the style, color, and size of fonts
- Create tables
- Create navigation through hyperlinks
- Design forms for gathering data from users
- Include other media types on your page, such as Flash or video clips

Environment needed to use HTML

Unlike some of the languages mentioned later in this chapter, you need nothing more than a text editor to create HTML files and a Web browser to view them. Of course, I believe that using Dreamweaver to create your HTML files is easier than using a text editor because Dreamweaver offers you a graphical environment in which to create them.

Example of HTML code

Here is a bit of HTML code, which defines a page, a title, some text, and a link to www.wiley.com, Wiley Publishing's Web site:

```
<HTML>
<HEAD>
<TITLE>A Very Simple Web Page</TITLE>
</HEAD>
<BODY>
To go to Wiley's website, <a href = www.wiley.com>click
here</a>.
</BODY>
</HTML>
```

In this example, I've capitalized all the tags even though HTML is not case sensitive. Tags usually occur in pairs, with the second one containing a slash to indicate the end of that tag. Figure 4.1 shows what this Web page looks like in a browser.

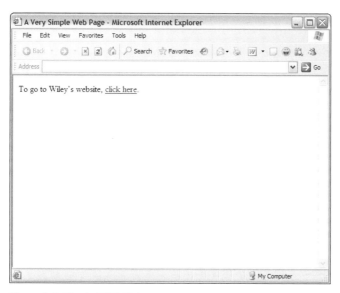

Figure 4.1. Simple HTML Web page

How Dreamweaver supports HTML

Nearly all the tags used in HTML are easily accessible through the Dreamweaver interface. You don't need to type them in yourself if you don't wish to. In fact, you never even need to see the HTML being placed in your page if you work in Design view.

XHTML

XHTML stands for Extensible Hypertext Markup Language. It is a markup language written in XML, intended to be a reformulation of HTML in XML, making it an XML application. When properly formatted, XHTML will be correctly interpreted by HTML browsers and XML tools.

How Dreamweaver supports XHTML

XHTML has a number of very specific rules. Dreamweaver can make both new pages and existing pages XHTML compliant by modifying code to conform to XHTML rules.

Some XHTML rules

Here are three of the many rules XHTML must follow:

- A DOCTYPE declaration referencing one of the three Document Type Definition files must be in the file before the `<html>` tag.
- The file must have head, title, and body HTML tags.
- Unlike in HTML files, all tags and attributes must be lowercase. Attributes must be enclosed in quotation marks.

There are a number of other rules that Dreamweaver adheres to when creating or modifying existing files to XHTML.

CSS

CSS stands for Cascading Style Sheets. CSS code helps you create a set of styles for all the HTML elements in your page and apply those to other pages on your site by typing only one line to include them. With Dreamweaver, you don't even have to type that one line. CSS styles are discussed in greater detail in Chapter 18.

Environment needed to use CSS

Just like HTML, you don't need any special Web server software. Web browsers interpret CSS files when they access the page. Newer browsers correctly interpret CSS, but a number of older browsers do not.

Example of CSS code

In the simple example of CSS code that follows, any text surrounded by the `<H1>` tag would appear red in a 10-point font size:

```
<style type="text/css">
<!—
H1 { color: red; font-size: 10pt;}
-->
</style>
```

How Dreamweaver supports CSS

Creating CSS in Dreamweaver is extremely easy. You can create your page in Design view and never have to type any CSS commands. Most of the work can be done through the Property Inspector, covered in more detail in Chapter 8.

JavaScript

JavaScript is a scripting language that works on most browsers. It can be used for a variety of tasks including validating forms, adding interactivity to Web pages, and communicating with media elements such as Flash. For more JavaScript applications, see Chapter 3.

Environment needed to use JavaScript

JavaScript is a client-side language, meaning that the browser interprets it. You need no special servers. You should get an idea of what browsers your visitors might be using, however, so that you can use the correct JavaScript code to reach as many people as possible.

Example of JavaScript code

The following JavaScript function opens an alert box:

```
<script language="Javascript">
<!—
alert ("This is a JavaScript alert box. How exciting!")
</script>
```

Watch Out!

Microsoft IE doesn't actually support JavaScript. Microsoft supports its own language, called Jscript, which is very much like JavaScript, but may not be exactly the same. Test your code on a number of different browsers to make sure it works!

How Dreamweaver supports JavaScript

JavaScript is used often on the Web and has been tightly integrated in the Dreamweaver interface. In addition to being able to validate your code and help debug it, Dreamweaver can automatically generate JavaScript for common tasks. Chapter 22 discusses in detail how to use JavaScript with Dreamweaver.

ColdFusion Markup Language (CFML)

ColdFusion Markup Language is a server-side Web scripting language. It is primarily used to create dynamic pages and database-driven pages. CFML is designed to support dynamic page creation and database access in a Web server environment.

Environment needed to use CFML

To run code written in ColdFusion, it is necessary to purchase the commercial product ColdFusion Web Application Server from Macromedia.

Example of CFML code

If your code were being served from a ColdFusion Web Application Server, you would be able to put a tag like this one anywhere in your HTML page:

```
<CFOUTPUT>
Date: #dateformat(now())#
</CFOUTPUT>
```

You would then see the current date output on the page, like this:

```
Date: Oct 10, 2005
```

How Dreamweaver supports CFML

Dreamweaver provides code hints, built-in program reference material, and syntax highlighting for CFML. Dreamweaver also offers language-specific database connection code.

Visual Basic

Visual Basic is a programming language created by Microsoft. It was originally created from the BASIC language. It became one of the first products to offer an extensive graphical programming environment. Its first primary use was to build Windows executables, but it has now been rolled into the Microsoft .NET framework.

Environment needed to use Visual Basic

To run Visual Basic code created in Dreamweaver, you will need to use Microsoft Internet Information Server 5 (IIS) with the .NET Framework as your Web server.

How Dreamweaver supports Visual Basic

Dreamweaver provides code hints, built-in program reference material, and syntax highlighting for Visual Basic. Dreamweaver also offers language specific database connection code.

C#

Like Visual Basic, C# is a programming language created by Microsoft. C# is a blend of the C language and Visual Basic.

Environment needed to Use C#

To run C# code created in Dreamweaver, you will need to use Microsoft Internet Information Server 5 (IIS) with the .NET Framework as your Web server.

How Dreamweaver supports C#

Dreamweaver provides code hints, built-in program reference material, and syntax highlighting for C#. Dreamweaver also offers language specific database connection code.

JSP

JSP stands for Java Server Pages. JSP uses small programs run on a Web server, called servlets, to control the content of a Web page and create dynamic Web applications.

Environment needed to use JSP

JSP servlets must be run from a Web server with a JSP server such as Apache Tomcat.

Example of JSP code

The following JSP code outputs the current time and date:

```
<%
 java.util.Date date = new java.util.Date();
%>
The time and date is now <%= date %>
```

How Dreamweaver supports JSP

Dreamweaver provides code hints, built-in program reference material, and syntax highlighting for JSP. Dreamweaver also offers language-specific database connection code.

PHP

PHP stands for Hypertext Preprocessor. PHP is a server-side scripting language. PHP scripts are executed on the server. Most important, PHP is free to download and use.

Environment needed to use PHP

PHP must be served from a Web server that can understand it. Apache and IIS can both work with PHP if they have had modules installed to support it. Most Web hosting companies support it, so it is generally a good choice for a Web programming language.

Example of PHP code

This code will output text to the Web page:

```
<?php
 $var = "This is text written by PHP code.";
 echo $var;
?>
```

Inside Scoop

Because PHP is free, it can easily connect to MySQL (a popular free database), and is so widely supported by Web hosting companies, it may be a good choice for your Web site. To find out more, visit php.net.

How Dreamweaver supports PHP

Dreamweaver provides code hints, built-in program reference material, and syntax highlighting for PHP. Dreamweaver also offers language specific database connection code.

Adding other types

You can edit other languages in Dreamweaver, such as Perl, but you will not have any of the language-specific features of Dreamweaver available to you in the editing environment. You can choose to associate an external editor with Dreamweaver for unsupported programming languages.

If you are going to use Homesite on Windows, or BBEdit on the Mac, the editor will be integrated into Dreamweaver. All other editors will open in their own programs.

To select an editor, choose Edit ⇨ Preferences. Select the File Types/Editors category on the left. The Preferences dialog box should look like the one shown in Figure 4.2.

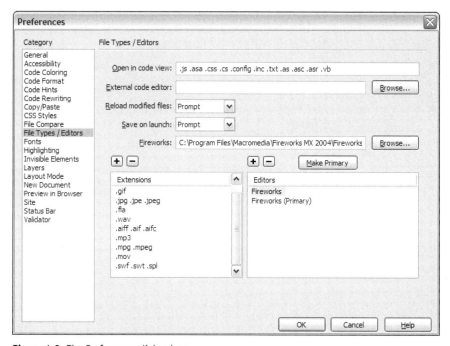

Figure 4.2. The Preferences dialog box

If we wanted to select Windows Notepad as the external editor of choice for Perl files, we would change these settings as follows:

1. Look for the file extension in the Extensions column. In this case we are looking for .pl. If it isn't there, as in this case, click the plus sign (+) above the Extensions column. Now type in our extension, **.pl**.

2. With our new extension selected in the left column, click the plus (+) sign above the Editors column.

3. In the File Browser dialog box that appears, locate the executable program you want to use as your editor.

4. Open your new file in Dreamweaver and choose Edit ⇨ Edit with ... The name of your external editor will be listed.

That's it. Now the editor of our choice will be available whenever we open a .pl file in Dreamweaver.

Just the facts

- HTML, CSS, and JavaScript require no special Web server.
- Dreamweaver provides code correction, syntax highlighting, and reference material for its supported languages.
- ColdFusion, Visual Basic, C#, JSP, and PHP are server-side languages requiring Web servers capable of processing them.
- You can modify the Preferences under File Types/Editors to associate an external editor to an unsupported language.

Getting to Know Dreamweaver

GET THE SCOOP ON...
The built-in tour ▪ The included tutorials ▪
Jump-starting your project with samples ▪ Customizing
your code view ▪ Managing FTP sessions

PART II

Starting Dreamweaver: Choosing the Right Project

The first time I started Macromedia Dreamweaver, I was perplexed. First, I was presented with a dialog box that wanted me to decide if I was a "Designer" or a "Coder." If I chose coder, would I be able to create tables in a graphical environment and avoid typing in tedious HTML table tags? If I chose designer, would I be able to write code at all? I chose one, I don't remember which, hoping that I could figure out how to switch workspace views in the program later on. After I made that choice, the huge menu of choices I was presented with on the Start Page further daunted me. I thought I would be using Dreamweaver to create a new Web page. But now I had to decide, did I want a page with JavaScript? With ASP? Or maybe I'd choose one of the many "Create from Samples" links available to me. And I was even presented with a tour and tutorials to distract me from beginning work on my simple page.

After I spent time investigating all the options, I was generally quite pleased. Exploring the tour gave me a general idea of what Dreamweaver had to offer me. And while not all of the tutorials were useful, some of them saved me a great deal of time.

Viewing the tour

As of this writing, there is a single tour that is focused on features of Dreamweaver (see Figure 5.1) and consists of eight sections, which fall into one of three categories:

- Efficiency
- Best Practices
- Integration

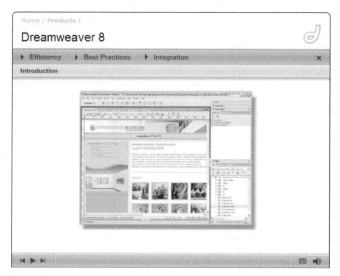

Figure 5.1. Dreamweaver tours

The entire tour is worth watching. It emphasizes the new features of Dreamweaver 8. I anticipate that Macromedia will be adding more tours in the future.

Going through the tutorials

I found the tutorials provided by Macromedia to be both appropriate and thorough. Figure 5.2 shows the dialog box with the listing of topics and tutorials that open when you click Help ⇨ Getting Started with Dreamweaver.

These tutorials fall into three main categories: informational topics, general topics, and setup instructions. I will discuss each type in the next sections.

Figure 5.2. Dreamweaver tutorials

Informational topic tutorials

These tutorials include "Introduction," "Learning Dreamweaver," and "Dreamweaver Basics." The "Introduction" topic has some excellent information on installing and running Dreamweaver, but if you are viewing the tutorials, you probably have already set up the Dreamweaver program correctly.

"Learning Dreamweaver" contains information about the Dreamweaver documentation and help system. "Dreamweaver Basics" briefly covers the various panels and controls that make up the Dreamweaver interface.

The "Quick Site Setup" tutorial is one of the more complete and important tutorials. Although it doesn't tell you why you need to set up a site, it does tell you how to do it. In this book you can find a discussion on reasons for creating a site in Chapter 7.

General topic tutorials

The general topic tutorials include instructions on how to:

Hack

These tutorials are well written but extremely dense. The same material presented is covered in this book in a more evenly paced, step-by-step fashion.

- Set up a Site
- Create a Static Page
- Edit Code
- Link and Preview Pages
- Develop a Web Application
- Install a Web Server

These tutorials contain a great deal of information presented in a very few pages. They basically build upon each other in the order in which they are presented. Before you can edit code, you must create a page. Before you can link and preview pages, you must be able to edit code.

Setup instruction tutorials

Much like the general topic tutorials previously mentioned, the setup tutorials are full of information, but the information is presented very quickly. The topics are:

- Setup for a Sample ColdFusion Site
- Setup for a Sample ASP.NET Site
- Setup for a Sample ASP Site
- Setup for a Sample JSP Site
- Setup for a Sample PHP Site

Create New

By now you are probably ready to start creating a new page. In this section, I'll briefly discuss the various options located under the Create New menu of the Start Page.

Inside Scoop

These setup tutorials are language specific. Unless you are going to need to use one of the specific languages mentioned above, you don't need to read through these setup instructions.

HTML

You will probably choose the HTML link more often than any of the others on the Start Page. When you click it, in the Code view window you are presented with a basic page with the following code already in place:

```
<!DOCTYPE HTML PUBLIC "-//W3C//DTD HTML 4.01
Transitional//EN"
"http://www.w3.org/TR/html4/loose.dtd">
<html>
<head>
<meta http-equiv="Content-Type" content="text/html;
charset=iso-8859-1">
<title>Untitled Document</title>
</head>
<body>
</body>
</html>
```

If you are in Design view, you are presented with a blank, white page. In the Code view you begin inserting your HTML code between the <BODY> and </BODY> tags. In Design view you are creating your page graphically, and anything you insert on the page is placed between the same body tags, but is not visible to you until you switch views. See Chapter 6 for more information on switching between Design and Code views.

ColdFusion and PHP

When you select either of these, the Code view is exactly the same as that of the HTML option mentioned previously.

ASP JavaScript

When you create a new ASP JavaScript, Dreamweaver adds this line to the beginning of the basic HTML code listed previously:

```
<%@LANGUAGE="JAVASCRIPT" CODEPAGE="1252"%>
```

Inside Scoop

The only real difference between selecting HTML, ColdFusion, and PHP file types from the Create New menu is seen when you choose File ⇨ Save to save these files. Then the appropriate extension for each of the file types is added to the filename.

ASP VBScript

This is the line used when you select ASP VBScript:

```
<%@LANGUAGE="VBSCRIPT" CODEPAGE="1252"%>
```

ASP.NET C#

This is the line used when you select ASP.NET C#:

```
<%@ Page Language="C#" ContentType="text/html"
ResponseEncoding="iso-8859-1" %>
```

ASP.NET VB

This is the line used when you select ASP.NET VB:

```
<%@ Page Language="VB" ContentType="text/html"
ResponseEncoding="iso-8859-1" %>
```

JSP

This is the line used when you select JSP:

```
<%@ page contentType="text/html; charset=iso-8859-1"
language="java" import="java.sql.*" errorPage="" %>
```

CSS

Unlike the rest of the file types, creating a new CSS document causes a blank page to open in Code view with a single comment at the top:

```
/* CSS Document */
```

Dreamweaver Site...

Clicking the Dreamweaver Site... button at the bottom of the Create New menu opens a new dialog box, shown in Figure 5.3.

This wizard walks you through the process of creating a site, either locally or remotely, where your actual files are stored. Setting up your local or remote site is discussed in Chapter 7.

More

The More link opens the New Document dialog box. This is the same dialog box that opens when you select any of the Create from Samples links on the right-hand side of the Start Page. In the next section, which deals with creating with samples, I will give you an overview of the New Document dialog box.

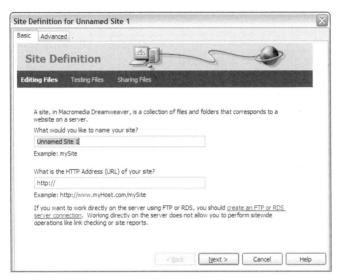

Figure 5.3. The Dreamweaver Site Definition dialog box

Create from Samples

When you select any of the Create from Samples links on the right-hand side of the Start Page, or the More... link at the bottom of the center column, the New Document dialog box opens, as shown in Figure 5.4. This dialog box also opens when you choose File ⇨ New.

CSS Style Sheets

One of the most useful sample types Dreamweaver provides you with is the CSS Style Sheets. When you click CSS Style Sheets on the left-hand side of the New Document dialog box, you are given a long list of CSS Styles from which to choose, as well as a preview of them, as shown in Figure 5.5.

Hack

The Create from Samples options on the Start Page are one of my favorite features of Dreamweaver. If you have to create a simple page quickly, or just want to mock something up, these wizard-like interfaces give you an easy way to have something ready to run in very little time.

Hack

Take advantage of the CSS Style Sheets whenever you are creating your own. The major HTML element appearances are already defined for you and you can simply change what you wish instead of creating a style sheet from scratch.

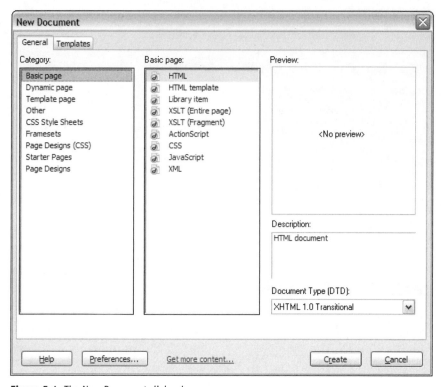

Figure 5.4. The New Document dialog box

Framesets

If you need to use frames, the Frameset styles in the New Document dialogue will quickly get you started. When you choose a frame sample, Web pages for all of the frames are created for you.

Starter Pages

Starter Pages are new to this version of Dreamweaver. They consist of sets of pages for hypothetical businesses. These include sites for businesses in these industries:

- Entertainment
- Health and nutrition
- Lodging
- Personal training
- Restaurant
- Spa
- Travel

Each industry has five starter pages, consisting of a calendar, catalog, home page, product page, and text page. Macromedia has kept the design of these starter pages simple, but still quite attractive. If you have no inspiration for your own site, these starter pages are a good place to start. You can customize them to your liking quite easily.

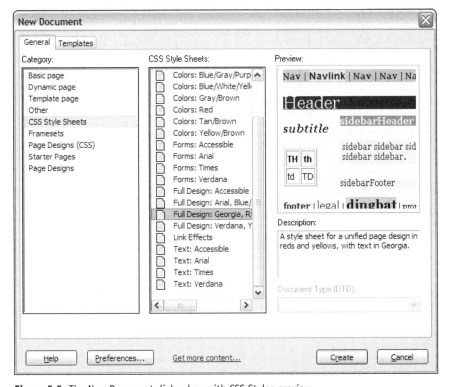

Figure 5.5. The New Document dialog box with CSS Styles preview

Page Designs (CSS)

The Page Designs (CSS), shown in Figure 5.6, take the CSS Style Sheets one step further by defining layers on the page and decorating them with lines or borders. You may recognize some of the designs from sites you have visited.

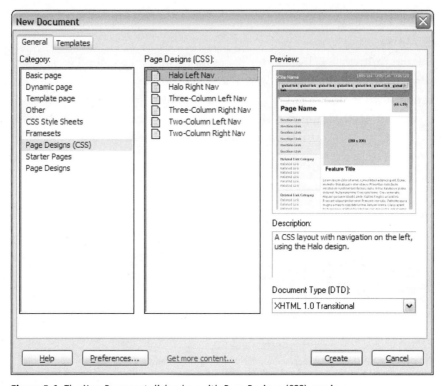

Figure 5.6. The New Document dialog box with Page Designs (CSS) preview

Page Designs

Unlike the Page Designs (CSS) category I previously mentioned, the Page Designs category contains samples of pages with no CSS. These are strictly

Inside Scoop

After you have finished the tours and tutorials, you may want to turn off the Start Page and simply use the New Document dialog box each time you create a new document.

HTML code. In many cases, they are not an entire Web page, but only pieces of code that can be cut and pasted together to form a static page.

Extend

Macromedia encourages interaction between the users of its products. A number of links in the Dreamweaver interface send you to the Macromedia user community Web site, called Macromedia Exchange. You have already encountered two of those links: One is at the bottom right of the Start Page, and the other is at the bottom center of the New Document dialog box and simply reads "Get more content."

Dreamweaver Exchange

On the Dreamweaver Exchange page, shown in Figure 5.7, you will find a listing of over a thousand plug-ins developed for Dreamweaver and the MX line of products.

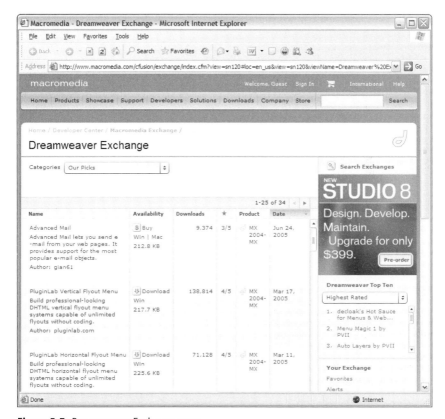

Figure 5.7. Dreamweaver Exchange page

Watch Out!

As you explore the various plug-ins on the Dreamweaver Exchange site, be aware that some of them are shareware and cost money. Their prices are not presented on the main display page, so it's generally a good idea to click the name of the product and read more about it before downloading.

Preferences

The first time I used Dreamweaver 8, I couldn't figure out why there was no small yellow symbol on the Design view screen to represent my JavaScript code. In the previous version there was always one; why not in this version? I began hunting around and found the option to turn it on buried in the Preferences dialog box, shown in Figure 5.8.

Dreamweaver has an extensive set of preferences. There are 20 individual Preference screens, accessible by choosing Edit ➪ Preferences. Some of the options are obvious, but some are definitely worth knowing about. In this section, I will give an overview of what is in each screen and my recommendations for what settings you may want to use.

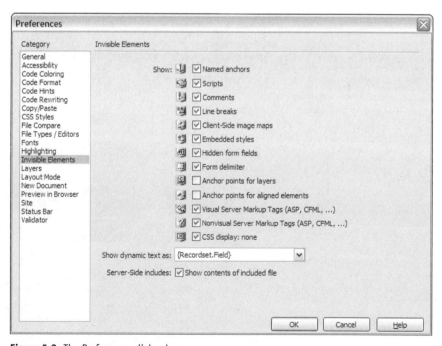

Figure 5.8. The Preferences dialog box

General

- **Open documents in tab:** This only shows up on the Mac and allows you to open each document in the same window with tabs to navigate between them.

- **Show start page:** This controls whether or not the Start Page appears when you first open the program.

- **Reopen documents on startup:** If this is checked, you can leave documents opened and saved in Dreamweaver when you close the program. The next time you open it, the same documents automatically opens.

- **Warn when opening read-only files:** When checked, you are warned if the file you have opened for editing is read-only.

- **Update links when moving files:** When you set up a Dreamweaver site, this controls how links in pages you create in that site are handled when you move a file.

- **Show dialog when inserting objects:** Most objects you insert into your Web page have attributes. Dreamweaver has a dialog box associated with nearly every object you insert. When checked, this option causes the appropriate object dialog box to open when you insert a new object.

- **Enable double-byte inline input:** A number of languages require longer byte codes than the English alphabet. This option allows you to enter double-byte text directly in your page without conversion.

- **Switch to plain paragraph after heading:** When you create a heading in the Design view and press Enter, two things can happen. If this is checked, a `<p>` tag is automatically inserted. If this is not checked, the heading tag continues to the next line.

- **Allow multiple consecutive spaces:** When you have multiple spaces in a row in your Web page, browsers ignore these and interpret them as a single space. If this is checked, Dreamweaver inserts the code ` ` for each space, so each space is detected by the browser.

- **Use `<strong>` and `<em>` in place of `<b>` and `<i>`:** When checked, Dreamweaver replaces your uses of `<b>` (bold) and `<i>` (italics) with `<strong>` and `<em>`, respectively. These are more standard HTML tags, and do not change the way the bold or italics look in browsers.

Watch Out!

There will probably be times when you do not want CSS formatting. Make sure you deselect the Use CSS instead of HTML tags check box, or you will probably have to do quite a bit of extra work recreating the page without CSS. This has happened to me a few times!

- **Use CSS instead of HTML tags:** When checked, CSS code is automatically inserted into your page when you are using Design mode to format and add content to your page.

- **Warn when placing editable regions within** <p> **or** <h1>-<h6> **tags:** Editable regions in Dreamweaver templates do not allow you to create more paragraphs in the region. When checked, this warns you about that.

- **Maximum number of history steps:** History steps are great. This box specifies the number of times you can undo changes to your page using Edit ⇨ Undo.

- **Spelling Dictionary:** The language the spell checker uses is specified here.

Accessibility

The Accessibility preferences are mainly used to indicate whether or not to open dialog boxes with accessibility options when you insert certain object types. An example of the image accessibility dialog box is shown in Figure 5.9.

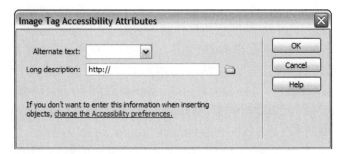

Figure 5.9. The Image Tag Accessibility Attributes dialog box

Inside Scoop

I typically use a high number of history steps. On more than one occasion this has saved me a great deal of pain when I saved a document after I made a code mistake.

Code Coloring

When you are creating an HTML page and working in the Code view, you may notice that Dreamweaver colors HTML commands blue and plain text black. These colors are set in the Code Coloring preference page. You can also use this page to dictate what a large number of other Web programming languages will look like in the Code view.

Code Format

Use this page to define how Dreamweaver automatically formats code in Code view. Here are the settings you can change:

- **Indent:** Check to indent your code, and use the text box to specify how many spaces to indent.

- **Tab size:** When Tab is pressed, move over the number of spaces specified.

- **Automatic wrapping:** Purely cosmetic, this inserts a line break after the number of spaces specified in the column text box.

- **Line break type:** This is a very important box to check if you intend to edit your files on systems other than the type you created them on. Windows line breaks are different than Unix breaks, for example, and to edit on one system and then another may cause problems with the editor not recognizing the line breaks.

- **Default tag case, Default attribute case:** This doesn't generally matter for HTML, but some languages, such as XHTML, demand a certain case.

Inside Scoop

Dreamweaver uses the file extension to figure out which code color scheme to use. For example, to use the PHP code color scheme, save your file with an extension of .php.

Code Hints

As you type code in Dreamweaver, the editor pays attention to what you are typing. With Code Hints configured, you can specify prompts that you get as you type.

- **Close tags:** You are given three options here. Whenever you type an opening HTML tag, such as , the editor can be configured to prompt you with the close tag, in this case , at various times. The first radio button causes it to appear after you type </ and the second after you finish typing the final > on the opening tag. The third option turns this off entirely.

- **Enable code hints:** If you uncheck this, you do not get any code hints at all. You can delay the time it takes for them to appear with the slider.

- **Menus:** This is a specific list of options, including HTML, CSS, and JavaScript tags, that are enabled with code hints if checked.

Code Rewriting

In this page are a series of code elements that you may wish Dreamweaver to rewrite for you if you add them to your page. I typically do not allow Dreamweaver to rewrite my code because I would prefer to figure out what is incorrect in it so I don't repeat that mistake next time.

Copy/Paste

If you ever copy text from a Word document or PDF or Web page, this preference page lets you specify how Dreamweaver handles it. I generally use the Text only option, unless I'm copying from another Web page, in which case I prefer Text with structure plus basic formatting. I always leave Retain line breaks and Clean up Word paragraph spacing checked.

CSS Styles

This page is mostly concerned with how Dreamweaver-generated CSS rules are written. CSS can be written in two ways, longhand and short-hand. The difference is quite simple. When using CSS in longhand to define an object, some text for example, every CSS rule for how that text should look is defined, even if you want to use default values. When using shorthand, only the rules you want to change from default are specified. Longhand CSS is generally better, because ambiguity in shorthand CSS can produce unexpected results.

File Compare

If you have two versions of the same file, this dialog box lets you select a program on your system that does file compare operations. Dreamweaver doesn't have any built-in file comparison tools.

File Types/Editors

For any media types you are putting in your page, the File Types/Editors preference page lets you specify what external program will edit the media if you choose to edit it in Design view. Some common examples of this would be attaching Macromedia Flash to SWF files and some type of sound recorder program to WAV files.

Fonts

These font selections dictate how the fonts appear in the Dreamweaver Code and Design views. They do not affect how fonts appear on the Web as defined by your HTML or CSS tags. I use the default selections.

Highlighting

These highlighting colors dictate what these various regions look like in Design view as you are coding your page. They have no bearing on the live page in a browser.

Invisible Elements

This page is a list of various "invisible elements" in a Web page. They are tags and code that are present in the Code view, but not actually represented by anything in the Design view. I prefer to have all of these visible in Design view so I can tell where they are and that they are there at all. At a minimum, I recommend you check the boxes concerned with scripts and forms.

Layers

The Layers preference page specifies how Dreamweaver creates layers when they are created automatically using Insert ⇨ Layer.

- **Visibility:** Layer visibility can be set to default, visible, inherit, or hidden.

- **Width, Height:** This is the default size of the automatically created layer.

- **Background color:** This is the background color of the automatically created layer.

- **Background image:** A background image can be specified.

- **Nest when created within a layer:** If the layer you draw is inside another layer, this specifies whether that layer is nested in the outer layer or a distinct layer.

- **Add resize fix when inserting a layer:** Netscape 4 has a layer problem when the window is resized. If this is checked, JavaScript code is added to your page to fix this problem.

Layout Mode

Layout mode allows you to graphically design tables in Design view. The options on this page define how layout mode will look.

- **Autoinsert spacers:** If you create a long column without any content, this option inserts a transparent spacer image in the space.

- **Spacer image:** You can select the spacer image you wish to use here or use a default image.

- **Cell outline:** This is the color of the cell outline.

- **Table outline:** This is the color of the table outline.

- **Table background:** This is the color of areas of the table without layout cells.

New Document

Simply stated, use this preference page to select the most common type of page you are creating. Then, when you select New Document, it is the default type. You can specify some other type-specific settings here as well.

Inside Scoop

If you need old versions of Netscape browsers for testing, I highly recommend the site `http://sillydog.org/narchive`.

Preview in Browser

If you know your audience, you should know what browsers they are using. This dialog box lets you set a list of browsers in which to test your pages. The browsers you list in this dialog box is available to you when you click the Earth icon in the bar just above the Code or Design view of your document. Each browser in this list needs to be available on your system.

Site

These are some extremely important settings for specifying how Dreamweaver works with a remote site you have set up.

- **Always show:** This specifies on which side local or remote files are shown.

- **Dependent files:** When loading a page that contains references to other files, this asks if you want to load the dependent files as well.

- **FTP connection:** This is how many minutes your FTP connection stays open once initiated.

- **FTP time out:** This is how long until Dreamweaver gives up when trying to initiate a connection to a slow or unresponsive FTP server.

- **FTP transfer options:** If you have wandered off just as the FTP is querying you through Dreamweaver for information, this is how long Dreamweaver waits before sending default information to the FTP server.

- **Firewall host, Firewall port:** Use these to specify your proxy server and port (if not the default 21) if you are behind a firewall.

- **Save files before putting:** If checked, files are saved locally before they are put on the FTP server.

- **Prompt before moving files on server:** If files are being moved, not copied, you get a message if this is checked.

- **Manage Sites:** This opens the Manage Sites dialog box.

Status bar

In the status bar of the page you are working on you see the current page height and width with a drop-down list of standard page sizes, and a download speed estimate. You can customize what appears in this status bar with this preference page.

Validator

Dreamweaver has a validator that looks through your code and points out possible problems and errors. This page lets you choose from some languages and browser extensions to decide what should be validated. The Validate button is located on the bar at the top of the current document to the right of the title text box and the Browser Check button.

Just the facts

- The tour and tutorials provided with Dreamweaver can help you get up to speed with the interface and its features.

- Be sure to investigate all of the document types presented on the Start Page.

- The Start Page can be turned off and File ⇨ New can be used instead.

- The Macromedia Exchange Web site offers plug-ins that can extend your Dreamweaver software.

- Dreamweaver is extremely customizable. Some of the customizations specify how files are saved, how code is colored in the editor, how code is auto-finished, and how FTP connections to remote sites are handled.

Choosing Your View

Macromedia Dreamweaver has many toolbars, menu items, buttons, and property bars. You will probably end up using 10 percent of the controls 95 percent of the time. It's that aggravating other 5 percent of the time when you need to know that Dreamweaver has a control button or property for something you are trying to do. As long as you know that Dreamweaver can do it, you don't have to remember where the control for it is. You have at your disposal this book and Dreamweaver's own built-in help commands to help you find that elusive toolbar button, menu option, or property.

This chapter takes you on a tour of all the menus, toolbars, and properties. As you go through it, focus on what Dreamweaver has to offer and not necessarily on the exact location of everything. You'll quickly learn where the most commonly used 10 percent of the controls are, and you'll know that somewhere in the interface Dreamweaver has a control for that one thing you think you'll have to do just once in a while.

Picking the right view

There exists an elusive Dreamweaver dialog box, shown in Figure 6.1. You will only see it if you are on a PC, the very first time you run Dreamweaver.

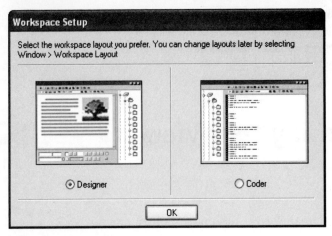

Figure 6.1. The Workplace Setup dialog box

You are commanded to select the workspace you prefer. Right now! There's no getting out of it: Are you a designer or a coder?

Relax. Just pick one. You can change your workspace easily, as often as you wish. After you have started the software, simply choose Window ⇨ Workspace Layout and play with the options you see there to figure out what works best for you. So when you are asked that question the first time you start the program, pick either designer or coder; it won't matter in the integrated and flexible world of Dreamweaver.

Controlling your view

The workspace you choose does not matter as much as the view you are in. Dreamweaver has three views: Code, Design, and Split. In this section, I will explain these three views and show you how to switch between them.

Dreamweaver allows you to create Web pages in two ways: by typing code, or by laying out the page elements graphically. Figure 6.2 shows you the Code view of a basic HTML page. This page simply contains some text, a table, and an image.

You can also create your Web pages graphically, in a point and click environment. This is called Design view and is shown in Figure 6.3. This is the same page as shown in Figure 6.2.

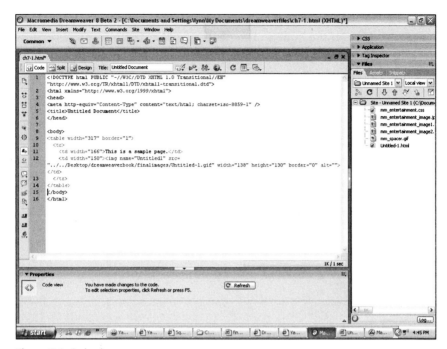

Figure 6.2. Code view

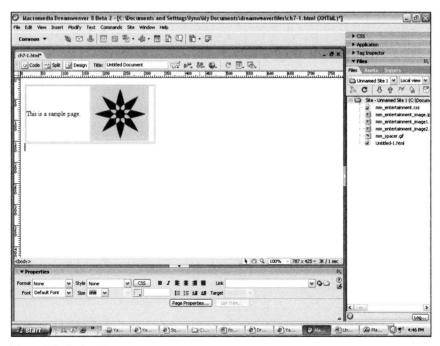

Figure 6.3. Design view

Finally, there is the view that I use the most often, the Split view. This view gives you both the code in the page as well as the graphical version of it. You can see the Split view of the same page as shown in the previous two figures in Figure 6.4.

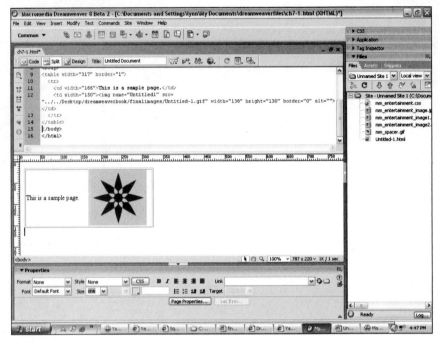

Figure 6.4. Split view

Changing views is simple. Start the Dreamweaver program and choose Create New ⇨ HTML. If this is your first time running the program, you will probably be in Split view. To change the view, click the Code, Split, or Design button at the top left of the document, as shown in Figure 6.5.

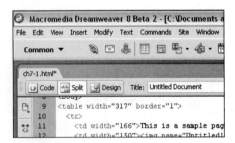

Figure 6.5. View change buttons

Hack

You can also change views with the menu option View. You will see the three view modes listed with the currently selected one checked.

Menus

Dreamweaver has the standard menus you see on most applications as well as ones containing largely HTML customizations. I will go through the various menus, primarily focusing on Dreamweaver-specific items, and not listing more standard menu items found in most software.

File menu

Here are the File menu options and an explanation of what each does.

- **New:** Opens the New Document dialog box, as shown in Figure 6.6. This is a dialog box you should spend time experimenting with. The Starter Pages are new to this version of Dreamweaver and are a very good place to start if you are still coming up with your page design.

- **Open in Frame:** If your Web page is made up of frames, you can select one and open the saved document within that frameset.

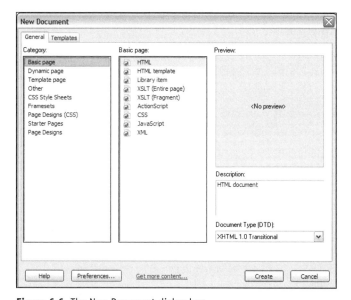

Figure 6.6. The New Document dialog box

- **Save to Remote Server:** You can set up a connection to a remote Web server using the Site ⇨ New Site dialog box; this option then lets you save your file to that remote server.

- **Save as Template:** By using this option, you can turn your Web page into a template that can be reused as the basis for multiple pages.

- **Revert:** While you are working on your page, if you have made so many bad changes that you can't use the current version, this option re-opens the last saved version of the current file. This is especially useful when you are coding and break your program horribly but can't figure out what you did.

- **Print Code:** This prints the Code view of the page.

- **Import:** You can import several types of data into your Web page, including XML document data and tabular data, Word documents, and Excel documents.

- **Export:** This allows you to export XML data, CSS styles, and tabular data.

- **Convert:** This changes the DOCTYPE line in your file to define the specific type of document.

- **Preview in Browser:** This is a great menu option. The page you are currently working on can be easily previewed in the browser you choose by selecting this.

- **Check Page:** This option allows you to check your page for a number of potential problems. Areas checked include accessibility, links, and markup.

- **Compare with Remote:** If you have the same file locally and also on a remote site, this option tells you what is different between them.

- **Design Notes:** This handy feature allows you to add documentation about your page or site that you don't want actually published to the Web. This information is available to anyone editing the site with Dreamweaver, but not viewable by the outside world.

Inside Scoop

You can also preview your work in a browser by clicking the button with the Earth icon on the title bar of the editor window.

Edit menu

These commands are used primarily to modify the code in the Code view.

- **Paste Special:** This allows you to paste HTML text into your Design view in a variety of ways. You can paste just the text, or the text with all formatting as it appeared when you copied it.

- **Select Parent Tag:** This command selects the pair of HTML tags surrounding the currently selected object as well as anything in them.

- **Select Child:** In the Design view, you can select an object and use this command to select the first "child" object, or nested HTML element, in it.

- **Go to Line:** In the Code view, the lines of code are numbered. This command takes you to the line number you specify.

- **Show Code Hints:** Code Hints are shown in a box that pops up for auto-completion as you are typing HTML or script code in the Code view page.

- **Code Hint Tools:** These are three tools to save you some time in creating your code. They are all designed to work in the Code view window. The first is the **Color Picker,** which inserts the hex value of the color you choose into your HTML file. The **URL Browser** allows you to use the Select File dialog box to pick a file. That file path and name is then inserted as text in your Code view window. The **Font List** is a list of the commonly used font families for Web pages. Selecting one inserts those names as text in your HTML file.

- **Indent Code:** In your Code view window, this command easily allows you to indent control structures or selected text in your code.

- **Outdent Code:** "Outdent" may not actually be a word, but it is a useful command. If you have an indented section of code you no longer need indented, select it and use this command.

- **Balance Braces:** In blocks of scripted code, this command adds or removes braces as needed to match up the number of right and left braces.

- **Repeating Entries:** Repeating entries are areas you define to contain the same content in multiple locations on the page. These menu options allow you to make changes to your repeated entries.

- **Code Collapse:** In Code view, Code Collapse allows you to hide portions of your code for ease of editing. For example, if you have a table on your page but don't need to edit it, you can hide it by selecting the first <TABLE> tag and choosing Edit ⇨ Code Collapse ⇨ Collapse Full Tag. You will see the open tag followed by an ellipsis (...). To expand your code, double-click the opening tag or ellipsis and the code appears again.

- **Edit with External Editor:** If you have an image, text, or multimedia content that you wish to edit with the program of your choice, you can open the content in that other program with this dialog box.

- **Tag Libraries:** This opens the Tag Library Editor, a handy place to look up and specify how you want your tags to appear when inserted in Code view.

- **Preferences:** This opens the very large Preferences menu. This dialog box is covered in more detail in Chapter 5.

View menu

Here are the nonstandard View menu options and an explanation of what each does.

- **Code, Design, Code and Design:** These three menu options switch your view, just as the buttons on the title bar of the editor window do.

- **Switch Views:** This toggles you between Code view and Design view. If you are in Split view, it does not change your view.

- **Refresh Design View:** This redraws the Design view window, useful if you have made a change to the code that was not reflected in the Design window.

- **Head Content:** When you are in Design view, this command opens a bar with icons on it representing the lines of code in the HEAD portion of your Web page.

- **Noscript Content:** If you use a <NOSCRIPT> tag in your HTML, this command allows you to preview this content in your Design view.

- **Table Mode:** This command offers three ways of viewing and manipulating tables in Design view. **Standard Mode** displays tables very much as they will appear on your final Web page but with the table and cell borders visible. **Expanded Mode** makes the table seem

Inside Scoop

For the best code-writing experience, I recommend using the following options from the Code View Option menu when coding: Word Wrap, Line Numbers, Syntax Coloring, and Auto Indent.

larger in Design view to make it easier for you to modify the shape of it. **Layout Mode** allows you to actually draw the table in Design view.

- **Visual Aids:** The visual aids are visual representations of CSS elements, layer outlines, table sizes and borders, image maps, and invisible elements such as forms or scripts. If checked, these things are visible in the Design view window.

- **Style Rendering:** This menu option lists media types and gives you the opportunity to see how your design will look if viewed in one of these.

- **Code View Options:** For use while coding, any of these elements checked will appear in the Code view window.

- **Tracing Image:** If you have created a Web page design in Photoshop or another graphics program, you can use Tracing Image to place a screenshot of that image in your Design view window and use it to build the actual design in Dreamweaver. You must **Load** the image, and then you can use the **Align, Adjust,** and **Reset** options to place it where you need it. As you work, you can uncheck **Show** to give you the actual view of the page you are working on.

- **Plugins:** This refers to Web browser plug-ins. If you insert a Macromedia Flash movie or other file in your page that requires a plug-in, you can preview it in the Design view window with the Plugins commands.

Insert menu

These commands place HTML objects, snippets (bits of code you manually save), and template objects in your page. These same objects can also be inserted using the toolbars discussed in the next section. It is generally easier to use the toolbar buttons than this menu.

- **Tag:** You know there's a tag to do that thing you are trying to do, but you just can't remember it. Use this command to help jog your memory and insert it into your code.

- **Image:** This command opens the Select Image Source dialog box and inserts the selected image into your page. You can also type the URL of an image here. This is generally poor form unless you own the image and the domain where it is located.

- **Image Objects:** You can insert four different Image Objects. The **Image Placeholder** is useful if you are still waiting on a final image, but know what size it will be and where it will be on the page. The **Rollover Image** option inserts JavaScript code and an image that will be swapped with another when the mouse moves over it. Inserting a **Navigation Bar** is basically creating multiple Rollover Images that all have links associated with them and reside side by side in a table. Finally, the **Fireworks HTML** allows you to insert images and associated HTML generated by the Macromedia Fireworks program.

- **Media:** Use this menu item to easily insert Flash animations, other types of Flash files, and Java applets into your page.

- **Table:** This inserts an HTML table in your page. You can specify the table size, border thickness, cell spacing and padding, header, and alignment at the time of creation.

- **Table Objects:** This menu allows you to modify an existing table or add just part of the HTML code for a table.

- **Layout Objects:** These consist of layers, div tags, and tools you can use to visually draw tables when you are in Layout mode.

- **Form:** This inserts a form and various elements belonging in a form such as text fields and drop-down boxes.

- **Hyperlink:** You can easily create hyperlinked text on your page with this command.

- **Email Link:** This creates a "mailto:" hyperlink on your page.

- **Named Anchor:** This adds an anchor tag to your page.

- **Date:** This command inserts the current date and optionally the time as text on your Web page in a variety of date formats.

- **Server-Side Include:** Selecting this allows you to locate a Server-Side Include file and reference it in the current page.

- **Comment:** This inserts an HTML comment into your Code view window.

- **HTML:** This menu contains a number of common HTML elements for insertion.

- **Template Objects:** This inserts a variety of template objects into your page.

- **Recent Snippets:** This command allows you to insert a saved snippet into your Code view page. To save a snippet, select the code you wish to save and right-click and select **Create New Snippet** from the menu. After you have created it, it appears in the **Recent Snippets** menu.

- **Customize Favorites:** You can modify the Favorites toolbar with this option.

- **Get More Objects:** This option opens a browser window and connects you to the Macromedia Exchange site to locate add-on objects.

Modify menu

These commands are used to change properties of the page or items on the page.

Text menu

These commands are used to control the appearance of HTML text. When used in the Code view window, they insert HTML tags. When used in the Design view window, they change the appearance of the text.

- **Indent:** This indents a selected block of text.

- **Outdent:** If an indented block of text is selected, choosing this removes the indent.

- **Paragraph:** This menu option opens a submenu with paragraph insertion options, including various sizes of headers and pre-formatted text.

- **Align:** Use this to specify what alignment to use on the selected text: left, center, right, or justified.

- **List:** This command creates a list out of selected text, or inserts a list at the cursor location if no text is selected.

- **Font, Style, CSS Styles, Size, Size Change, Color:** Respectively these specify font appearance, including the font face, font style (HTML), font style in CSS, size, relative size, and color.

- **Check Spelling:** This command is self-explanatory, but it's worth mentioning that you should be using it every single time you have any text on a Web page. Misspelled words look careless, and even if you don't notice them, rest assured visitors to your Web site will.

Commands menu

This menu contains controls for recording and replaying commands, as well as some miscellaneous functions.

- **Start Recording, Play Recorded Command, Edit Command List, Get More Commands:** These menu options allow you to automate a series of actions you perform in Design view.

- **Apply Source Formatting, Apply Source Formatting to Selection:** These commands format the code in your page as specified in the Preferences dialog box. See Chapter 5 for more information.

- **Clean Up XHTML:** This command cleans up XHTML code so that it meets XHTML requirements.

- **Clean Up Word HTML:** If you have ever created an HTML document from Word and then viewed the source, you can appreciate just how wonderful this command is.

- **Add/Remove Netscape Resize Fix:** When using layers with Netscape 4, Dreamweaver can insert JavaScript code to fix a known bug with the browser. This command adds code if it isn't there and removes the code if it is.

- **Optimize Image in Fireworks:** If you have Macromedia Fireworks installed, this command opens the Fireworks image optimizer with the image from your Web page, giving you an opportunity to adjust the number of colors if a GIF or the compression if a JPG.

- **Create Web Photo Album:** This command seems a bit out of place here. You can specify a directory on your computer with images and this automatically creates a Web photo album from them.

- **Format Table:** This command applies formatting preferences to a selected table.

- **Sort Table:** You can select a column in your table and sort the table contents on that column.

- **Insert Mark of the Web:** This inserts this line of code in your Web page:

```
<!-- saved from url=(0014)about:internet -->
```

This line tells IE to run active content from the Internet zone, which keeps the IE security warning from appearing. You can find more information at `http://msdn.microsoft.com/workshop/ author/dhtml/overview/motw.asp`.

Site menu

These menu options are used to control Web content remotely, as well as provide version control for projects where multiple people are working on the same set of files.

- **New Site, Manage Site:** Use these commands to access the site management dialog box. See Chapter 7 for more information about site setup.

- **Get, Check Out, Put, Check In, Undo Check Out, Locate in Site:** These commands are all used for managing remote files when more than one developer is working on them. This is Dreamweaver's built in version control system.

- **Reports:** Dreamweaver Reports can help you optimize and fine-tune your site. This dialog box lets you pick which reports to run and run them.

- **Synchronize Sitewide, Check Links Sitewide, Change Link Sitewide:** These commands work with the entire site. Synchronizing your files allows you to make sure the latest versions of all files are on the remote and/or local server. Checking links sitewide checks all the links and makes certain they are valid. Change link sitewide looks for a particular link all over your site and changes it in all instances.

- **Advanced:** Among other options, this menu gives you access to the FTP log. This can be useful to confirm uploads and troubleshoot FTP connection problems. This menu is discussed in more detail in Chapter 7.

 Inside Scoop

The Extension Manager is used to import bits of code into the Dreamweaver program for easy insertion in pages created with Dreamweaver. This code can be HTML and JavaScript commands, as well as new Property inspectors and panels.

Window menu

For the most part, these menu items open and close the various panel windows.

- **Workspace Layout:** This is used to switch between workspace views, as well as save your own customized view.

- **Hide Panels/Show Panels:** This toggle command hides or shows all the panel windows.

Help menu

These are standard Help menu items, with the exception of the Manage Extensions command.

- **Manage Extensions:** This opens the Extension Manager dialog. Use this command to add Dreamweaver extensions you have downloaded from the Macromedia Dreamweaver Exchange site.

Toolbars

The toolbars exist primarily to let you quickly insert various common HTML elements in your code by clicking the appropriate button instead of having to painstakingly type out the code.

Common

The Common toolbar, shown in Figure 6.7, contains the following buttons for inserting common HTML elements:

- **Hyperlink:** Creates a hyperlink of whatever element is currently selected.

- **Email Link:** Inserts a mailto link.

- **Named Anchor:** Inserts an anchor.

- **Table:** Inserts a table.

- **Insert Div Tag:** Inserts a div tag.

- **Images:** This button has a submenu containing a variety of image objects and hotspots.

- **Media:** This button has a submenu containing various types of Flash, Shockwave, and Java applets.

- **Date:** Inserts a date into the current page.

- **Server-Side Include:** This opens a file dialog box to let you choose an Include file.

- **Comment:** An HTML comment tag is inserted in the page. Any text typed inside it will not be viewable in a browser.

- **Templates:** This opens a large submenu of template insertion options.

- **Tag Chooser:** If you don't see the tag you want listed, or can't quite remember it, click this button to open the Tag Chooser dialog box.

Figure 6.7. Common toolbar

Layout

The Layout toolbar is shown in Figure 6.8. These buttons allow you to visually create tables, divs, and layers in Design view. The buttons on the far right allow you to work with tables in Layout mode, allowing you complete control over the way they look.

Figure 6.8. Layout toolbar

Forms

The Forms toolbar, shown in Figure 6.9, contains buttons for all the HTML form elements. In order, these are:

- **Form:** Creates an empty form.
- **Text Field:** Creates a text field.
- **Hidden Field:** Adds a hidden field. This will not be visible in a browser.
- **Textarea:** Adds a large text box to allow multiple lines of text to be added.
- **Checkbox:** Creates a checkbox.
- **Radio Button:** Creates a radio button.

- **Radio Group:** Creates a group of radio buttons.

- **List/Menu:** Adds a drop-down list box.

- **Jump Menu:** Adds a drop-down list box with JavaScript code attached. If an option is selected, the Web page will go to the specified URL for that option without a button being pressed.

- **Image Field:** Used for creating image buttons.

- **File Field:** Adds a field with a button for browsing files on the local machine.

- **Button:** Creates a basic button.

- **Label:** Adds a Label tag with text.

- **Fieldset:** Adds a Fieldset tag. This is used for separating parts of a form.

Figure 6.9. Forms toolbar

Text

The Text toolbar, shown in Figure 6.10, contains buttons for controlling the appearance of HTML font and other text elements. In order, these are:

- **Font Tag Editor:** This opens a dialog box allowing you to change the font face, size, and color.

- **Bold:** Creates boldface text.

- **Italic:** Creates italicized text.

- **Strong:** Creates boldface text.

- **Emphasis:** Creates italicized text.

- **Paragraph:** Inserts a new paragraph.

- **Block Quote:** Creates a block quote.

- **Preformatted Text:** Overrides any font tags around the text and displays the text as is.

- **Heading 1, Heading 2, Heading 3:** Creates headers.

- **Unordered List, Ordered List:** Creates lists. Unordered lists are bulleted; ordered lists are numbered.

Figure 6.10. Text toolbar

HTML

The HTML toolbar, shown in Figure 6.11, contains some common HTML tags. In order, these are:

- **Horizontal Rule:** This adds a horizontal line across the page.

- **Head Tag:** Contains a number of common tags that can be put in the HEAD section of the HTML page.

- **Tables:** Contains a submenu with tags used in tables.

- **Frames:** Contains a submenu with tags used to create framesets.

- **Script:** Contains a submenu with a script, noscript, and server side include (SSI) tag.

Figure 6.11. HTML toolbar

Application

The Application toolbar, shown in Figure 6.12, contains elements used for connecting to databases and interacting with data. Creating applications in Dreamweaver is covered in more detail in Chapter 24. In order, these buttons are:

- **Recordset:** After setting up your site and server, use this to connect to your database.

- **Stored Procedure:** Access a stored procedure.

- **Dynamic Data:** Use these to populate common form elements with data from a database.

- **Repeated Region:** Define a region in your page to contain database data. These can be used in multiple places in your pages.

- **Show Region:** You can specify which records to show based on specific criteria.

- **Recordset Paging:** These options allow you to create pages that navigate a range of records.

- **Go To Detail Page, Go To Related Page:** These can be used to create detailed record pages that can be selected from a list of records.

- **Display Record Count:** Displays the number of records returned after a query is executed.

- **Master Detail Page Set:** Allows you to create a master page to use for all record detail pages.

- **Insert Record:** Use this to insert a record into a database.

- **Update Record:** Allows you to update a record currently in a database.

Figure 6.12. Application toolbar

Flash Elements

This simple toolbar, shown in Figure 6.13, inserts a Flash element into the page.

Figure 6.13. Flash Elements toolbar

Favorites

The Favorites toolbar is a customizable blank toolbar where you can add the buttons for those objects you work with the most.

Properties

Each time you select an object in your page, both in Code and Design views, the Properties panel changes. The Properties panel contains all the attributes of the current object, and allows you to change them. Figure 6.14 shows the Properties panel when an image is selected.

This is a quick overview of the Properties panel. The Properties panel will be covered in detail when each object type is discussed during the course of the book.

Figure 6.14. The Properties panel

Just the facts

■ You have the option of working in Code view, Design view, or Split view.

■ The Dreamweaver interface contains a huge number of menu commands. Some are duplicated in the toolbar buttons, some are not.

■ The toolbars contain HTML, media, and database tag buttons that allow for easy insertion of code.

■ The Properties panel allows you to easily change the attributes of objects in your page.

GET THE SCOOP ON...
What a site is ▪ Creating your site ▪ Modifying your site ▪
Linking to a remote site ▪ Keeping track of your files

Setting Up Your Site

Chapter **7**

By now the Macromedia Dreamweaver interface should be starting to feel a little more familiar. You are getting comfortable with the idea of building your Web site using Dreamweaver. Now you just need to know what tools are available in Dreamweaver to help you manage an entire site.

Dreamweaver's basic structure is called a site. In Dreamweaver, when you set up a site, you can give it a name, create a file directory structure on your local machine, and create a mirrored version of the site on your remote Web server. With Dreamweaver, you can also lock the remote copies of your files, allowing multiple developers to work on a single site without fear of overwriting each other's work. Dreamweaver can also keep your local copy of your site synchronized with your remote version.

All about sites

You probably think of a site as a collection of Web pages, images, and interconnected links and code. That's partly accurate for our purposes. When we talk about a site in Dreamweaver, we really mean that collection of Web pages, images, and interconnected links and code, but located on a Web server. This is a significant detail. Every reference made to sites in Dreamweaver assumes that your files ultimately reside on a server. This makes sense, of course. Why build a Web site if you don't intend to make it visible via a Web server at some point?

Dreamweaver's site-building strategy centers around local files on your machine and remote files somewhere else on a Web server. Every site you build on Dreamweaver can have two sets of files: the ones you work on, and the ones you publish. You never work directly on files being served on the Web. This is quite a good practice. Doing this ensures that you never accidentally erase a file you have no copy of.

Having local and remote files also makes it simpler for more than one person to work on a site at the same time. You each check out the file you want to work on and check it in when you are done.

Before you begin creating your site, you should make some decisions about it. Here are a few important things to consider.

Can you sketch your site flow?

If the answer to this is no, then you need to do some planning. Before you can build your site, you need to have a clear picture of how all the pages of the site work together. Figure 7.1 shows two proposed simple site flow drawings of a site I have created for this book.

CompleatTraveler.com

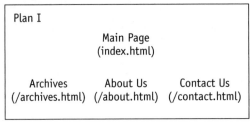

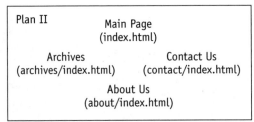

Figure 7.1. CompleatTraveler.com site flow plans

CompleatTraveler.com is going to be an online travel journal belonging to a fictional couple. In this example, there are two possible options. The top one places all the site pages in the same directory. The bottom

Watch Out!

When you use FTP or Dreamweaver's built-in FTP to move your files to the live server, the more files you have, the slower the response time. When you have very large numbers of files, FTP operations can get really slow.

one puts each subpage in its own subdirectory. Each plan has some good points. For a small site, putting all your files in the main directory might make sense. Creating links is easier; you don't need to specify a subdirectory. Creating your navigation is a little easier; you don't ever have to navigate into subpages. But putting all your pages in a single directory is a bit like putting all your paperwork in the same file folder. When you start getting more paperwork, it gets more difficult to manage.

When I build sites, I generally stick with Plan II. I prefer my subpages to go in their own subfolders.

Where will you store media?

Obviously you can just drop your GIFs and JPGs in the same directory as your HTML files. That will work, and it's easy enough. But I recommend creating a separate folder to hold all your images. You can name it something obvious that you won't forget, like "images." By putting your images in a separate folder, you are giving yourself a better-organized site.

Be aware, though, that if you are building a very large site with lots of images, having a single image folder might not make sense. As mentioned before, too many files in a single directory can cause FTP programs to behave sluggishly.

What features will be in your site?

Hopefully you know what all your site pages and features will be before you begin. If not, figure it out. Also, think about the future. Your site may end up growing. Do you have a plan for when things are added? If you have dropped all your files in one big directory, adding new files can cause problems. What if you have accidentally named a new file with the

Inside Scoop

Putting all your images in a single directory keeps you from inadvertently using the same name for an image twice. This saves you confusion should you ever need to find the image.

Hack

Modifying a Web server to correctly serve Flash movies (SWF files) is relatively simple on the most common servers, Apache and IIS. You can easily find documentation on the Web to fix the problem or to send to your site administrator.

same name as an old one? And if you need to dig up files to add navigation to your new pages, locating them in the midst of all those other files can be a challenge.

Where will you host the site?

I've mentioned some technologies that Dreamweaver supports in previous chapters. When deciding where you will host the site, you need to know beforehand what technologies you will use and what technologies the particular Web host has available.

For CompleatTraveler.com, I've decided that I need MySql and PHP. I will be using Macromedia Flash on the site, so the Web server I will be using must be configured to do so. Most Web servers are configured for Macromedia Flash, but occasionally you may run across one that isn't.

I want to make sure that the hosting service offers me several e-mail addresses for the site. I also want enough storage space. I always make sure I have much more than I need.

For CompleatTraveler.com, I opened an account with Aplus.Net. I didn't know anything about them, but I asked several friends for recommendations and compared the features and the price. Aplus seemed like the best choice for me.

Creating your site

You've answered some basic but important questions. Now it's time to create your site so you can begin building it! I will walk you through the creation of CompleatTraveler.com so you can see how to create your own site.

Watch Out!

When looking for a hosting service, be skeptical of "Top Ten Best Web Hosts" lists. Most of these sites are just advertisements in disguise, no matter how objective they may seem. Your best bet is to look for an unbiased source of information.

You will first need to open the Site Definition dialog box, shown in Figure 7.2.

There are two ways to open this dialog box. You can choose the menu command Site ⇨ New Site, or you can click the Dreamweaver Site link that appears on the Start Page when no files are open. The Site Definition dialog box has two tabs. Opening with the menu option shows the Advanced tab, and the Start Page link with the Basic tab. Obviously you can switch between them. For our purposes click the Advanced tab, as shown in Figure 7.2. Notice that the Category field on the left is Local Info. If you have something else selected, change it. The following is a description of all the fields of the Local Info category and how they should be filled out.

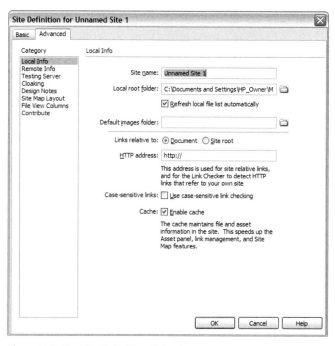

Figure 7.2. The Site Definition dialog box

- **Site name:** This is a name for your own reference, to help you differentiate among multiple sites. It does not appear anywhere on the actual Web site. I name mine CompleatTraveler.

- **Local root folder:** This is the location of your files on your computer. This has no bearing on the location of the files on the Web server.

Select a folder where you wish to store your working files. To simplify file paths for the examples in this book, I am using C:\CompleatTraveler\. I generally leave the Refresh check box checked. This keeps my Files panel list up to date. If your machine seems to be slowing down, unchecking this may improve performance. Keep in mind that the Files panel view you get may not be accurate. You may have to refresh the view by clicking the Refresh button.

- **Default images folder:** When you add an image to your Web page, if that image is in some folder on your machine outside of the root folder, the image is copied to the folder specified in this text box. It can save you time, but if you are just trying out images and unsure which you want, it can lead to many unnecessary copies of images. For my site, I leave it blank.

- **Links relative to Document or Site root:** Generally this should be set to Document.

- **HTTP address:** Enter the URL of your Web site here. When your site is being validated, this allows Dreamweaver to check any URLs in your site that use relative links for accuracy. I enter http://compleattraveler.com.

- **Case-sensitive links:** If you are using a UNIX-based Web server, you will probably check this box. Most Web servers are not case sensitive. Check with your site administrator to determine this. For my site, I leave it unchecked.

- **Cache:** I leave this checked. Having a cache speeds up a number of site operations in Dreamweaver and needs to be checked for the Assets panel to function.

After you have finished filling everything out, click OK. The local part of your new site has been created. Figure 7.3 shows the newly created CompleatTraveler in the Files panel. If you don't see the Files panel, choose Window ⇨ Files to open it. If it is checked, it should be visible.

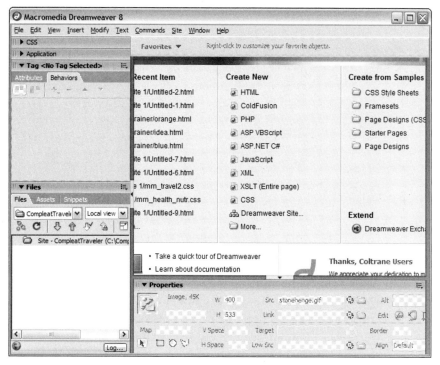

Figure 7.3. Files panel with site

Modifying your site

Now that you have created your site, I'll show you how to edit it and set up some additional information for it. To access all of the topics in this section, you use the Advanced tab of the Site Definition dialog box, shown in Figure 7.2. Open it now by choosing Site ⇨ Manage Sites. A list of sites you have created appears in the Manage Sites dialog box, shown in Figure 7.4.

From this dialog box you can create new sites and edit current ones. You can also duplicate sites. This copies the entire site and all settings to a new location and name that you specify. You can remove sites, and export and import sites to and from Dreamweaver on another computer.

Figure 7.4. The Manage Sites dialog box

Editing your site

To edit the site, select it on the left side of the Manage Sites dialog box. Click the Edit button on the right. The Site Definition dialog box opens with all the information we previously entered visible. While we are here, we can set more information about our site.

Design Notes

Using the Advanced tab of the Site Definition dialog box, click Design Notes. Design Notes are text files associated with particular Web pages you create. You can use Design Notes to keep information about a page, such as things that you need to do to it, or documentation for a script in the page. The Design Notes settings are as follows:

- **Maintain Design Notes:** If this is checked, you are able to add Design Notes for each file you create.
- **Clean Up:** This button looks for "orphaned" Design Notes. Perhaps you have deleted a page on your site, but the Design Note for it still exists. Clicking this button removes extraneous notes.
- **Upload Design Notes for sharing:** If this is checked, your Design Notes are uploaded when you upload your files to a remote server. They will not be viewable on the Web. This allows you to share information with other developers working on your site with you.

Site Map Layout

Dreamweaver creates a Site Map for you based on the pages in your site. The Site Map Layout, shown in Figure 7.5, contains settings for it.

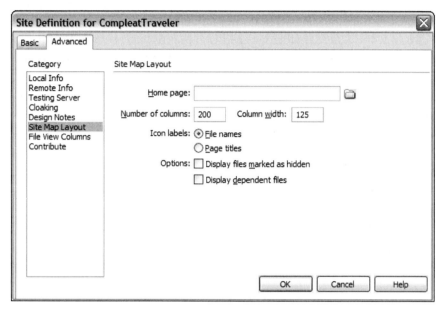

Figure 7.5. Site Map settings

I haven't created any pages in my site yet, but I can fill out these settings.

- **Home page:** This is the landing page of your Web site. For CompleatTraveler, I enter index.html. I haven't created a home page yet. When I finish filling out the Site Map settings I am asked if I want to create index.html. At that point, I click OK and it is created for me.

- **Number of columns, Column width:** These define the Site Map Layout. For now, I use the default settings; I can always change these later.

- **Icon labels:** You can either display the filename or the page title of each page on your site. I prefer the filenames for now, but I can come back when I've created all my pages and change it. Using page titles can work well if your titles are descriptive enough.

- **Options:** You can choose to include "hidden" files, typically support files such as JS or CSS files, or any files you choose to hide. You can also show file dependencies in your site map; for example, index.html using main_page.css. For now I leave this unchecked.

When you are finished, click File View Columns under the left Category menu. You may get the warning that index.html does not exist and be asked if you wish to create it. Click OK.

To view the Site Map, locate the Files panel. There are two drop-down lists on the top of the panel. The one on the left lists your sites, the one on the right lists the various views. Click the right-hand drop-down list and choose Map view. At this point, you should only see one file, index.html. This gets more interesting as we add more files. The Files panel is discussed in more detail in Chapter 9.

File View Columns

This page, shown in Figure 7.6, controls the way the Files panel displays the files in your site.

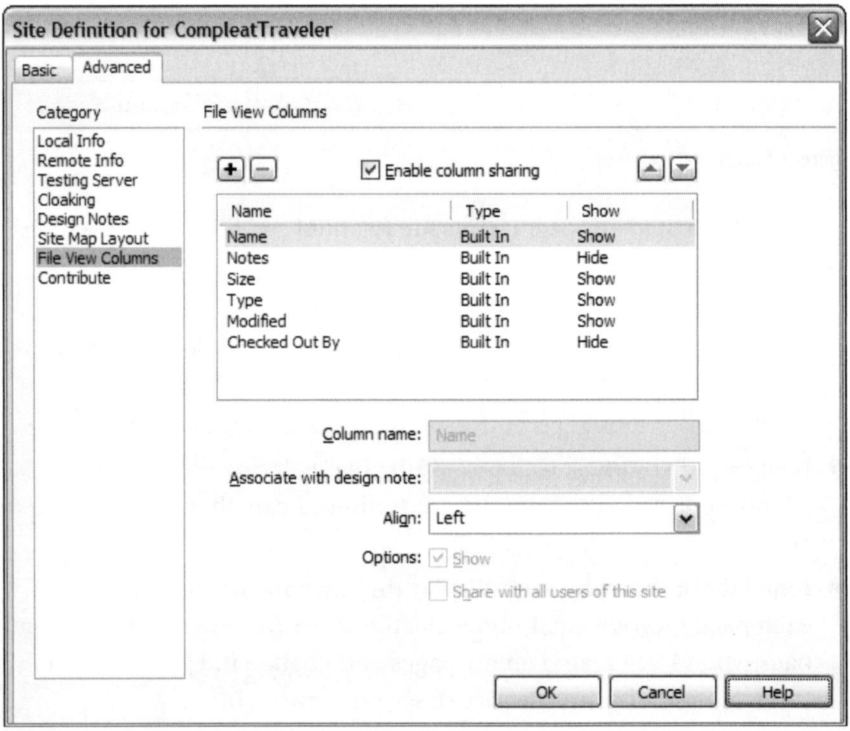

Figure 7.6. File View Columns settings

The Files panel is discussed at greater length in Chapter 9. For now, you can see what columns you can display in the panel. Notice that you can create columns of your own, associated with particular design notes.

Contribute

Click the Contribute category on the left of the Site Definition dialog box. This page activates Dreamweaver features that work with another Macromedia product, Contribute. Unless you have the Contribute software, you should leave this box unchecked.

Using a remote server

We have set up our site on the local server, now we need to set up the copy of the site that will be live on the Web. I use my Web hosting service's FTP settings to set this up for CompleatTraveler.com.

Setting up Remote Info

To set up our remote server, you will use the Advanced tab of the Site Definition dialog box, shown in Figure 7.2. Open it now by choosing Site ⇨ Manage Sites. Select your site from the dialog box and click the Edit button. The Site Definition dialog box should be getting familiar to you now. Click the Remote Info category on the left side. You see a single drop-down option. This page changes as you change this setting. The settings are:

- **None:** Select this if you do not have a remote server.
- **Local/Network:** You may be running a Web server from your current machine, or somewhere on your network.
- **FTP:** If you are uploading files to a remote server, select this. For my purposes, I choose FTP. This is the most common access method. The page now looks like Figure 7.7.
- **RDS:** If you are using ColdFusion, select this for your remote server.
- **Microsoft Visual SourceSafe:** Obviously, if you use Visual SourceSafe, select this.
- **WebDAV:** IIS and Apache servers with appropriate modules can use this.

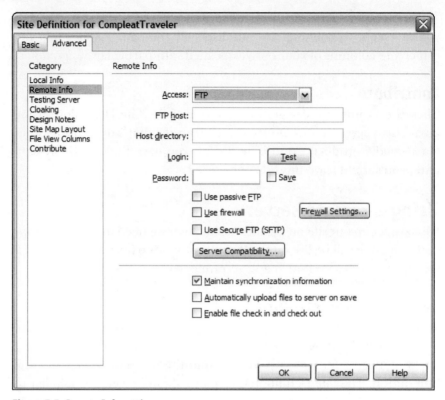

Figure 7.7. Remote Info settings

- **FTP host:** This is the FTP server on your Web host. Usually it is named with your domain name, something like ftp.yourdomainname.com. Check with your site administrator if you are not certain.

- **Host directory:** This is the directory on your FTP site where any Web pages you upload are viewable on your site. Some commonly used names for this directory include html, www, or public_html. You may not have a host directory at all. If you want to leave this blank, you will have a chance to view what directories are on your FTP server so you can choose the right one. Again, if you aren't sure what it is, contact your Web host.

- **Login, Password:** You should have been provided with a login name and password to use to connect to the FTP site. Enter them here.

- **Test button:** Click this button to test your connection. On Windows XP, you may get the message box shown in Figure 7.8. Click Unblock to allow Dreamweaver to communicate with your FTP server. You

Inside Scoop

If you are the only user on your computer and it is located in a safe place, you may choose to save your password. If you don't save it, you need to re-type it each time you connect to your FTP site.

should now see a message telling you whether or not your FTP connection is working. If it isn't, you may have the wrong server, or you may have mistyped your user login or password. If it still doesn't work, you may have to change the firewall settings; check with your site administrator.

Figure 7.8. Windows Security Alert

- **Save check box:** Uncheck this box if you don't want your password saved.
- **Use passive FTP:** If your firewall requires passive FTP, check this box.
- **Use firewall:** If your local machine is behind a firewall, check this box.
- **Firewall Settings button:** Click this button if your local machine is behind a firewall. This opens the Preferences dialog box, with the Site category selected. See Chapter 5 for more information.
- **Use Secure FTP (SFTP):** If your Web host uses SFTP, check this box.
- **Server Compatibility button:** This opens a small box with two options to try if you are having trouble transferring files.

Watch Out!

Not all FTP servers are created equal. Some FTP servers are not able to use performance optimization. If the Use FTP performance optimization box is checked, you may be unable to connect.

- **Maintain synchronization information:** If this is checked, Dreamweaver keeps track of what files need to be synchronized at all times, rather than having to check when you choose to synchronize. For more information on synchronizing your site, look at Chapter 9, the Files panel.

- **Automatically upload files to server on save:** Generally I don't check this option. Often I am experimenting when I save files, and not ready for them to be put on the live server.

- **Enable file check in and check out:** Check this option if you intend to use Dreamweaver's file check in/out system. This is especially good for sites with multiple developers.

Testing Server

If you intend to use live data or any Web server-based programming languages, for example, PHP, you probably want to set up a Testing Server. This is a server that is not publicly accessible on the Web, either because it is password protected or exists behind a firewall or on your local machine. You can use the Testing Server settings to tell Dreamweaver where it is. This allows Dreamweaver to let you preview your dynamic content while you are developing it.

To access the Testing Server settings, click the Advanced tab of the Site Definition dialog box and choose Testing Server from the Category list.

Cloaking

You can cloak files on your site. This keeps them from being uploaded to your Web server with the rest of your site. Perhaps you want to store your .png image files or your .fla Flash files somewhere in your site, but don't want them uploaded. Cloaking lets you specify which file types not to upload when synchronizing your site.

To specify which files you want cloaked, click the Cloaking category of the Site Definition dialog box. Use the check boxes to enable cloaking, and the text box to list which file types to cloak. You can also cloak entire folders and specific files using the Files panel. This is discussed in more detail in Chapter 9.

Checking files in and out

There are two ways to check files in and out. One way uses the Files panel and is discussed in Chapter 9. The other way uses the files you currently have open in Dreamweaver and uses the Site menu.

To activate file checking in and out, make sure the Enable file check in and check out check box is selected on the Site Definition dialog box (under the Remote Info category). Dreamweaver makes checking files in and out incredibly easy for you. When you check the Enable box, you will see text boxes in which to enter your name and e-mail address. These are used to keep track of who is checking out which files.

Before you can check files in or out, you need them to exist on your remote server. Begin by creating a page on your local site. To do this, make sure your current site is selected in your Files panel. Then just choose File ⇨ New to create a page. When you are ready, simply save it. It appears in your Files panel under the current site.

Once you have some files on your local site, you need to transfer copies to your remote site. Assuming you are connecting appropriately, select the file or files you want on your remote server and choose Site ⇨ Put. Copies of your files are placed on your server.

Putting and Getting files

The check in/out system exists on top of the Putting and Getting of files.

As you work with files on your local machine, the remote server does not automatically receive the changes to them. When you are ready for the file you are working on to be sent to the remote server, choose Site ⇨ Put. When you want to get the most recent version of a file that exists on the remote server, choose Site ⇨ Get. The file that is currently open in Dreamweaver is replaced with the version that exists on the Web server.

Watch Out!

Checking files out exists to keep track of who is working on the current file, not to monitor changes to it. To actually change a file, you should check it out, make your changes, use the Put command, and check it back in again. Conversely, you should use the Get command to get the most recent version of the file after you check it out.

Inside Scoop

If you want the remote server to automatically get the new versions of local files each time you save them, open the Site Definition dialog box, choose Remote Info, and check the Automatically upload files to server on save check box.

Check out

On your Files panel, you should see the files you have created and put on your remote server. Files should have either a check mark or a padlock icon next to them. If they have a padlock, that means they are currently checked in. To check out a file, begin by opening the file. You are opening the local copy of the file, and it is not yet checked out. Now choose Site ⇨ Check Out. The file you currently have open is now checked out to you. Figure 7.9 shows a file named about.html checked out. Notice the check sign next to it in the Files panel.

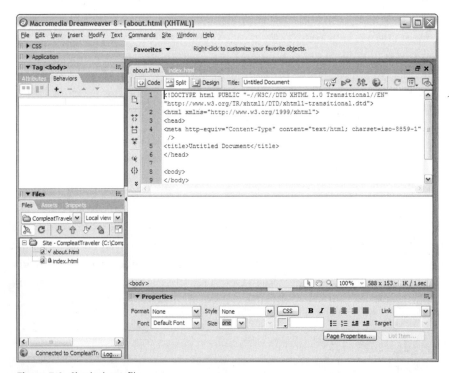

Figure 7.9. Checked-out file

Check in

To check the file back in, simply choose Site ⇨ Check In. If you have made changes to the file, make sure you use the Put command to put the changed file on the live server.

Just the facts

- Plan out your site to help you figure out a file structure.

- Decide what features you need for your site to pick the appropriate Web hosting setup.

- Find out what settings and information you need to connect you to your remote Web host, including the site directory for the Web server.

- Use Put and Get to move your files to and from your remote Web host.

- Checking files in and out keeps track of who has last worked on what files.

Chapter 8

Understanding Properties, CSS, and Application Panels

The Macromedia Dreamweaver interface is made up of editing panes and panels. Lots of panels. And each panel has options. Lots of options. The Properties panel is by far the single most useful panel in the Dreamweaver program. Each time you select an HTML object in design or code view, the Properties panel contents change to reflect the choice.

Two other panels are also extremely useful, the CSS panel and the Application panel. The CSS panel is also one of the most crucial. Not only can you view all the currently set styles in your page, you can easily modify them with this panel. Creating CSS styles becomes extremely simple. You don't need to laboriously seek out the rule that is being applied to a specific element in your page: You can simply select it, and Dreamweaver's CSS panel will display the rule for you. The Application panel allows you easy access to dialog boxes that connect you to your databases. It also allows you to view database tables and assists you in connecting to your data.

Properties panel

The Properties panel is the panel on the bottom of the Dreamweaver interface, just underneath the Code and Design view windows. Dreamweaver refers to this panel as the Property Inspector, and it is used to modify the properties of the currently selected object in the file open in your Dreamweaver workspace. In this section, I'll discuss the Properties panel for a number of the more common HTML elements.

Page

The Page Properties dialog box is shown in Figure 8.1.

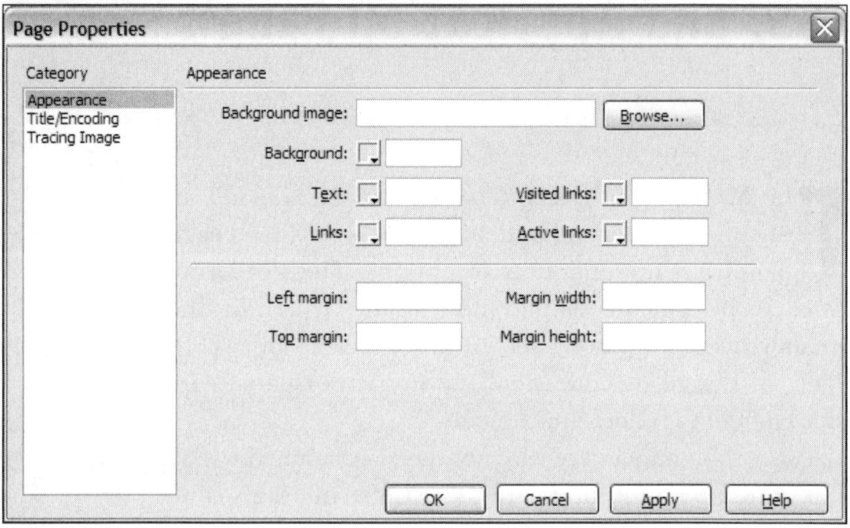

Figure 8.1. The Page Properties dialog box

Most of the properties are accessible in the Properties panel when you select the HTML tag or click the object in the Design view. The page properties are more difficult to get to. Instead of opening in the Properties panel, page properties open in a separate dialog box. There are two ways to open the page properties. You must have a page open for editing. You can choose Modify ⇨ Page to open the Page Properties dialog box, or you can press the Page Properties button on the Properties panel. You can see this button in Figure 8.2.

Once you have opened the Page Properties dialog box, you can set certain properties for the entire page. Here are the options when you have the Appearance category selected from the menu on the left.

- **Background image:** No doubt you have seen Web pages with background images. They used to be everywhere, but now they are not used very often, possibly because people noticed that they made text rather difficult to read. If for some reason you want one, you can select it here.

- **Background:** Set the background color of the page here. You can enter a hex value directly or you can click the color chooser and Dreamweaver fills in the hex value for you.

- **Text:** This sets the text color on the page. If this is not set, text will be black.

- **Links:** This sets the color of text links. If this is not set, they will be blue.

- **Visited links:** This sets the color of visited links. If this is not set, they will be purple.

- **Active links:** This sets the color of links when they are being clicked. If this is not set, they will be red.

- **Left margin:** This is how many pixels your page content will be away from the left side of the browser window. This tag only works on IE.

- **Top margin:** This is how many pixels your page content will be away from the top of the browser window. This tag only works on IE.

- **Margin width:** This is how many pixels your page content will be away from both sides of the browser window. This tag only works on Netscape.

- **Margin height:** This is how many pixels your page content will be away from the top and bottom of the browser window. This tag only works on Netscape.

There are more options on the Page Properties dialog box under the Title/Encoding category.

- **Title:** This is where you can enter the page title. You can also enter it in the Title Properties panel that appears when you select the `<TITLE>` tag in the Code view.

- **Document Type (DTD):** Use this to select the document type definition.

Hack

To actually preview your margins, you have to click the Preview in Browser button. Dreamweaver does not allow you to preview the margins in the Design view.

Inside Scoop

The tracing image can be a mock of the Web page created in Photoshop. Using the image, you can create a Web page that looks identical to the image, but is more functional than a large image on a Web page would be, as well as providing a faster download.

- **Encoding:** This controls which character encoding is used in your page. This is useful if you are using an alphabet with special characters.

- **Unicode Normalization Form:** This box lets you select a form for UTF-8.

- **Include Unicode Signature (BOM):** This lets you include a Byte Order Mark (BOM) in the document, required for UTF-16 and UTF-32.

There are more options on the Page Properties dialog box under the Tracing Image category.

- **Tracing Image:** You can select an image to be used to help you lay out your page. This image appears as a background and you can lay out tables, layers, images, and content over it. This image does not appear on the final page; it only appears in the Dreamweaver editing environment.

- **Transparency:** You can make the tracing image more muted to help you see the content you are placing over it more clearly.

Title

The Title Properties panel has only a text field in it for you to enter the title of your page. Click the <TITLE> tag in the Code view to make this panel appear.

Text

The Text Properties panel is shown in Figure 8.2.

Figure 8.2. Text Properties panel

Click any non-HTML text in between the <BODY> tags in the Code view to make this panel appear. The options you can set are:

- **Format:** Select a standard HTML heading or paragraph format to apply to your text.

- **Style:** Any named CSS styles available in this page or an associated CSS file appear here. You can select one to apply it to the text.

- **CSS:** This button populates the CSS panel with editable information about the current style. See the section "CSS panel" later in this chapter for more information.

- **Bold, Italic:** Make your text bold or italicized with these buttons.

- **Align Left, Center, Right, and Justify:** Use these buttons to adjust the centering and justification of your text.

- **Link:** Turn the selected text into a link to this URL.

- **Font:** Set the font.

- **Size:** Set the size of your font.

- **Color:** Set the color of your text here. You can type in the hex value or use the color chooser to pick a color and Dreamweaver adds the hex value for you.

- **Bulleted, Numbered List:** Use these buttons to create a bulleted or numbered list. You can also select lines of text to convert them to a list.

- **Indent, Un-indent:** Use these buttons to indent or un-indent selected text.

- **Target:** If you have defined a link, this button lets you choose the target window for that URL.

- **Page Properties:** This button opens the Page Properties dialog box, discussed in the previous section.

Image

The Image Properties panel is shown in Figure 8.3.

Figure 8.3. Image Properties panel

After you insert an image or image placeholder, you can click anywhere in the <IMG> tag to display the Image Properties panel. The options you can set with this panel are:

- **Image Name:** This is the text box under the image file size with no label. Put a name here if you need to reference the image with code; for example, to use it in a JavaScript rollover.

- **W and H:** These stand for the pixel width and height of the image. These should be automatically filled out for you when you insert the image. If not, click the blue arrow next to them and Dreamweaver inserts them.

- **Src:** This is the path to the image.

- **Link:** If your image is a link to another page, enter the URL here.

- **Alt:** Enter a short description of the image here for users to see when they mouse over the image and for accessible browsers.

- **Class:** Any named CSS classes available in this page or an associated CSS file appear here. You can select one to apply it to the image.

- **Edit:** There is a series of buttons to allow you to perform various image editing tasks. With these buttons you can open your image in Fireworks for editing, optimize your image in Fireworks, crop, resample, change brightness and contrast, and sharpen. If you are

---

Watch Out!

In general, you should not change the width and height values. If your image is too large, you should instead resize the image in an image editing program. Resizing the image in the HTML leads to lower-quality images, and the file size is no smaller. Resizing with an image editor maintains the quality and reduces the file size.

using an image placeholder instead of an image, the Edit button does not appear. Instead, you will see a Create button.

- **Map:** Enter a name for an image map in the text box, and then use the three buttons underneath to draw sections on your image. After you draw a shape for mapping, click the arrow to the left of the shapes, then click the map shape. The Properties panel changes to let you enter a URL and target window for the mapped shape. To return to the image properties, simply click an unmapped portion of the image in Design view, or anywhere in the <IMG> tag in Code view.

- **V Space, H Space:** These add the designated number of pixels of space around your image.

- **Border:** If you want a border around your image, you can specify the thickness of it in pixels here. If you have added a link to your image, you should set this value to 0 if you don't wish to have a border around it.

- **Align:** This drop-down menu contains a number of alignment options for your image.

Table

The Table Properties panel is shown in Figure 8.4.

Figure 8.4. Table Properties panel

After you insert a table, click the <TABLE> tag to display the Table Properties panel. You can click a TD or TR in the table to open a different Properties panel with properties that apply just to that particular TD or TR. First I will mention the table properties, shown in Figure 8.4, and then the TD and TR properties.

Inside Scoop

These values can be expressed in pixels or in a percentage of the page width and height if you wish your table to stretch.

- **Table Id:** Put a name here if you need to reference the table with code.

- **Rows, Cols:** These are the number of rows and columns in the table.

- **W, H:** Define the width and height of the table here, if necessary. If the actual content in the table is wider or taller than the values here, they are ignored.

- **CellPad:** This is the number of pixels of padding in each table cell.

- **CellSpace:** This is the number of pixels between each cell.

- **Align:** This drop-down menu contains a number of alignment options for your table.

- **Border:** This is the border size of your table. If you don't want your table to have a border, set this to 0.

- **Class:** Any named CSS classes available in this page or an associated CSS file appear here. You can select one to apply it to the table or create one.

The bottom half of the panel has a series of buttons for use in adjusting the width and height of your table.

- **Bg color:** Set the background color of your table here. You can type in the hex value or use the color chooser to pick a color and Dreamweaver adds the hex value for you.

- **Bg Image:** If you wish to use an image as a background for your table, enter the path and name of the image here.

- **Brdr color:** If your table borders aren't set to 0, you can customize the border color in this box.

Most of the TD and TR properties are the same as those found in the Text Properties panel. I will mention a few specific to table elements here. Access the Properties panel for these by clicking the HTML tags for them in Code view.

- **Horz, Vert:** These control how TD or TR content is aligned within the cells.

- **W, H:** The width and height of the cell is set here.

- **No wrap:** Check this if you don't want the content in your cell to wrap to the next line, making your cell taller.

- **Bg Image, Bg Color, and Brdr:** Just like the table, an individual cell or row can also have a background image, colored background, or border.

Script

The Script Properties panel is shown in Figure 8.5.

Figure 8.5. Script Properties panel

You can click the <SCRIPT> tag to display the Script Properties panel. The options you can set with this panel are:

- **Language:** This drop-down box lets you choose a variety of JavaScript versions, as well as VBScript for the script language.
- **Type:** Use this to indicate whether the script is client or server side.
- **Source:** If you wish to use a script in another file, you can put the path here; for example, if your JavaScript functions are in a .js file.
- **Edit:** Clicking this button opens an editor window where you can enter the code to go between the <SCRIPT> tags in your page.

Div

After you insert a div, you can click the <DIV> tag to display the Div Properties panel. This panel has few options.

- **Div ID:** Put a name here if you need to reference the div with code.
- **Class:** Any named CSS classes available in this page or an associated CSS file appear here. You can select one to apply it to the div or add one.

Inside Scoop

I don't recommend clicking the Edit button on this Properties panel to open the Script Editing dialog box. This dialog box does not highlight syntax as the Code view does.

Layer

The Layer Properties panel is shown in Figure 8.6.

Figure 8.6. Layer Properties panel

A layer is a specific kind of <DIV> tag. To create a layer choose Insert ⇨ Layout Objects ⇨ Layer. You can click the <DIV> tag that is defining the layer to display the Layer Properties panel. Here are the settings:

- **Layer ID:** If you intend to use code to manipulate this layer, this is where you can give it a name to reference in your code.

- **L, T:** This stands for left and top and defines where the upper left corner should be on the page.

- **W, H:** This is the width and height of the layer.

- **Z-Index:** You can place a layer over other content on the page, or over other layers. The Z-Index is used to determine the stacking order of layers.

- **Vis:** You can hide layers and use code to make them visible when some user event occurs. Use this to specify if this layer is hidden or not.

- **Bg image:** Use this to locate a graphic to use as the background image of the layer.

- **Bg color:** Set the color of your layer here.

- **Class:** Any named CSS classes available in this page or an associated CSS file appear here. You can select one to apply it to the layer div or add one.

- **Overflow:** Unlike a table, a layer won't automatically stretch if the content is too large for the specified height and width. This option specifies how the layer should handle content when it overflows the layer.

- **Clip:** The L, T, R, B stand for left, top, right, and bottom. These four values define a rectangle. If you set these, only the layer content inside that rectangle is visible on the page.

CSS panel

This section is more about the CSS panel operation than it is about CSS and Dreamweaver. I will give you an overview of the panel and explain its features. To get a better understanding of what CSS is and how Dreamweaver works with it, check out Chapter 18.

CSS Styles tab

Begin by locating the CSS panel. If it is not visible, chose Window ⇨ CSS Styles. Figure 8.7 shows the CSS panel with the CSS Styles tab selected and the All button clicked.

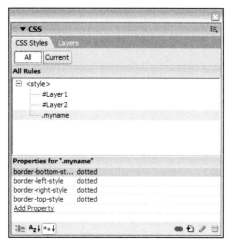

Figure 8.7. All button, CSS Styles tab

This shows you a list of all CSS elements you have defined in your page. You also see a list of elements from external .css files you have linked to your page.

The bottom half of the panel displays an editable list of properties for the currently selected element. It is here that you can easily edit any of the properties without having to track down the code and do it in the

Inside Scoop

Double-click an individual style in the upper pane to open the CSS Rule Definition dialog box. This dialog box gives you all related properties for the currently selected element. It's often faster than working with the bottom pane.

Design view. On the left is the property list, on the right are the corresponding values. Click either one to change it. You can even add new properties.

The Current button "zooms in" on the currently selected style to give you more information about it. Select an element in your page and click the Current button. Figure 8.8 shows the CSS panel with the CSS Styles tab selected and the Current button clicked.

There are three panes visible. The top one lists all the properties for the currently selected style. The middle pane has two buttons on the right side of it. These look like blue polygons. Click the first button to show information about the currently selected property. Basically, you see where the property definition is found. Click the second button to show a cascade of rules for the second tag. This means that all rules on the page that surround the current rule are displayed here, starting with the big ones like body definitions and ending with the current rule. The bottom pane is the same here as when the All button is clicked.

Figure 8.8. Current button, CSS Styles tab

Bottom buttons

With either Current or All, you should see a number of buttons along the bottom of this panel. These are used to change the way information in the bottom Properties pane is displayed.

- **Show category view:** This displays the CSS properties in a category view.

- **Show list view:** This lists all the properties alphabetically.

- **Show only set properties:** This shows only the properties currently set in the page.

- **Attach Style Sheet:** Clicking this opens a file browser for you to locate an external style sheet CSS file.

- **New CSS Rule:** This opens the CSS Rule Definition dialog box. If this is a new rule, nothing is set.

- **Edit Style:** This also opens the CSS Rule Definition dialog box. Information in it is pre-filled from current settings.

- **Delete CSS Rule:** The current rule is deleted.

CSS Styles tab menu

With the Styles tab selected, click the menu button on the upper right of the panel. As if all the previous options weren't enough, you see a list of even more options for working with the CSS Styles. These are:

- **Go to Code:** This is an easy way to go directly to the CSS code in the page where it lives.

- **New:** Just like the New CSS Rule button on the bottom of the panel, this opens the CSS Rule Definition dialog box.

- **Edit:** Just like the Edit Style button on the bottom of the panel, this opens the CSS Rule Definition dialog box.

- **Duplicate:** Use this to duplicate the current rule and its attributes.

- **Rename:** Use this to rename the rule.

- **Apply:** This option is always grayed out so it's not clear what it does.

- **Delete:** Deletes the current rule.

- **Use External Editor:** You can open an external editor for .css files. This is set up in the Preferences menu under File Types/Editors. See Chapter 5 for more information.

Watch Out!
I don't recommend renaming the panels, and I think that they are reasonably grouped by default. If you do rename or regroup them, they won't match the images and names in this book any longer, so be careful!

- **Attach Style Sheet:** Just like the Attach Style Sheet button at the bottom of the panel, this opens a dialog box to let you attach a style sheet to the current page.

- **Export:** This option lets you export your styles into a .css file.

- **Design-time:** You can have certain styles that appear during design-time, but not in the browser. More about this can be found in Chapter 18.

- **Help:** Opens Dreamweaver help for the current menu.

The rest of the menu items are concerned with organizing your workspace. You can move individual panels around, group them in different ways, and even rename them.

Layers tab

Figure 8.9 shows the CSS panel with the Layers tab selected.

This panel is much simpler than the CSS Styles panel. You are presented with a list of all layers on the page, along with their Z-indices. You can click to the left of a layer under the image of an eye to hide it in Design view. When the eye is closed, the layer is hidden. Click again to open the eye and view the layer. You can rename the layer by clicking its name. Finally, you can change the Z-index of the layer, altering the stacking order on the page.

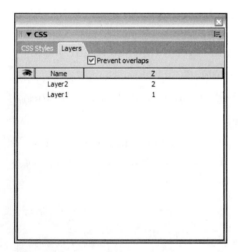

Figure 8.9. Layers tab

Bright Idea

When you are in the middle of creating SQL queries, leave this panel open with your current table fields visible. It will help you remember exactly what you named everything and help you avoid mistakes.

Application panel

As in the CSS panel section, this section is more about the Application panel operation than it is about creating database applications in Dreamweaver. To get details on creating applications in Dreamweaver and using this panel, check out Chapter 24.

The Application panel contains information about dynamic code and database connections on your site. Each panel has a plus (+) button for adding panel specific options, and a minus (-) button for removing them.

Databases

Begin by locating the Application panel. If it is not visible, choose Window ⇨ Databases. Figure 8.10 shows the Application panel with the Databases tab selected.

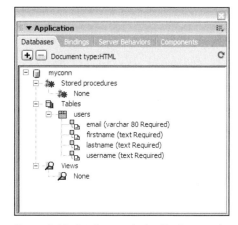

Figure 8.10. Databases tab, Application panel

This panel is used for viewing databases you have connected to. You can navigate into individual tables and view field definitions.

Bindings

Figure 8.11 shows the Application panel with the Bindings tab selected.

Figure 8.11. Bindings tab, Application panel

This panel is where you can see what connections, known as bindings, exist and edit them. The connection code is placed in your page for you. You can also insert dynamic data items using the Insert button on the bottom of the panel.

Server Behaviors

Figure 8.12 shows the Application panel with the Server Behaviors tab selected.

This panel has a huge menu of server behaviors you can add to a page, or edit once placed on a page. This is where you can create SQL queries and place the results on your page. You can also use this panel to create update pages, insert pages, and access control pages.

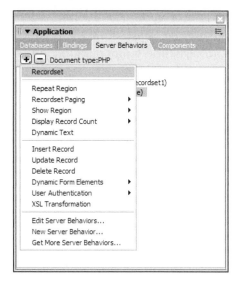

Figure 8.12. Server Behaviors tab, Application panel

Components

Figure 8.13 shows the Application panel with the Components tab selected.

Figure 8.13. Components tab, Application panel

This panel is primarily used for JSP Java Beans and ColdFusion components. To use it, your document type must be CFML or JSP. This panel lets you insert and edit code. Specific information about creating applications in Dreamweaver can be found in Chapter 24.

Just the facts

- Properties panels contain editable properties for HTML tags.
- Properties panels exist for most HTML tags. Select the tag in Code view to access the appropriate properties panel.
- Use the Dreamweaver CSS panel to find, add, edit, and delete CSS content.
- Use the Application panel to control, create, add, edit, and delete database bindings and dynamic code.

GET THE SCOOP ON...
Inspecting tags ▪ Using the Tag Chooser ▪ Files panel ▪
Results panel ▪ Other useful panels

Understanding Tag Inspector and Files Panels

Chapter 9

I n the last chapter I discussed the CSS, Application, and Property panels. I hope you aren't tired of panels, because Macromedia Dreamweaver has a few more you haven't seen yet. These include the Tag Inspector, Files, and Results panels.

These panels are an integral part of the Dreamweaver interface. The Tag Inspector panel lets you take a close look at the attributes assigned to your tags as well as attributes available but not assigned. The Files panel is crucial for keeping all your files organized both on local and remote sites. It also allows you to create, edit, and add code snippets and library items to your pages. The Results panel displays such useful information as browser check errors, search results, and syntax errors. And that's not all, there are the History, Frames, and Code Inspector panels. Take a deep breath and think to yourself, "I love panels!"

Tag Inspector panel

The Tag Inspector allows you to see tags in your page in a property sheet. This panel and the Properties panel share some common attributes. Both let you change the most common properties of the currently selected tag. But while the Properties panel has a smaller set of properties displayed, the interface to change them is more robust. With the Properties panel, if you want to change the path to an image, the file browser opens. With the Tag Inspector, you have to know the path and type or paste it in the right-hand column. You can open the Tag Inspector panel by choosing Window ⇨ Tag Inspector. The panel has two tabs, Attributes and Behaviors.

Attributes tab

The Attributes tab shown in Figure 9.1 is an example of the attributes you would see if you clicked on an <IMG> tag in your page.

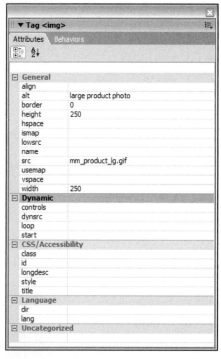

Figure 9.1. The Attributes tab of the Tag Inspector panel

Inside Scoop

Don't let the word attributes fool you. Attributes are the same thing as properties. For example, setting the width attribute to 200 in the Tag Inspector does exactly the same thing as setting the W text box in the Properties panel to 200.

As you might guess, to use the Tag Inspector, you need to select a tag to inspect. In Code view, simply click inside a tag to select that tag. If it is a tag that has an open and close tag, for example, the <TD> tag in a table, you have to be a bit more specific. Take a look at this code:

```
<td height="64" id="tagline" valign="top"
align="center">
<font face="Arial, Helvetica, sans-serif">
I love panels!
</font>
</td>
```

I've put each HTML tag on its own line so I can more easily explain how to choose a tag. If you click the text "I love panels!" the Tag Inspector shows the attributes for the <FONT> tag. To see the attributes for the <TD> tag, you would have to click anywhere before the <FONT> tag begins or after it ends.

In Design view, you click the visual representation of the tag, if you can. Some tags simply are not accessible from Design view. Your best bet is to use Split view to locate the tag you are after.

To set a value for a particular attribute, simply click the column to the right of the attribute you wish to change. Type in the value, and click somewhere else. Your code now reflects this change.

The panel has two buttons just under the word Attributes on the tab. The first is the category view button, and the next, the one with the A Z, and down arrow on it, displays a list view; that is, an alphabetically ordered list of all the attributes.

This panel actually has some hidden powers that make it quite useful. You can rename attributes by clicking the attribute name and editing it, or much more importantly, you can create new attributes. Creating new attributes is easy, and useful. If the code that Dreamweaver generates doesn't have a certain attribute you need for a tag, you can remedy that. To do this:

1. You have to have a tag selected. Pick a tag, any tag, in a currently opened page.

2. You can do this in either category or list view. If you are in list view, click in the left cell at the very bottom of the list right under the last attribute listed. If you are in category view, click under the word "Uncategorized."

3. Type the new attribute name on the left, and the value you want for it on the right.

Try it, and then take a look at the Design view of the tag you edited. In Figure 9.2, I show an attribute I have created, and just above it, the <IMG> tag in which it appears.

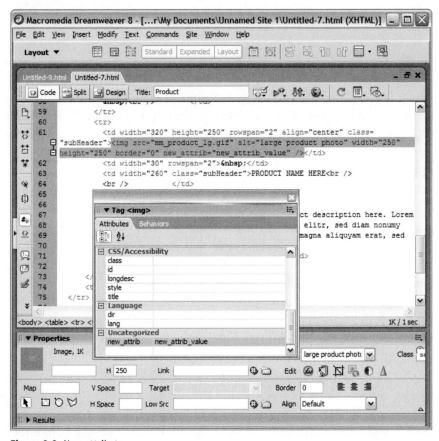

Figure 9.2. New attribute

The attribute you created is added to the currently selected tag in the format your_attribute_name = "your_attribute_value". Adding an attribute only changes the currently selected instance of the tag. For example, my edited attribute "new_attrib" only appears in the particular image tag I changed, not every image tag on the page.

Deleting an attribute you have created is easy, too. Simply select the attribute name and delete it. It is removed, along with any value you have assigned to it.

Watch Out!

If you decide to change an attribute name, make sure it's not an attribute you need. I don't change attribute names; I generally create new ones.

When you change the value of attributes, you may notice a lightning bolt symbol to the right. This is used to insert dynamic data for a value. For example, if you were storing the location of an image as a field in a database table, you could reference it here instead of actually having to know the height by number.

The last piece of the Attributes tab puzzle is the menu. This is located on the upper right of the panel. There are two options worth mentioning: the Edit Tag option and the Tag Library option.

Edit Tag opens the Tag Editor for the current tag. The Tag Editor is a dialog box with a robust set of options for the currently selected tag. You can also get to this dialog box at any time by right-clicking any object and choosing Edit Tag in either Code or Design view. As with the Attributes settings, changes made to this panel apply only to the currently selected tag.

Finally, there is the Tag Library Editor dialog box. In this incredibly full dialog box, you can add, edit, and delete tags and their attributes and import or export tag libraries. You are given complete control over what kind of data a tag accepts and whether to use uppercase or lowercase. Not only can you edit the specific tag, but all properties of that tag are also editable and listed under it.

Behaviors tab

The Behaviors tab of the Tag Inspector is used to examine behaviors attached to tags on your page. What are behaviors, you ask? Behaviors are specific JavaScript events and corresponding actions that Dreamweaver allows you to easily program through the Behaviors tab, shown in Figure 9.3.

Watch Out!

This section is all about Behaviors, not to be confused with Server Behaviors, which are in a completely different panel. Server Behaviors are server-side dynamic code bits. Behaviors, without the word "server," define bits of JavaScript code that operate on the client-side.

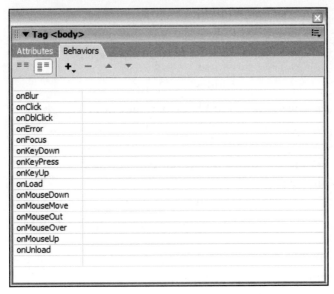

Figure 9.3. The Behaviors tab of the Tag Inspector panel

To open the Behaviors tab, choose Windows ⇨ Behaviors. You will see a list of events associated with the currently selected tag. Each event can have one or more actions associated with it. These events and actions are discussed in more detail in Chapter 22. For now, you should just become familiar with the panel and its operation.

Adding an action to a behavior is easy. You simply click the behavior you want to add an action to and then click the plus (+) button. The actions available in this menu and not grayed out are the ones that can be applied to the current tag.

You can also enter more than one action to the same behavior. Suppose you want to play a sound when the user clicks on an image on your page, and you also want to pop up a message box. You can use the OnMouseDown event for the sound action, and then add a new event by clicking under the last event in the list and using the drop-down to select OnMouseDown. Then you simply use the plus (+) button to add the message box action.

You can easily delete an action by selecting it and clicking the minus (-) button. Finally, you can add your own JavaScript to your events by choosing Call JavaScript and adding your own function name. Again, don't worry too much about the details of the code side of this panel, just become familiar with its operation. Jump ahead to Chapter 22 for more information on the events and actions.

Just like the Attributes tab, there are two buttons to change the view of the items in this panel. These are located to the left of the plus (+) button. The first shows set events and hides all the events except for those with actions defined. If you click this button with no actions set, your list will be empty. The second button shows all events, with blank boxes on the right if there are no actions yet defined.

Using the Tag Chooser

We're going to depart from panels for this section, but never fear, we'll return to them in the next. But it's time to discuss a very panel-like tool, the Tag Chooser.

The Tag Chooser is not your typical dialog box, because it can be left open while you use it repeatedly. It's also not quite a panel, since you can't dock it into the Dreamweaver interface. It also isn't listed under the Window menu. To open the Tag Chooser, you must first find a location in your Code or Design view where you intend to place a tag. Click there and choose Insert ➪ Tag to open the Tag Chooser, shown in Figure 9.4.

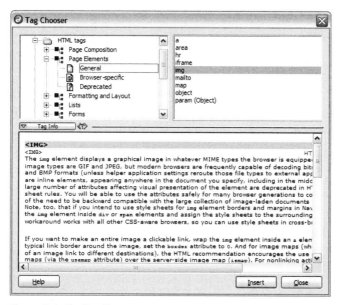

Figure 9.4. The Tag Chooser

On the left are folders that you can navigate by clicking the plus signs to expand them. Notice that not only does the Tag Chooser have HTML tags, it also has CFML, ASP.NET, JSP, Jrun, ASP, PHP, and WML tags. Whew! And some of these folders categorize the tags. As you expand the language folders on the left, the list of available tags shows up on the right. Click one, and reference material relating to that tag appears in the bottom pane. If you don't see the reference information, click the Tag Info button just above the Help button.

If you find a tag you want to insert in the list, highlight it and click Insert. If the tag has properties associated with it, such as an <IMG> tag, clicking Insert opens an actual dialog box, Edit Tag, which you've seen before. If the tag has no related properties and appears as a pair of tags, for example, <nobr></nobr>, it is immediately inserted.

The Tag Chooser is really useful if you think you know the right tag to use but aren't sure. You can locate it in the list and read the reference material about it. You'll learn everything you could possibly want to know about that tag, and more. And now, back to more panels!

Files panel

If I had to pick a favorite panel, I would choose the Files panel. With this panel, you can control your local and remote files, manage your assets, and insert any of a large number of predefined code snippets. We'll start with the Files tab.

Files tab

The Files tab always displays a list of the files contained in the current site you are working with. See Chapter 7 for more information on setting up your site. If you are not working in a site, you will see a list of files in the current directory. The Files tab of the Files panel is shown in Figure 9.5.

Inside Scoop

Don't be alarmed if some of your pages don't show up on the site map. The site map only shows links two levels deep.

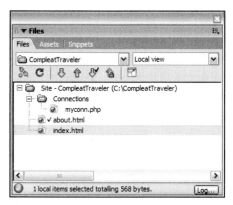

Figure 9.5. The Files tab of the Files panel

This panel has lots of bells and whistles. I'll begin with the drop-down boxes across the top. On the left is a drop-down menu containing a list of all your Dreamweaver sites, as well as a list of top-level folders and a file browser. Here is where you select the site or folder containing the files you wish to work with.

On the right is another drop-down menu. This is where you choose which version of your site you wish to see. Local view displays files on the machine you are currently using. In Chapter 7, I discussed creating a site on a remote server. If you wish to see the files on that server, choose Remote view. If you have set up a testing server and wish to see those files, choose Testing Server. Finally, to get a sense of how your pages connect, choose Site Map to see a visual representation of pages and links.

There are seven buttons across the top of the Files tab. Here's what they are:

- **Connect to remote host/Disconnect from remote host:** If you have a remote server defined, use this to toggle the connection to it.

- **Refresh:** If you add or delete files to your file system or site, sometimes the changes aren't reflected immediately. This refreshes the window and updates the file list.

- **Get File:** This sends a copy of the currently selected file to the remote server.

- **Put File:** This retrieves a copy of the currently selected file from the remote server.

- **Check Out:** This checks out the currently selected file.

- **Check In:** This checks in the currently selected file.

- **Expand to show local and remote sites:** This button opens the Files tab in a separate pane. It gives you a more complete view of the information to be found in the Files tab, but doesn't really offer anything new.

At the bottom of the Files tab is an icon on the left and a Log... button on the right. Clicking either one of these does the same thing; both open the Background File Activity dialog box. This contains a record of files recently uploaded, downloaded, checked in, or checked out as well as the time and date it occurred.

Assets tab

The Assets tab is to the right of the Files tab on the Files panel. Either click the tab or choose Window ⇨ Assets to open the panel, shown in Figure 9.6.

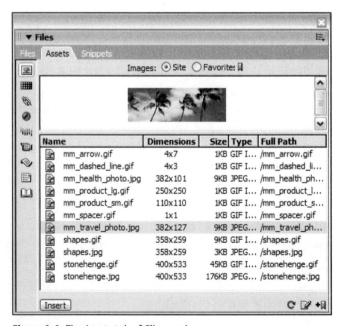

Figure 9.6. The Assets tab of File panel

The Assets panel allows you to easily view all the assets associated with your site in one place. Assets include images, Macromedia Flash movies, and Java applets. It also includes some nonasset listings of things such as colors and links used in your site. You have to have a page from the currently selected site open in Code or Design view.

Starting with the top of this panel, notice the radio buttons Site and Favorites. Select Site to see all of your assets. Select Favorites to see a list of assets you have chosen as your favorites. You create your own list, based on your favorite assets that you want to find quickly, by selecting an asset and clicking the button on the lower right, with a purple ribbon and plus (+) sign on it. Now the asset appears in both views.

On the left-hand side of the panel are the asset types. Clicking one of these displays assets of that particular type. Here are the types:

- **Images:** This lists all GIF, JPEG, and PNG files.

- **Colors:** These are not precisely assets, but rather a list of colors from CSS and HTML settings in your site. This includes colors such as text, link, and background colors used in your site.

- **URLs:** All the links used in your site appear here.

- **Flash:** This is a list of all Flash files used in your site.

- **Shockwave:** This lists all Macromedia Shockwave files in your site.

- **Movies:** This lists MPEG and QuickTime.

- **Scripts:** If you have created separate files containing JavaScript or VBScripts, those are listed here. You will not see scripts listed that are inside your HTML files.

- **Templates:** Templates you have used in your site appear here. See Chapter 10 for more information on templates.

- **Library:** The Library is a repository for assets that will be reused. Modifying a library item updates it on all pages where it is used. More information on the library follows.

Assets tab Library

I am giving the Library its own little section here because it is a bit more complex and important than the rest of the Assets tab buttons. This section gives you an overview of using the Library; Chapter 10 actually walks you through using it. When you create a Library, Dreamweaver creates a folder with references to your assets. Then, when you want to change an asset, you can alter it once, in the Library, and then everywhere it appears in the site is updated.

Inside Scoop

I recommend using Code view to select items. That way you know precisely what you are adding and won't end up with code you didn't mean to save.

When you use insert a library item into one of your pages, Dreamweaver references the version stored in the Library folder it created.

Here are the actions you can perform on the Library:

- **Add an item to the Library:** It's easy to add items to the Library. Simply select what you wish to add either in Code or Design view and drag it into the Library pane. You can also click the New Library Item button on the bottom right of the panel. It's the second one and has a plus (+) sign. You should then give the item a meaningful name.

- **Insert a Library item into a page:** This is very simple. Click at the location you wish to insert the item in your page, and then click the Insert button on the bottom of the panel. You can also drag the item to the page.

- **Edit a Library item:** Editing an item is simple, too. Locate it in the Library panel and either double-click it or click the Edit button on the lower right, the one with a pencil and paper icon. The code that makes up your Library item appears in a separate document. Make your changes and then save, just as you would any other document. You are then asked if you want to update it in the pages in which it is referenced, along with a list of those pages. If you do, you see the Update Pages dialog box, shown in Figure 9.7.

  To see the log of the library file updates, check the Show log box.

- **Delete a Library item:** Highlight the Library item you wish to delete, and click the garbage can button on the lower right of the panel.

Watch Out!

Deleting a library item does not delete it from the pages it is in on your site. It does remove your ability to edit it through the Library panel, and each instance of the code now stands on its own and has to be edited separately.

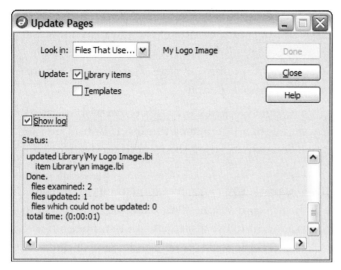

Figure 9.7. The Update Pages dialog box

Snippets tab

The Snippets tab is to the right of the Files and Assets tabs on the Files panel. Either click the tab or choose Window ⇨ Snippets to open the panel, shown in Figure 9.8.

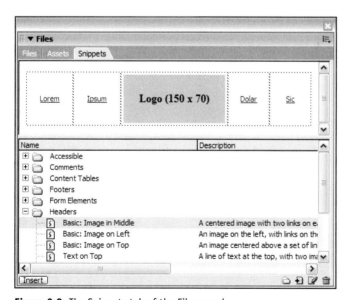

Figure 9.8. The Snippets tab of the Files panel

Snippets are simply bits of code that you can save and reuse. You can create your own snippets or use some of the ones Dreamweaver has stored. Some snippets actually consist of two parts and can be used to surround some content on your page. Here are the actions you can perform in the Snippets panel:

▪ **Insert a snippet into a page:** Click at the location you wish to insert the item in your document and then click the Insert button on the bottom of the panel. You can also drag the item to the page or double-click it.

If your snippet has two parts, you can select some content on your page and surround it with your snippet. For example, if you wish to format a text string and want to use a snippet, your snippet has a first and last part. You select the text you want to format, and the first part of your snippet goes before the text, and the last part goes after it.

▪ **Create a snippet:** To create a snippet, click the Create button on the bottom right, the one with a plus (+) sign. The Snippet dialog box opens, shown in Figure 9.9.

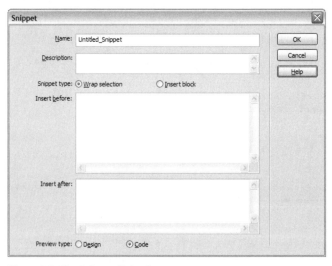

Figure 9.9. The Snippet dialog box

Name your snippet and give it a meaningful description. The description appears to the right in the Snippet panel to help you locate it again in the future. Select a Snippet type. If you choose

Wrap selection, you can put part of the code before and part of the code after whatever is selected in your document when you insert the snippet. Insert block places a single block of code in your document on insertion. Select a preview type. This defines what the snippet looks like in the preview pane at the top of the Snippet panel. If your snippet is HTML code, you probably want to choose Design. If it's something like a JavaScript function, you should choose Code.

■ **Edit a snippet:** Editing a snippet opens it in the Snippet dialog box shown in Figure 9.9. Simply select the snippet you wish to edit and click the Edit button on the lower right, the one with a pencil and paper icon. Editing a snippet has no effect on any uses of it in pages. To use an edited snippet, you have to replace the old version with the new one.

■ **Delete a snippet:** Highlight the snippet you wish to delete and click the garbage can button on the lower right of the panel. Deleting a snippet does not remove it from pages where you have placed it.

Results panel

To open the Results panel, choose Window ➪ Results. This opens the panel shown in Figure 9.10. It is located below the Properties panel.

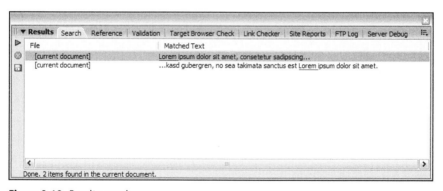

Figure 9.10. Results panel

The Results panel contains quite a number of tabs. These are Search, Reference, Validation, Target Browser Check, Link Checker, Site Reports, FTP Log, and Server Debug. In the following sections I'll give you a brief look at the Search and Reference tabs. The rest of the tabs are discussed in more detail in other chapters. Here is a brief description of each:

- **Search:** This tab displays the results of text and code searches.
- **Reference:** This displays information about a selected tag, tag attribute, or keyword.
- **Validation:** The results of validation checks are reported here. More information on validating your code is in Chapter 11.
- **Target Browser Check:** The results of checking your code for compliance with a specific browser are reported here. More information on browser-checking your code is in Chapter 11.
- **Link Checker:** The results of running the Link Checker, discussed in Chapter 11, are displayed here.
- **Site Reports:** If you have any site reports set up, this is where you see the output. To set up a site report, choose Site ⇨ Reports.
- **FTP Log:** The FTP Log contains the history of all FTP transfers of files on your site.
- **Server Debug:** This is a Windows-only ColdFusion debugger.

Search tab

The Search tab is the tab opened by default on the Results panel. If you don't see it, choose Window ⇨ Results to open the panel shown in Figure 9.10. This tab is used to display results from code and text searches of your document. To try it out, open an HTML file with some images in it, and double-click the green arrow on the upper right side of the panel. You can also choose Edit ⇨ Find and Replace. I discuss the Find and Replace dialog box in Chapter 16, but for now, choose Find in: Current Document, Search: Specific Tag, and choose img for the tag. Click the minus (-) button next to With Attribute. Now click the Find All button. This dialog box closes and your Search panel has the results of this search listed. Double-click the listing, and it is selected for you in your document. You can also save your search results as an XML file by clicking the button that looks like a diskette.

Reference tab

The Reference tab is to the right of the Search tab. If you don't see it, choose Window ⇨ Reference to open the panel shown in Figure 9.11.

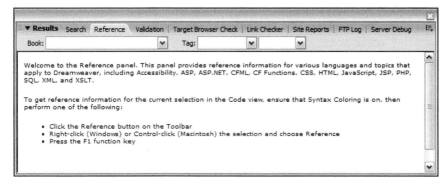

Figure 9.11. Reference panel

The easiest way to see the Reference material about a particular tag or attribute is to click inside the tag and then press Shift and F1 simultaneously. The Reference panel will now contain information about that tag. You can also use the drop-down box on the top middle to choose a specific tag, and the one to the right to choose a specific attribute of the currently selected tag.

Other panels

There are two more panels that are not linked to a panel set. These are the History and Frames panels.

History panel

Choose Window ⇨ History to open the panel shown in Figure 9.12.

The History panel keeps a running list of all changes you have made to your document. It allows you to get detailed information when you undo and redo edits to your document by choosing Edit ⇨ Undo and Edit ⇨ Redo. It also lets you backtrack quite easily if you need to undo more than one edit at a time.

Inside Scoop

The number of edits which are listed in this panel is set in the Edit ⇨ Preferences ⇨ General under Maximum number of history steps.

Figure 9.12. History panel

To go back any number of edits, simply slide the slider bar on the left up as far as you need to. To repeat edits, highlight the edits you wish to repeat and click the Replay button. You can select multiple edits by holding down the mouse button and dragging across the edits you wish to select.

You can use the menu on the upper right and choose Clear History. This clears the list, but keep in mind that you won't be able to undo those edits any longer once you have cleared the list.

Frames panel

If you are using Frames in your site, the Frames panel is an easy way to select the current frame you wish to work in. This is discussed in detail in Chapter 20.

Code Inspector

The Code Inspector isn't precisely a panel. It is a detachable copy of the Code view. It has all the same buttons and options. It exists because it may

Inside Scoop

You can actually have both Code view and the Code Inspector up, but there is no real reason to do this. Changes you make to one occur in the other at the same time.

be useful for you at times to work in Design view and have your Code view off to the side. To open the Code Inspector, simply choose Window ⇨ Code Inspector.

Timelines panel

The Timelines panel is used to add animation to layers in your document. It is discussed in Chapter 15.

Just the facts

- The Tag Inspector lets you closely examine the attributes of tags and modify them.

- The Files panel lets you view and control the content on your local and remote sites.

- The Results panel shows the results of searching, reference look-up, and various syntax checks of your code.

- The History panel lets you precisely control how you undo edits to your document.

- The Code Inspector gives you a detached Code view to work in.

GET THE SCOOP ON...
Creating templates ▪ Applying and removing templates ▪
A look at template code ▪ Editing templates ▪
Library privileges

Using Templates and Libraries

Chapter 10

A template is a reusable page layout. It contains regions that are not editable, such as a footer bar, and regions that are, such as text content inside the page. Templates let you control what can and cannot be edited in a Web site. Templates are effective when you have multiple users working on the same site and you want to tightly control the layout of pages.

Templates not only let you control what regions can be changed, but they also allow you to simultaneously update every page using the template. This is an incredibly handy feature. For example, I might add a page to my Web site. Without templates, I would have to change my navigation bar on every single page of the site, one at a time. With a template, I can edit my template just once and then republish my site.

You should use a template if you have a site with many pages that all will have the same design, with the only major difference between the pages being in the text or images in the center of the page. You probably won't get much out of using templates if your site has only a few pages or none have a consistent look and feel.

Creating templates

To create a template, begin by designing the page you will use to create the template. For the sake of this book, I've chosen one of the starter pages provided by Macromedia Dreamweaver. I will either create a site, or use an existing site. In my example that follows, I use a starter page from Dreamweaver and create a template page for my site, www.compleat traveler.com.

1. **Create your static page:** Begin by opening a starter page. Choose File ⇨ New, click the General tab, and pick Starter Pages from the Category on the left, as shown in Figure 10.1. I choose the Travel – Text Page from the list on the right.

2. **Save this file as a template:** After you select a starter page and click Create, a Save As dialog box opens. From the Save as type drop-down box, choose Template files (*.dwt). DWT stands for Dreamweaver template. Give your file a meaningful name, then click Save.

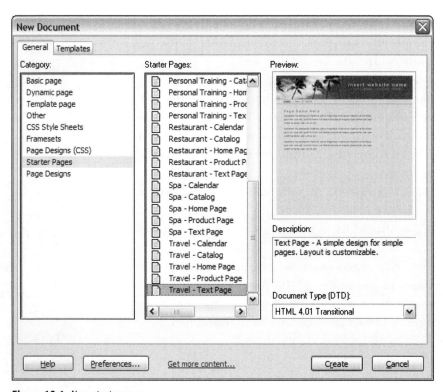

Figure 10.1. New starter page

Inside Scoop

To easily access your template at any time, simply open the Assets panel and click the Templates button. It is the next-to-the-bottom button on the left-hand side of the panel.

3. Copy Dependent Files: The Copy Dependent Files dialog box opens if this page has files not in your current site. Click Copy to move them to your current site.

4. Use the Common toolbar to create a template: Open the Common toolbar if it isn't already open. Locate and click the Templates button. It is the second-to-the-last button on this toolbar. Select Make Template from the menu.

5. Click OK on the warning dialog box: You'll see a dialog box telling you that you have no editable regions. Click OK. We will set editable regions shortly.

6. Fill out the Save As Template dialog box: Give your template a description and a name, then click Save. Mine is called Compleat_main. Click Yes on the Update Links dialog box that opens.

How to create editable regions

Your template won't do you much good if you don't create editable regions. There are three types of regions:

- **Editable:** These regions can be edited in individual pages with the template applied to them.
- **Optional:** These regions appear if a condition in the code is met.
- **Repeating:** These regions can be repeated multiple times in a templated page.

Most of the time, you will be creating editable regions in your template. Here is how I made the center text in my CompleatTraveler template editable:

1. Select the code you wish to make editable. In my case, I selected the text in the center of the page.

2. Click the Templates button on the Common toolbar. This time, select Editable Region from the drop-down list.

3. The New Editable Region dialog box opens, as shown in Figure 10.2. You can also see the selected text on the page behind the dialog box. Give the region a name. I named mine "center_text." Click OK.

4. Save your template. Choose File ⇨ Save.

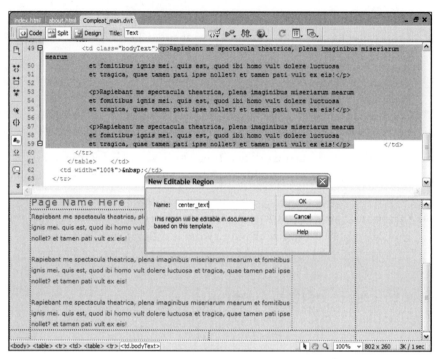

Figure 10.2. The New Editable Region dialog box

How to create optional regions

Optional regions exist so that you can set some kind of parameter in your template that has to be met for regions to appear in the page. You can set up if...else statements to control whether or not the region is visible. An example of when you might use an optional region is if you wanted only users who had signed in to your site to see some particular content. Or perhaps you want certain code to show only at a particular time of day. The New Optional Region dialog box, shown in Figure 10.3, allows you to create conditional statements for these optional template regions.

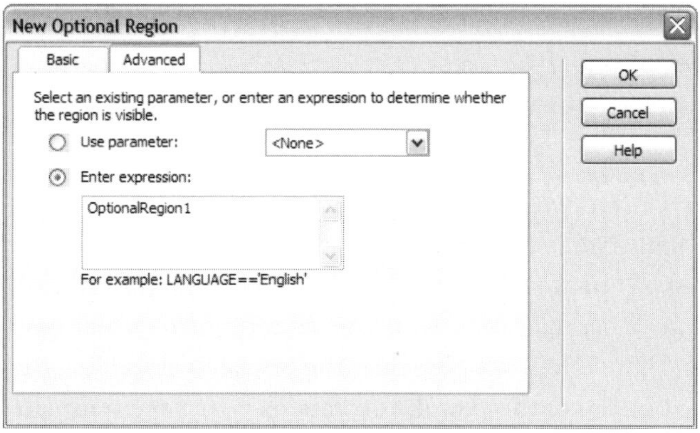

Figure 10.3. The New Optional Region dialog box

Here is how to create an optional region:

1. Select the region to make optional.

2. Click the Templates button on the Common toolbar. This time, select Optional Region from the drop-down list.

3. On the Basic tab, enter a name for a parameter to be used to control the optional region. If you want the optional region to be hidden by default, uncheck the box.

Here is an example of the code that is inserted into your template. This example assumes that you named your optional region "test_optional."

```
<!-- TemplateBeginIf cond="test_optional" -->Text to
display if test_optional is true.<!-- TemplateEndIf -->
In the head section of each page using this template,
you will find this editable code:
<!-- TemplateParam name="test_optional" type="boolean"
value="true" -->
```

To make your text not appear, change the value to "false."

How to create repeated regions

Here is how to create repeated regions:

1. Select the code you wish to make a repeated region.

2. Click the Templates button on the Common toolbar. This time, select Repeated Region from the drop-down list.

3. The New Repeated Region dialog box opens. Give the region a name, then click OK.

4. Save your template. Choose File ⇨ Save.

Applying and removing templates

Applying your new template is very simple. Locate the template you just created under the Assets panel. You need to click the Templates button on the left-hand side to see it. Then, with the document to which you wish to apply the template open, simply select the template and click the Apply button on the bottom of the panel. You can also drag the template into the document.

Your document now looks like your template. You can only edit the regions that are not grayed out; the rest of the page is protected.

Removing templates from your pages is simple, too. Open the page with the template you wish to remove. Choose Modify ⇨ Templates ⇨ Detach from Template.

What does template code look like?

When you have created a template and view it in Code view, the beginning of your page will have code like this:

```
<html><!-- InstanceBegin
template="/Templates/Compleat_main.dwt"
 codeOutsideHTMLIsLocked="false" -->
```

This defines the beginning of the template. It is placed just after the open HTML tag. The end of the templated page has this line:

```
<!-- InstanceEnd --></html>
```

While this allows you to put content outside of the template tags and inside the HTML tags, nothing placed there would be visible on the page.

You will also see sections of code very much like this:

```
<!-- InstanceBeginEditable name="center_text" -->
<p>This is some text that is editable in my page. </p>
 <!-- InstanceEndEditable -->
```

This is the code around an editable region. The code between the `InstanceBeginEditable` and the `InstanceEndEditable` is, as you can probably guess, editable. But if you try to edit code outside of a region like that, you can't. You can select and copy it, but you can't paste it. Notice that the code not in the editable region is grayed out.

In Design view, notice that your cursor becomes a black circle with a line through it whenever you try to click anywhere but in an editable region on the page.

Editing templates

Editing your template is just like editing any other document. You need to locate it in the Assets panel and double-click it or choose Edit from the menu on the upper right corner of the panel. If I wanted to add another region or make changes to the static portion of the template, I would simply make my changes here and choose File ➯ Save. The Update Pages dialog box appears, as shown in Figure 10.4.

This dialog box allows you to update all pages that use the template you just edited by clicking Done. You can also click the Show log box to see the status of the updates.

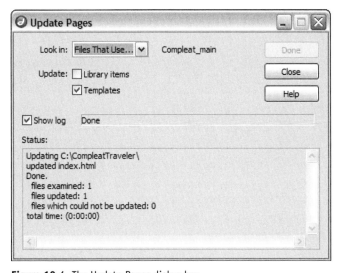

Figure 10.4. The Update Pages dialog box

Inside Scoop

Unless you are simply curious, you never need to worry about how the library stores code and references to files. Editing library content can be done directly from the Assets panel, so you never need to browse to a particular folder to edit a library item.

Creating libraries

We talked a bit about the Library panel in the last chapter. Here, we'll take a closer look at what a library is — why you should (or shouldn't) use one and adding, editing, and removing content from your library.

What is a library?

A library is a site-specific repository of reusable assets. You would create a library if you have an HTML table you use in a number of different locations, for example. If you needed to edit that table, having it stored in a library would allow you to simply edit it and then press a button to update all your pages that used it.

The library stores code and references to files in a master file. It is in this file that changes are made when you edit library items, and it is from this file that library items are referenced in your code.

Having a site library is a good idea if your site is large and images, tables, Java applets, Macromedia Flash movies, or even text paragraphs are used repeatedly and need to be easy to find.

If your site is just a few pages and you don't reuse anything, a library probably won't do you much good. And if you change your mind, a library is easy to add to your site at any time.

How do I create a library?

Your library already exists. It is empty until you add some content. To see it, choose Window ⇨ Assets and click the Library button on the left side of the panel. It is the last button, the one that looks like an open book. Figure 10.5 shows the empty Library panel. Notice the Library button on the left.

Figure 10.5. Library in the Assets panel

Here is how to add items:

1. Select the tags, text, image links, or other content in your page that you wish to turn into a library item.

2. Click the New Library Item button with a plus (+) sign, located on the bottom of the Assets panel. You can also choose Modify ⇨ Library ⇨ Add Object to Library. You can also simply drag the selected code into the Library window.

3. Name your new item and press Enter.

If you want to create a library item that doesn't yet exist in your document, you can. Simply make sure you have nothing selected in your page and click the New Library Item button. You can then name your item and when you are ready, edit it.

How do I use library items?

Pick where in your page you wish to put the library item. You can put it in either the Design view or the Code view. Either drag the library item into your page or click the Insert button on the bottom of the Assets panel.

Hack

You can insert a copy of the contents of a library item without actually linking it to the library. To do this, hold the Ctrl key while clicking and dragging the item with the mouse; on the Mac, the Option key.

Once the library item is in your page, you can "disconnect" it from the library if you wish. This means that when you edit the library item and update the pages, this instance of it is not changed. To do this, click the library item in your page and open the Properties panel. Click the Detach from Original button.

How do I edit library items?

The real power of using the library is your ability to update all types of content on pages without having to go to individual pages and do so.

Here is how to edit an item in the library:

1. Select a library item to edit.

2. Open it for editing by either double-clicking it or clicking the Edit button on the bottom right of the panel. It's the button that looks like a pencil and paper.

3. The library item opens on the page. See Figure 10.6 for an example of a rather silly library item being edited. You can make any changes you wish to the item in this file.

4. After you finish, choose File ⇨ Save.

5. The Update Library Items dialog box appears, allowing you to decide if you want to update any pages in which the library item appears.

You can rename items in the library. This does not unlink them from their instances in your pages, so it is generally safe to do this. Select the library item you wish to rename and click the menu button on the upper right hand corner of the Assets panel. Click Rename. Your library item name is now selected and editable. Type the new name and press Enter.

At this point, you are asked if you wish to update your files. This process changes the name of the referenced library object to the new name.

Inside Scoop

You can update your pages containing library items at any time, should you choose not to do it when you save an edited library item. Simply choose Modify ⇨ Library ⇨ Update Pages.

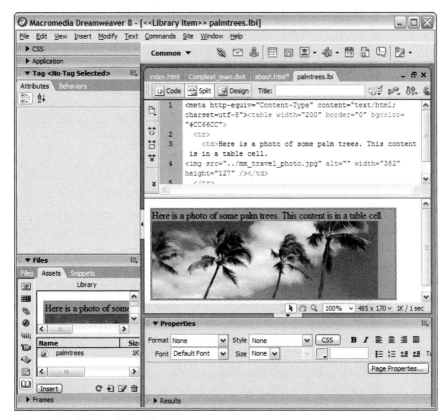

Figure 10.6. Editing a library item

How do I delete library items?

Before you delete library items, you need to know that deleting them will not delete them from your documents. Nor is there an easy way to do so, other than going to each page and cutting it out by hand, or using some sort of site-wide find/replace. Still, you may need to delete an item, so it's simple enough. Select the item you wish to delete and then click the garbage can button. Poof, it's gone.

Inside Scoop

Unlike templates, library item code can be edited directly. However, unless you detach it from the library item, it is updated when the files are updated and any changes you have made are overwritten.

But wait! You didn't mean to do that! All may not be lost. Find a page where you used that library item. You'll be able to tell because the code in the page will look something like this:

```
<!-- #BeginLibraryItem "/Library/palmtrees1.lbi" --
><table width="200" border="0" bgcolor="#3399CC">
<tr>
<td>Here is a photo of some palm trees. This content is
in a table cell.
<img src="mm_travel_photo.jpg" alt="" width="382"
height="127" /></td>
</tr>
</table>
<!-- #EndLibraryItem -->
```

Notice the comments with the #BeginLibraryItem and #EndLibraryItem. This is it, and if you haven't changed the editor settings for Dreamweaver, it should be highlighted a pale yellow.

Once you've located the code, open the Properties panel. If you don't see it, you can choose Window ⇨ Properties. Click anywhere in the highlighted code and the Properties panel looks like the one shown in Figure 10.7.

Figure 10.7. Properties panel for library item

Now simply click the Recreate button to add this back to your library.

Just the facts

- Templates allow you to create a consistent site design that is easily updated site-wide.
- Multiple users can edit templated sites and are restricted to editing only regions you specify as editable.
- There are three types of regions in a template: editable, optional, and repeating.

- The site library lets you store assets that can be used in multiple pages in your site.

- If you edit a library item, you change all instances of it without having to individually update the content.

- The contents of a library item can be detached from the library so that it stands alone and is not changed when the library item is edited and files are updated.

GET THE SCOOP ON...
Using the Code, Design, and Split view buttons ■
Browser checking ■ Validating code ■ File Management ■
Preview/Debug in Browser

Understanding the Editor Pane

The Editor pane is the big center area in the Macromedia Dreamweaver interface where you create and edit your pages. In previous chapters I've described features of the pane, but only in passing. There are a number of features associated with it that can only be accessed by clicking buttons or using menus attached to it. It deserves its very own chapter to cover these features and help you get the most out of it.

The Editor pane is primarily used to edit code. In Code view, you can use syntax highlighting, word wrap, and line numbers to help you easily edit your code. You can also preview and edit your pages graphically using Design view. Split view lets you view both the code and the design simultaneously. Meet your friend, the Editor pane.

Code, Design, and Split view buttons

By now you have figured out how the Code, Design, and Split view buttons work The Editor pane with these buttons is shown in Figure 11.1.

In this section, I'll tell you a few things about these views, and the Editor pane in general, that you probably don't know.

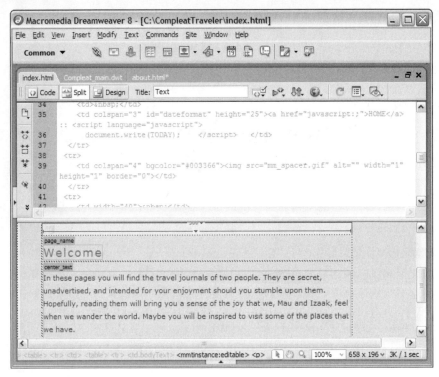

Figure 11.1. Editor Pane with view buttons

The three views

Let's start by going over what the three views are:

- **Code view:** Use the Code view, shown in Figure 11.2, to create code. This includes HTML, CSS, JavaScript, and code such as PHP, ASP, or CFML.

  The Code view offers you many helpful features in creating your code, including code highlighting, code collapsing and expanding, and multiple undo levels, and it is connected with the Find/Replace dialog box so that you can easily locate a particular bit of code.

  The Code view pane has buttons along the left-hand side specifically for helping you work with code. These are only present in Code view or Split view. See the upcoming section, "Code view buttons."

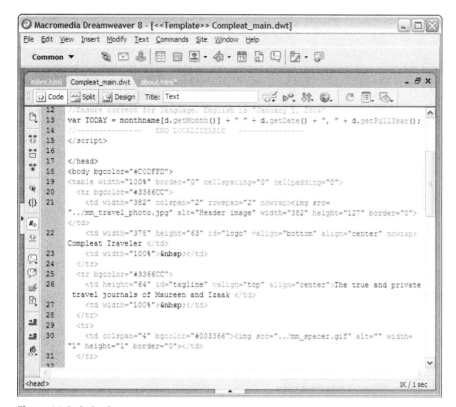

Figure 11.2. Code view

- **Design view:** This view offers you the chance to see your page almost as it will appear in a Web browser. Design view is shown in Figure 11.3.

  Certain things are missing; for example, JavaScript code isn't pre-viewable, but in general this view gives you a clear idea of what your page will look like. Design view offers you some distinct advantages over Code view. You can use a tracing image to assist you in creating your page.

  The Design view has a few special features on the status bar that are only present in Design view or Split view; these are discussed in the upcoming section, "Design view status bar."

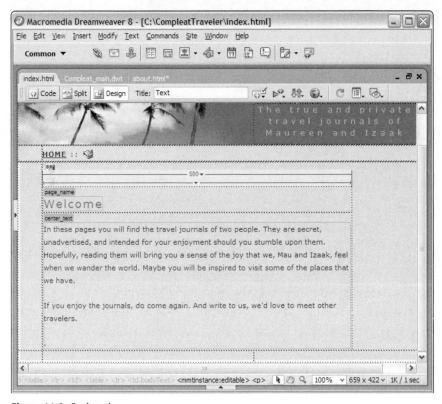

Figure 11.3. Design view

- **Split view:** Use the Split view when you want to see your page in both Code and Design views at the same time. Split view is shown in Figure 11.4.

    In Split view you can adjust the pane border between the Design and Code view panels to any height you wish.

Inside Scoop

After you make changes to files in the Editor pane, you see an asterisk next to their filenames just under the toolbar. This indicates that your changes are not yet saved. When you choose File ⇨ Save, the asterisk disappears.

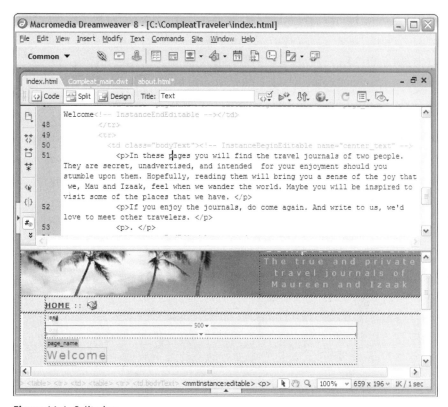

Figure 11.4. Split view

Context menu of the Editor pane

A context menu is any menu in Dreamweaver that opens by right-clicking (Windows) or Control-clicking (Mac). Right-click anywhere on or next to the Code, Split, Design view buttons on the Editor pane window to get to the context menu. This menu is shown in Figure 11.5.

The Editor pane context menu contains a list of four toolbars you can display on your Editor pane. These toolbars are also available by choosing

Inside Scoop

I generally use the default setting here and only display the Insert and Document toolbars. The other two toolbars are useful, but clutter up an already crowded workspace.

View ⇨ Toolbars. By default, the Insert and Document toolbars are selected. Here is a description of each toolbar:

- **Insert:** The Insert toolbar is the large toolbar across the top. For specific information on the Insert toolbar, see Chapter 6.

- **Style Rendering:** The Style Rendering toolbar lets you view your page in Design view in a number of different device styles. There is also a CSS view toggle button. This lets you see what your page will look like to a browser with no ability to view CSS information.

- **Document:** The Document toolbar is the most useful. It contains buttons to, among other things, change your view, validate your code, preview in browser, and manage files. These and the other buttons on this toolbar are discussed later in this chapter.

- **Standard:** This toolbar contains the standard file and edit icons you see on many applications.

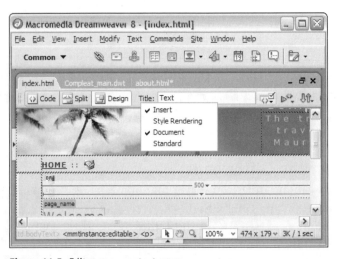

Figure 11.5. Editor pane context menu

Code view buttons

There are 15 buttons along the left side of the Code view window, as shown in Figure 11.6.

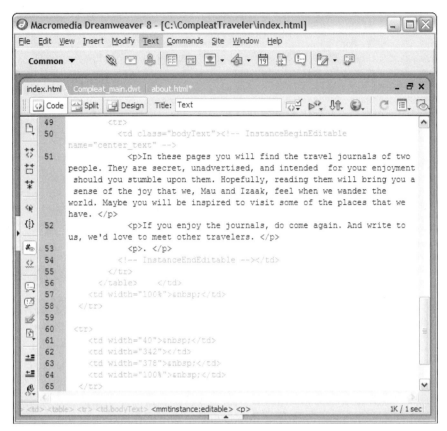

Figure 11.6. Code View buttons

Here are the buttons described in order from top to bottom:

■ **Open Documents:** This button looks like a piece of paper with a folded corner. Click this button to see a list of all documents you have open. The one with the check mark is the one that is currently on top in the Edit pane. To bring another document to the top, click its name. This accomplishes the same thing as clicking its tab in the Edit pane.

■ **Collapse Full Tag:** This button has two arrows above two angle brackets. Use the Collapse Full Tag button to temporarily hide sections of code when you are not working on them. To use this button, click in a tag in your code. This tag should be one with both an open and close tag. Click the button. Your tag is collapsed into the open angle

Bright Idea

You don't have to click a tag to use the Collapse Full Tag button. You can also click anywhere between two tags and the surrounding tags will be collapsed.

brace, the first seven characters in the tag, and an ellipsis. For example, if your tag looked like this:

```
<td>Some text here.</td>
```

Clicking the Collapse Full Tag button would result in it looking like this:

```
<td>Som...
```

Your collapsed tag is in a gray box. To see what is in it, move your mouse over the box. To uncollapse the tag, double-click it. You can collapse as many tags as you wish.

- **Collapse Selection:** The Collapse Selection button is the third one down and looks like two arrows above a rectangle. It works almost like the Collapse Full Tag button. The difference is that you select any code at all in your page and click this button. It is all compressed into the same gray box as previously. Just as with the Collapse Full Tag button, to see what is in it, move your mouse over the box. To uncollapse the selection, double-click it. You can collapse as many selections as you want.

- **Expand All:** This button looks like two outward pointing arrows over an asterisk. Clicking this button uncollapses all your collapsed tags and selections back to the normal view.

- **Select Parent Tag:** This button is the fifth from the top. It looks like two angle braces with an arrow between them. This handy button can be used to quickly locate and select the tags that surround text in your page. If you click some text in a table, for example, click this button and the <TD> tags around the text are selected. Click it again and the <TR> tags are selected. Click it one more time and the entire table is selected.

Inside Scoop

Collapsing your tag or selection in no way changes your HTML code. It is a visual effect to help you get code you aren't working with out of the way.

- **Balance Braces:** This button, which looks like two curly braces separated by a dotted line, is useful in script blocks in your code. Clicking this somewhere inside a script selects the surrounding braces or parentheses or brackets.

- **Line Numbers:** The Line Numbers button has a number sign on it. Click this button to display line numbers on the left side of your Code view. These can be useful when you choose Edit ⇨ Search to find something in your code, as Search returns line numbers in its results.

- **Highlight Invalid Code:** Click this button with the angle braces and red squiggly line underneath to highlight any invalid code in yellow.

- **Apply Comment:** The Apply Comment button looks like a cartoon talk bubble. It can be used to add a variety of different comment types into your code. To use it, select the text to which you wish to apply the comment, or the spot where you want to create a new empty comment, and choose the correct comment type. The HTML comment is first. The /**/ comment is used in JavaScript or CSS code and can span multiple lines between the asterisks. The // comment type is also for JavaScript or CSS, and comments out a single line behind it. Visual Basic code uses the single apostrophe type comment. The final option is used for a specific file type you are editing. If you are working on a file of a type other than HTML, and Dreamweaver recognizes it, this automatically inserts the appropriate comment type in your code.

- **Remove Comment:** This button removes a selected comment from your code.

- **Wrap Tag:** The Wrap Tag button is the fifth from the bottom. It looks like a pencil over an arrow shape. Select any code or text on your page you wish to surround with an HTML tag, then click the Wrap Tag button. A Wrap Tag drop-down box opens with a very long drop-down list of tags to choose from. Select one and press Enter, or if you prefer, you can type in appropriate attributes for the tag you have chosen.

- **Recent Snippets:** Clicking this button opens a list of snippets you have recently used in Dreamweaver. You can then easily select one of these or click the Snippets panel to open it so you can pick one not in this list. For more information on snippets, see Chapter 9.

Watch Out!

Don't confuse the indenting and outdenting buttons here with the HTML indent tags. The buttons here strictly change how your code looks in the editor by adding white space. They make no changes to the actual HTML code.

- **Indent Code:** Any code you have selected is indented when you click this button.

- **Outdent Code:** Click this button to remove the indents from any indented code you select.

- **Format Source Code:** This is the bottom button and looks like a paint bucket. Clicking this applies code formatting to code in the page. You can set your preferred code formatting in the Code Format Preferences dialog box. To get there, choose Edit ⇨ Preferences and click the Code Format category. You can also open this dialog box by choosing Code Format Settings from the menu attached to this button.

Design view status bar

We're now going to shift gears to the Design view. Take a look at Figure 11.7 of the Design view, and notice the icons and numbers along the bottom of this panel.

The items on the Design view status bar, from left to right, are:

- **Tag Selector:** On the bottom left you see a list of tags. This changes as you click around the page. This list represents tags that surround the current location you have clicked in the page. If you click one of these tags, everything inside that tag is selected. For example, if you click the <BODY> tag, you select the entire contents of the page from the open <BODY> tag to the close <BODY> tag.

- **Select tool:** This button looks like an arrow, and returns your cursor to normal after you have used the Hand or Zoom tools (see below).

- **Hand tool:** The Hand tool looks like a hand and changes your mouse cursor into a hand when you click it. This tool lets you drag the page around in the Design view. When your page is not zoomed in, it does nothing. If you zoom in, and not all of your page is visible in the Design view, you can use this tool to move it around. When you are done with it, you can click the Select tool to return the cursor to normal.

Inside Scoop

Zooming in or out in no way changes your HTML code or the appearance of your page in browsers. It is a visual effect to help you get a closer look at the layout of your page.

■ **Zoom tool:** Use this magnifying glass button to change your cursor to a magnifying glass and click anywhere on the page to zoom in. You can also hold down the Alt key with the zoom tool to zoom out.

■ **Set magnification:** This menu contains preset percentages to zoom in or out of your page; 100% brings it back to the actual size.

■ **Window size:** This menu lets you pick some preset sizes in which to view your page. This will not work in Windows if your Edit pane is maximized. Click the maximize button on the upper right of the edit pane to unmaximize. Now the preset sizes can be used.

These sizes can be edited to allow you to add a height and width for which you are specifically designing your page. Click the Edit Sizes link to add your own sizes or modify this list.

■ **Download Size/Download Time:** This pair of values on the far right side of the status bar gives you an idea of the current page size, including all images in it, and how long it will take your user to download it.

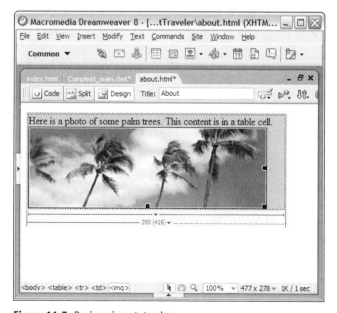

Figure 11.7. Design view status bar

Hack
You can set the Download Time to reflect the speed of your typical user's Internet connection. It's at the bottom of the Status Bar Preferences dialog box, accessible from Edit ⇨ Preferences. Click Status Bar in the category list on the left.

Changing the title

Changing the title of your page is ridiculously simple and can be done anytime by simply typing it into the Title text box to the right of the Code, Split, and Design view buttons. Type in your title and press Enter. This changes the <TITLE> tag in your page to reflect the change. If you have used a template, be aware that you must set the title of your page in the template document, unless you've made the <TITLE> section of your page an editable region. See Chapter 10 for more information on templates and editable regions.

Browser Check

Dreamweaver has a number of buttons to the right of the title text box. The first of these is the Browser Check button. You can use this button to check your current page for compatibility with specific browsers. You can use the Browser Check to make sure that all the HTML and CSS in your site is supported by your target browsers. Click on the button and the Results panel reports the results to you.

To begin using the Browser Check, first make sure the browsers you want to check against are included. To do this, click the Browser Check button and scroll down to the Settings option. Click it. The Target Browsers dialog box appears, shown in Figure 11.8.

Target Browsers		⊠
Minimum browser versions:		OK
☐ Firefox	1.0 ⌄	Cancel
☐ Microsoft IE for Macintosh	5.2 ⌄	
☑ Microsoft Internet Explorer	5.0 ⌄	
☐ Mozilla	1.0 ⌄	
☑ Netscape Navigator	6.0 ⌄	
☐ Opera	2.1 ⌄	
☐ Safari	1.0 ⌄	
		Help

Figure 11.8. The Target Browsers dialog box

Use this dialog box to set the browsers and minimum version numbers to check against. Every version of the browser from that minimum version to now is checked.

There are three different results you can get for browser incompatibility problems in your code:

- **You may get an informational message.** This lets you know that the browser doesn't support something in the page, but will not alter the appearance of the page in the browser.

- **You may get a warning.** This indicates that something in your page will not show up, or will not be displayed correctly.

- **You may get an error.** This means that your page content may not appear at all.

When you click the Browser Check button and choose Check Browser Support, you see code with possible problems underlined in red in Code view. To see the results for the entire page, along with line numbers and detailed descriptions, choose Window ⇨ Results and click the Target Browser Check tab. You can also click the Browser Check button and choose Show All Errors. You are presented with a list of errors, as shown in Figure 11.9.

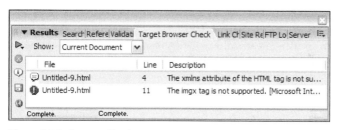

Figure 11.9. Browser Check errors

Double-click each one of these to be taken to the specific line in the code. There are a number of other actions you can take using the Results panel:

- **Run the check again:** Click the green arrow on the upper left of the Results panel. You can check specific documents, local files, or remote files with this button.

- **Stop the current check:** If the check is running, click the red X button to stop it.

- **Get more information:** Click the button with the "i" on it to get more information on a particular error.

- **Save the error report:** Click the disk button to save your report.

- **View the error report:** You can view the error report in a Web page by clicking the button with the globe.

Validate Markup

The Validate Markup button behaves in a similar fashion as the Browser Check. Use this button to check your current page for valid code. To begin using Validate Markup, first make sure that the languages you are using in your page will be included. To do this, click the Validate Markup button and scroll down to the Settings option. Click it. The Preferences dialog box opens with the Validator category chosen.

Use this dialog box to set the languages to check against. When you click the Validate Markup button you can choose to check the current file, selected files, or the entire local site. To see the results along with line numbers and detailed descriptions, choose Window ⇨ Results and click the Validation tab.

File Management

The File Management button is to the right of the Browser Check button. It can be used to control a number of file management tasks. These include Get, Check Out, Put, and Check In. These tasks can also be performed using the Files Panel, as covered in Chapter 7.

Probably the most useful menu item under this button is the Design Notes option.

Figure 11.10 shows the Design Notes dialog box. In this dialog box, click the Basic info tab. Choose a Status for the current page from the drop-down menu. Then, type any notes you wish pertaining to the page. Clicking the text box Show when file is opened opens the notes when

---

Hack

You can also get to Design Notes by choosing File ⇨ Design Notes. But because they are at the bottom of the long File menu, I find it easier to use the File Management button to get to them.

you open the file. This is a good way to remind yourself about something in the file, or something you need to do to it. It also allows you to tell other people working on the file things about it. You can also add key/value pairs using the All info tab. This might be something like Last edited by = Zebediah. To add these, enter the data in the bottom Name and Value text fields and click the plus (+) button. To remove a pair, select it and click the minus (-) button. Click OK when you are finished.

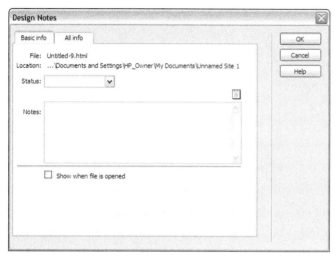

Figure 11.10. The Design Notes dialog box

Preview/Debug in Browser

Use this button to select which browser you would like to preview your page in. You can set the list of browsers by choosing the Edit Browser List option under this button. This opens the Preview in Browser category page of the Preferences dialog box. Here you can add and remove browsers. Keep in mind that you must have the browser installed on the local machine to preview your page in it.

After you click the Preview button, you are prompted to save the current page if it is not saved. Then it opens the page in the selected browser. Any server-side code in the page does not show up; this is simply a file being displayed in a browser, not being served through a Web server.

Just the facts

- Use the Code view buttons to control the appearance of your code while working with it in the Editor pane.

- Use the status bar buttons in Design view to zoom in and out, test the page dimensions, and check download time.

- You can check your HTML and CSS code against a number of browsers and versions.

- You can validate your markup code against a customized list of languages.

- Use the File Management menu to easily insert Design Notes.

- You can preview your page in any browser installed on your system.

Graphics, Media, and Text Layout

PART III

Inserting Images, Hotspots, and Placeholders

A picture's worth a thousand words, but in this chapter I say more than a thousand words about pictures. This chapter is all about the images in your pages. Macromedia Dreamweaver allows you to easily insert images and image placeholders in your page in Design view. Once your image is on the page, you can select it and use simple Dreamweaver buttons to edit and resize your image. Dreamweaver is integrated with Macromedia Fireworks and uses Fireworks to allow you to edit your image without ever having to save your work in Dreamweaver.

You can also visually create hotspots on your images, otherwise known as imagemaps. These areas can be drawn on your images to be used as links to other pages. These hotspots can also be used to trigger Dreamweaver behaviors. Behaviors are built-in JavaScripts that can be used for a variety of things including opening navigation menus and swapping images dynamically,

Inserting images

The short answer to the question, "How do I insert an image?" is to click the Image button on the Common toolbar, shown in Figure 12.1.

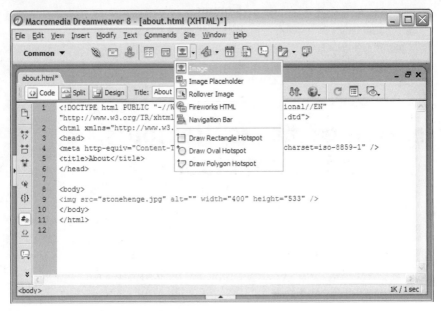

Figure 12.1. Image button

It's not quite that simple, however. Inserting images into your page basically means that you are creating and populating an HTML <IMG> tag, viewable in the Code view. You could simply type the tag and all the values and attributes that go in the tag, but you can instead easily insert images with Macromedia Dreamweaver and never have to type anything. You can also insert images without having to go into Code view if you don't wish to.

A basic <IMG> tag looks like this in the code:

```
<img src="images/stonehenge.jpg" alt="Stonehenge"
width="400" height="533" />
```

The src attribute is set to the location and filename of the image, the alt attribute is text that appears when the mouse cursor remains over the image for a few seconds and is used to provide information to browsers that can't see the image, and the width and height define the size of the image in the browser.

Instead of typing this in your Code view, you will find it simpler to use one of Dreamweaver's several ways to insert images:

■ **Use the Image button on the Common toolbar.** Figure 12.1 shows this toolbar with the Image button selected.

After you click the button, the Select Image Source dialog box appears, as shown in Figure 12.2.

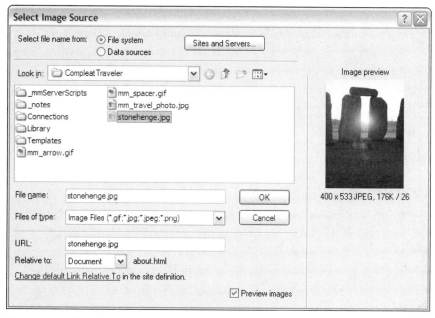

Figure 12.2. The Select Image Source dialog box

First, you need to locate the filename. Locate the file you wish to insert. Dreamweaver filters through the files and displays GIF, JPG, JPEG, and PNG image file types. Decide whether you want the file path of the image to be relative to the current document or relative to the site you are working in.

 Bright Idea

At a minimum, I recommend clicking the blue circular arrow next to the W and H text boxes in the Properties panel. This sets the width and height, respectively, of the image. It keeps the browser from having to figure out the image size, and helps you understand the difference between resizing and resampling, covered in the next section.

If you have accessibility options turned on in your Preferences panel, you may see another dialog box asking you to provide alternate text content for your image. Simply type in a descriptive name here, if you wish. Click OK. Your image is now in your document.

■ **Choose Insert ⇨ Image.** This is exactly the same process as clicking the Image button as previously discussed.

■ **Drag an image from the Files Panel, Assets Panel, or from your computer's files.** You won't see the Select Image Source dialog box if you drag your image into the page.

Now that your image is in your page, you can open the Properties panel and set additional attributes for it. Choose Window ⇨ Properties to open the panel, and then click the <IMAGE> tag in Code view or the image itself in Design view.

Modifying images

Dreamweaver offers you some limited image-editing abilities within the program. You don't need an image editor to perform these basic modifications to your image. In this section, I will show you how to resize, crop, adjust brightness and contrast, and sharpen your images without ever leaving Dreamweaver.

Resize and resample

In Dreamweaver, you can resize and resample images on the page. Resizing and resampling are two distinctly different activities.

When you resize, you are changing the height and width of the image in the HTML, but not actually changing the height and width of the image. When you resample, you shrink the image itself down to the size you want.

Take a look at Figure 12.3. This is the Design view of a page with a very large image of Stonehenge. It is too big for the page. In Figure 12.3, I have selected the image. Notice the three small square black handles. One is in the bottom right corner of the image, one halfway up the right side of the image, and one halfway across the bottom of the image. To resize this image, I simply click and hold one of these handles and drag the image to the size I want.

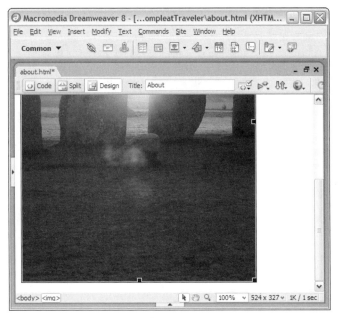

Figure 12.3. Image in Design view

But look at Figure 12.4 to see the downside of resizing!

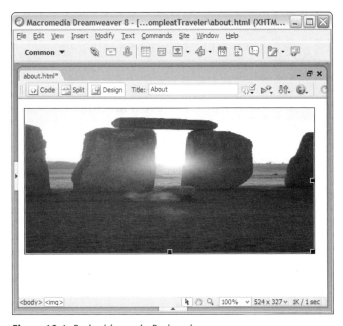

Figure 12.4. Resized image in Design view

Watch Out!

Resampling does alter your original JPG, GIF, or PNG file. Unfortunately, Dreamweaver doesn't make a new copy of the file and let you name it. Make sure you keep a backup copy of this image file just in case you need to resize it again later or use it elsewhere in a different size!

When you resize, you risk skewing your image. This is an extreme example, but the perceptive visitor to your site will notice even slightly skewed images and be less than impressed. To keep your image from skewing, hold down the Shift key as you drag the handle on the bottom corner.

Unlike resizing, resampling actually changes your image file to match the size you want it to be. The image quality is better with resampling, and the page loads faster for your users because you are actually shrinking the image, not just making the browser resize a larger image. I suggest you resample, rather than resize, whenever possible.

To resample your image:

1. Click the image to make the handles appear, as previously discussed.

2. Hold down the Shift key.

3. Click and drag the handle on the bottom right corner until the image is the size you want.

4. On the Properties panel, click the Resample button. It's located under the Alt text box and has a blue circular arrow. You can also choose Modify ⇨ Image ⇨ Resample.

5. You get a warning that this will change the actual file. Click OK.

Crop

Take a look at Figure 12.5 to see my resampled Stonehenge image.

My image has quite a bit of foreground in it. I'd like to center it on the rocks, and get rid of some of the bottom part of the image. Dreamweaver allows me to crop part of the image. To crop an image:

1. Select your image in Design view.

2. Locate and click the Crop button. It is located on the Properties panel under the Alt text box. It has a square crop symbol on it. You can also choose Modify ⇨ Image ⇨ Crop.

3. You get a warning that this will change the actual file. Click OK.

4. Your image now has a rectangle inside it representing the area to remain after cropping. This rectangle has drag handles on all corners and sides, as shown in Figure 12.6.

5. Drag the handles until you are happy with the cropped area.

6. Click the Crop button one more time to crop your image. It is now saved.

Figure 12.5. Resampled image in Design view

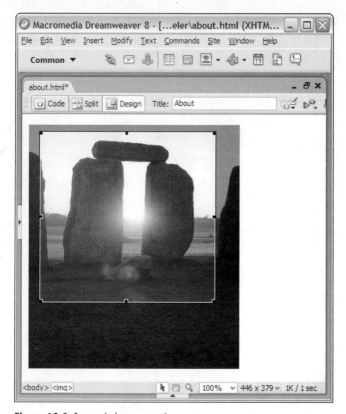

Figure 12.6. Image being cropped

Adjust brightness and contrast

If your image is too dark or too light, or if it is difficult to make out details in the image, you can use the Brightness/Contrast button to lighten or darken it or to add contrast.

To change the brightness or contrast of your image:

1. Click the image to select it.

2. On the Properties panel, click the Brightness/Contrast button. It's located under the Alt text box, and is a half-black, half-white circle. You can also choose Modify ⇨ Image ⇨ Brightness/Contrast.

3. You get a warning that this will change the actual file. Click OK.

4. The Brightness/Contrast dialog box opens. This dialog box has two slider bars. Use these to make your adjustments. There is also a Preview check box. Check this to see your image change as you move the sliders. When you are happy with how the image looks, click OK.

Sharpen

If your image is a bit blurry, you can use the Sharpen button to make it appear more crisp.

To increase the sharpness of your image:

1. Click the image to select it.

2. On the Properties panel, click the Sharpen button. It's located under the Alt text box, and is a blue inverted cone. You can also choose Modify ⇨ Image ⇨ Sharpen.

3. You get a warning that this will change the actual file. Click OK.

4. The Sharpen dialog box opens. This dialog box has a single slider bar. Use this to make your adjustment. There is also a Preview check box. Check this to see your image change as you move the slider. When you are happy with how the image looks, click OK.

Using Fireworks

Fireworks is Macromedia's image-editing program. It is a program that is distinct from Dreamweaver, but is made to work with Dreamweaver to help you with various image-related tasks. If you don't have the Fireworks program, you can skip this section.

Editing images with Fireworks

Suppose you have an image in a page in Dreamweaver that you wish to edit. With a single button click, Dreamweaver allows you to open an image that you have already placed in your code in Fireworks for editing.

Inside Scoop

You can also use Fireworks to optimize images you already have in a page. Just select the image and choose Modify ⇨ Image ⇨ Optimize Image in Fireworks. Your image appears in Fireworks' Optimize panel.

There you can make your changes and then click Done. Dreamweaver automatically updates the image in the page. Without using Fireworks, you would have to open your image-editing software, locate the image, make your changes, save it, and then update it in Dreamweaver.

To use Fireworks to edit an image in your current page:

1. Click the image to select it.

2. On the Properties panel, click the Fireworks button. It's located under the Alt text box, and is a yellow sphere with the Fireworks logo. You can also right-click on the image and choose Edit with Fireworks.

3. The Find Source dialog box opens, shown in Figure 12.7.

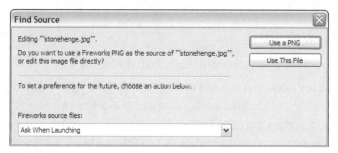

Figure 12.7. The Find Source dialog box

In this box you can locate the original PNG source of an image, if you have one. If not, you can use the current file referenced in the page.

4. Make whatever changes you wish. When you are done, click the Done button on the upper left part of the window around the image. You will be returned to Dreamweaver.

Create a Web photo album with Fireworks

Dreamweaver can work together with Fireworks to create a Web photo album. This consists of your images, thumbnail images, and Web pages with navigation. In this section, I will walk you through the creation of your own album.

To create your album:

1. Choose Commands ⇨ Create Web Photo Album. This opens the dialog box shown in Figure 12.8.

Inside Scoop

If you have quite a few files this process may take some time. Fireworks runs a batch process to take each image and resample a copy of it to create another small version of it for the thumbnail.

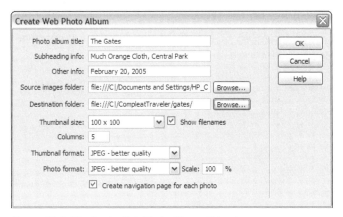

Figure 12.8. The Create Web Photo Album dialog box

2. Enter a Photo album title. Choose something descriptive, like Janey's Fifth Wedding.

3. Enter more detail in the Subheading if you wish.

4. Locate the folder containing your images and enter it in the Source images folder field.

5. Enter a Destination folder where you want your photo album files to be created.

6. Change the Thumbnail size and Columns if desired. Thumbnail size represents the pixel height and width of a preview image. The number of columns is how many thumbnails across the page are displayed.

7. Change the Thumbnail and Photo format settings if desired. JPEG is generally the best choice for photographic images. There are two more checkboxes on this dialog. You can choose to show the filenames of your images by checking Show filenames. You can also choose to create HTML pages with links to the previous and next image for each of the large images if you check the Create navigation page for each photo.

8. Click OK to create your photo album in Fireworks.

9. After Fireworks finishes, you are presented with the index page of your Web album in Dreamweaver. You can edit the appearance of this page if you like, as long as you keep the links on the thumbnails.

10. To see your album, open the destination folder and open the index.html file in a browser. You need only add these files to your Web server to make it live on the Web.

Figure 12.9 shows an example of a Web photo album I created as viewed in a Web browser.

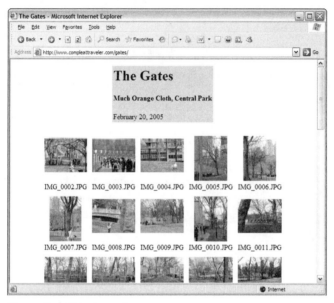

Figure 12.9. Web photo album

Creating hotspots

Dreamweaver refers to the linked areas in image maps as hotspots. Unlike the previous section, you don't need Fireworks to create image maps or hotspots in the images in your Web pages.

> **Inside Scoop**
>
> An image map consists of a block of HTML code with the coordinates of the hotspots listed as numeric values. As you add and edit hotspots, Dreamweaver manages and updates this block of code as needed.

Inside Scoop

If you make a mistake in creating a shape, click the arrow button and select the shape. You can try to drag the handles on it to fix it, or press Delete or choose Edit ⇨ Clear to start over.

To create hotspots:

1. Select the image in your Dreamweaver page where you will place the hotspots. Figure 12.10 shows a page in Design view with an image that has three areas that could use hotspots.

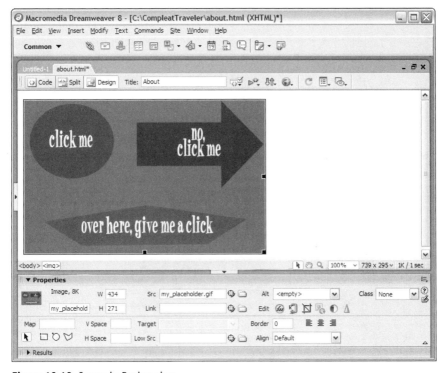

Figure 12.10. Image in Design view

2. Open the Properties panel. If it isn't visible, choose Window ⇨ Properties.

3. Locate the label Map in the Properties panel. Just underneath are the hotspot drawing tools. In Figure 12.10, you can see them on the bottom left corner of the Properties panel.

4. Type in a name for your image map if you wish. If you don't, it will be named for you using the image filename with the word "Map" after it.

5. Pick one of the three shapes under the Map text box. You can now draw on your image with them to select the clickable hotspot areas. The circle draws circles, the square shape draws rectangles. The polygon can be used to play connect the dots on odd-shaped images. Click the vertices, in order.

6. After you draw each shape, click the arrow button to the left of the shapes. Now you can select and edit your shape and move it around.

7. When you are done, click each shape. The Properties panel changes, as shown in Figure 12.11.

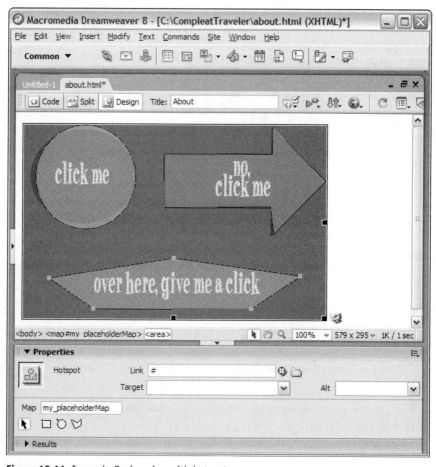

Figure 12.11. Image in Design view with hotspots

Bright Idea

If you know roughly what the predominant color in the final image will be, you can pick a background color here to match. This can be quite helpful if you still have some color design decisions to make in the rest of the page.

You need to enter a URL for the hotspot to link to. You can also enter alt text here, and a target window. If you change the target to _blank, the user gets a new browser window when he or she clicks.

You can modify your hotspots at any time, simply by clicking them in Design view and using the Properties panel to draw new ones.

Using an image placeholder

As you are designing your pages, there may be times when you know where an image needs to go, and you know exactly what size it needs to be, but you don't yet have the final image because someone may still need to decide about the image content, or it is still being worked on.

That doesn't need to keep you from designing your page. Dreamweaver has a layout tool called an image placeholder. You can place your image placeholder on your page until your actual image is ready.

To create an image placeholder:

1. Click at the location on the page where you want to place your image placeholder. You can use either Design or Code view.

2. Click the Image Placeholder button. This is located on the Common toolbar, under the Image button menu, or you can choose Insert ⇨ Image Objects ⇨ Image Placeholder.

3. The Image Placeholder dialog box opens, as shown in Figure 12.12.

Figure 12.12. The Image Placeholder dialog box

4. Choose a name for your placeholder image.

Watch Out!

If you publish your page with the placeholder image, browsers will see it as a broken image in your page.

5. Enter the correct width and height values for your future image.

6. Pick a background color. You can either use the color chooser or type in a hex value for a color if you know it. If you select a color from the chooser, Dreamweaver fills in the appropriate hex value for you.

7. Enter Alternate text if you wish. When you replace the image, this alternate text is still there, so it should apply to the final image, not the placeholder. Click OK.

8. Your image placeholder appears on your page. You can change the size if you wish by using the Properties panel or clicking and dragging the handles. Remember that the dimensions of your placeholder should be the same as the dimensions of your final image.

Now that you have your placeholder image in place, you can continue designing your page while the final image is being completed.

To replace the placeholder with a real image:

1. Select the placeholder.

2. Open the Properties panel for your placeholder.

3. Use the folder button next to the Src text box in the panel to locate the final file.

4. The placeholder is instantly replaced with the final image. If the height and width differ from the placeholder, the values change to match the new final image.

Editing image placeholders with Fireworks

Now that you know how to create them, these instructions can help you use Fireworks to put an image in place of an image placeholder.

When you are ready to replace your placeholder:

1. Select your image placeholder in your Dreamweaver page.

2. Click the Create button on the Properties panel. This button is under the Alt text box and has a yellow globe and Fireworks logo on it. You can also right-click on the image and choose Edit with Fireworks.

3. Fireworks opens with a blank canvas. Fireworks creates the new image as the same height and width as your placeholder.

4. Click Done when you are finished creating your image.

5. You are presented with a Save As dialog box. Save this image. This is actually the parent image, a PNG file, that can be used to create either a JPEG or GIF optimized image.

6. You get yet another dialog box, this time an Export dialog box. Pick the location where you want to save the optimized version of your PNG image. Click Save.

7. Dreamweaver becomes the active program again with the placeholder replaced with the new image.

Just the facts

- You can easily add images to your page with the Image button.

- Dreamweaver allows you to resize, resample, and crop your images without leaving the program and with no additional software.

- You can sharpen images and adjust brightness and contrast of your images inside Dreamweaver.

- Dreamweaver and Fireworks can be used together to create an online Web photo album.

- The Properties panel for images contains tools to allow you to create image maps and hotspots.

- Use an image placeholder to allow you to design around a final image you don't yet have.

Adding Media to Your Page

Chapter 13

Nearly every corporate Web site you visit today uses Macromedia Flash. Other sites have Java applets, or streaming video. With Macromedia Dreamweaver, you can easily place these media types in your code. This chapter explores which media types Dreamweaver actively supports and shows you how to use Dreamweaver to create the code to serve them to your visitors.

Flash media

Flash is everywhere on the Internet, and with good reason. Flash allows you to create animations and applications; and by doing so, add true interactivity to your Web site. Not only does Dreamweaver allow you to integrate easily Flash movies created using Flash, it also lets you create some limited types of Flash media.

I have grouped the various media types Dreamweaver supports that are Flash file types together in this section. To insert most of these Flash media types, you can use the Common toolbar and click the Media button, shown in Figure 13.1.

Inside Scoop

The only types of Flash media in this section that actually require the Flash program are generic Flash SWF files, discussed in the first subsection below, and the Flash Paper and Flash video media types. If you don't have Flash, the rest are fair game.

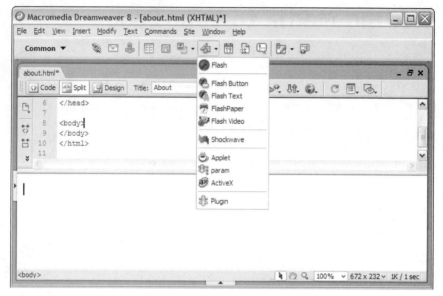

Figure 13.1. Media button on Common toolbar

I'll begin with the most obvious Flash media type: a Flash movie!

Flash

A basic Flash movie is any Flash animation or application that you create in the Flash environment. You have an SWF file, and you must put code in your page to call the file.

Here's how to insert the Flash file in your page:

1. Click in your page where you want to place the Flash file. This can be in either Design or Code view.

2. Locate the Media button, shown in Figure 13.1, on the Common toolbar. Click it and then choose the Flash menu option.

3. You see a Select File dialog box. Locate the SWF file you wish to insert in your page.

4. Your Flash file is inserted in your page. Figure 13.2 shows how it looks in Split view. In Code view there is a block of code surrounded by <OBJECT> tags. In Design view, you see a gray rectangle with the Flash logo in the middle of it.

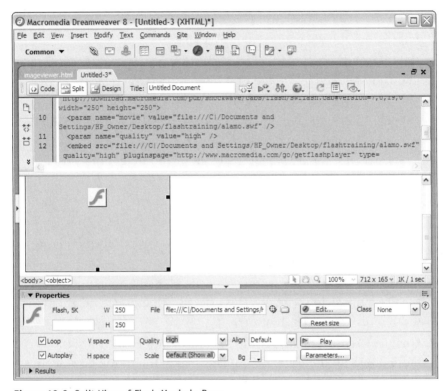

Figure 13.2. Split View of Flash Movie in Page

Let's take a closer look at the Properties panel for the Flash movie you just placed in your page. You can see it on the bottom third of Figure 13.2. Here are the settings:

■ **Name text box:** This is the unlabeled text box on the upper left, just under the word Flash. If you intend to use JavaScript to interact with this movie, you should give it a name. Otherwise, it can remain blank.

■ **W, H:** These are the width and height, respectively, of your Flash movie. Dreamweaver fills it in with the size you specified when you created the movie in Flash. The Scale setting, discussed a little later, controls how your movie looks when you change the width and height.

Inside Scoop

Because Flash is vector based, you can change the height and width and not suffer as much quality loss as you would with an image. However, it is still best to create your Flash file the size you want it to be in the page to achieve the best possible quality.

- **File:** This is the file path to your SWF file.

- **Edit:** If you have the Flash program, this button opens the Flash program and lets you locate the FLA file you used to create your SWF. You can then make the changes you wish to your file, and click the Done button. Your SWF will be replaced with the newly generated one with your changes reflected.

- **Reset size:** If you have changed the width and height of your Flash movie, this returns it to its original size.

- **Loop:** Check this if you want your Flash movie to play repeatedly in a loop.

- **Autoplay:** Check this if you want your Flash movie to begin playing when the user visits the page.

- **V space, H space:** These control how much padding to put around the Flash movie in the page. This does not change the height or width of the actual Flash movie.

- **Quality:** Use the Quality setting to control how clear your Flash movie looks on the page. Low quality makes the movie download more quickly, and high quality more slowly. The two auto settings can be used if you aren't sure of the bandwidth your users have. Use auto high if you think most users have a faster connection. This loads the best quality unless the download is taking too long, in which case the quality automatically drops for a faster download. Use auto low if you think your users have slow connections. If the download is going quickly enough, the movie automatically runs at a higher quality.

- **Scale:** If you have changed the height or width as described earlier, this setting controls how your movie displays in the new space. An example is shown in Figure 13.3.

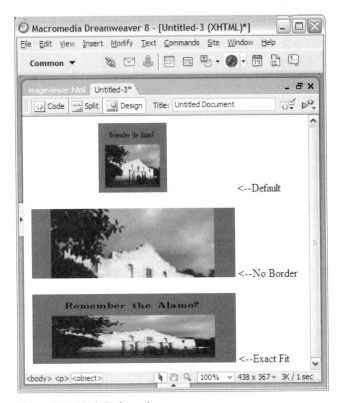

Figure 13.3. Flash Scale modes

In this example, I've taken the same 100 width by 100 height Flash movie and put it in my page three times. In each, I've changed the W setting in the Properties panel to 300. This shows how the three modes differ. From top to bottom, the modes are default, no border, and exact fit.

- **Align:** This contains a number of alignment options.

- **Bg:** When you set width and height and use the default Scale setting, as in Figure 13.3, the background color you choose here fills up the rest of the space that the Flash movie does not. In the previous example, if I had chosen a color here, I would see that color on either side of my movie filling up the 300 by 100 space.

- **Play/Stop:** Use this button to view your Flash movie actually playing in Design view.

- **Parameters:** If your Flash movie takes any parameters, click this button to open a dialog box where you can enter names and values of parameters.

Image viewer

The Flash image viewer is a built-in Flash application that allows you to view a slide show of images. You can specify in Dreamweaver which images you want the image viewer to display.

Figure 13.4 shows an example of the image viewer in a Web browser.

Figure 13.4. Flash image viewer

To create your own image viewer:

1. Create a page with any content you like and save it in the same directory as your images. Click in your page where you want to place the image viewer. This can be in either Design or Code view.

2. There are two ways to insert the image viewer. The first way is to locate the Flash elements toolbar, located under the menus and above the Editor pane. Click it and then click the Image Viewer button. The second way is to choose Insert ⇨ Media ⇨ Image Viewer.

Inside Scoop

You can only use JPG-, JPEG-, or SWF-based images in your image viewer.

3. A Save As dialog box opens. This is where you want to put the Flash image viewer. To make things simple, put it in the same directory as your images. You need to name it. You can call it anything you like, but imageviewer.swf is a good choice.

4. You see a Flash movie in your Design view. This is the image viewer, but it won't work quite yet. You have to enter the image names it will use. Begin by opening the Tag Inspector panel. Choose Window ⇨ Tag Inspector.

5. Click the Flash movie and notice that the Tag Inspector has now changed, as shown in Figure 13.5.

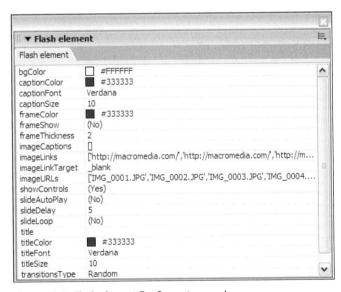

Figure 13.5. Flash element Tag Inspector panel

Inside Scoop

There are a number of fun options you can play with listed in the Tag Inspector panel when you select your image viewer in Design or Code view. Try changing the transitions, title, frame, font colors, and other parameters.

6. Locate the image URLs entry in the Tag Inspector panel. This line contains a list of the image names. You have to change those names to be your own filenames. Simply click in the box to change it. Use this format:

['yourimage1.jpg','yourimage2.jpg','yourimage3.jpg']

Surround each filename with single quotes (') and separate with commas. Put square brackets around the entire line.

7. Test your image viewer in Design view by selecting it and clicking Play in the Properties panel.

Flash button

If you would like to put a button in your page that is not the standard HTML-style button, you can use a Flash button. Flash buttons are pre-designed buttons in Dreamweaver that you can add to your pages. These buttons can be given URL links and targets, and have the added value of looking a little more interesting than standard buttons. Most also animate in some small way when the mouse cursor moves over them.

To add a Flash button to your page:

1. Click in your page where you want to place the Flash button. This can be in either Design or Code view.

2. Locate the Media button, shown in Figure 13.1, on the Common toolbar. Click it and then choose the Flash button menu option. The Insert Flash Button dialog box opens, shown in Figure 13.6.

3. Choose a Style from the list. A preview appears in the Sample area. Move your mouse over the preview to see what happens.

4. Type in the text you want on your button in the Button text box.

5. Choose a Font and a font Size.

6. Enter a link in the format www.putyourlinkhere.com.

7. Choose a Target window. If you want a new window to open when your button is clicked, choose _blank.

Watch Out!
You really can't put much text on your button, which is probably a good thing. The buttons are the size you see in the preview, and while you can use the W and H settings in the Properties panel to make them larger, the text you put in them is stretched.

Insert Flash Button

Sample:

> Button Text

OK

Apply

Cancel

Style:
| Beveled Rect-Blue |
| Beveled Rect-Bronze |
| Beveled Rect-Green |
| Beveled Rect-Grey |
| Blip Arrow |
| Blue Warper |

Get More Styles...

Help

Button text:

Font: Verdana   Size: 12

Link: Browse...

Target:

Bg color:

Save as: button1.swf   Browse...

Figure 13.6. The Insert Flash Button dialog box

8. Choose a Bg color. This should be the same color as the page background color underneath the button.

9. Pick a location to save the SWF file. This has to be moved to your Web server along with the Web page, so you may want to put it in the same folder or an image subfolder.

10. You can click the Apply button to preview the button in Design view before you close this dialog box. Click Apply and drag this dialog box to the side of your screen. You can then continue to make any changes you want.

To edit your button, simply click it in Design or Code view and click the Edit button in the Properties panel. Test your button using the Play button in Design view.

Inside Scoop

The Properties panel for your Flash button has much the same settings as the basic Flash movie Properties panel. Look in the previous section for specifics on these properties.

Flash text

Flash text is text that changes color when you roll over it and can be any font you have on your computer, unlike HTML text that depends on what fonts the people viewing your site have.

To add Flash text to your page:

1. Click in your page where you want to place the Flash text. This can be in either Design or Code view.

2. Locate the Media button, shown in Figure 13.1, on the Common toolbar. Click it and then choose the Flash text menu option. The Insert Flash Text dialog box opens, shown in Figure 13.7.

Figure 13.7. The Insert Flash Text dialog box

3. Choose a Font from the list and a Size for it. You can also choose bold, italic, left-justified, center, or right-justified.

4. Choose a Color for your font and a Rollover color for when the mouse cursor moves over it.

5. Type the text you wish to use in the Text box. If the Show font check box is checked, the Text box reflects the font choice and size you made. It will not change color in this box, but it will in your page.

6. Enter a link in the format www.putyourlinkhere.com.

7. Choose a Target window. If you want a new window to open when your text is clicked, choose _blank.

8. Choose a Bg color. This should be the same color as the page's background color underneath the text.

9. Pick a location to save the SWF file. This has to be moved to your Web server along with the Web page, so you may want to put it in the same folder or an image subfolder.

10. You can click the Apply button to preview the text in Design view before you close this dialog box. Click Apply and drag this dialog box to the side of your screen. You can then continue to make any changes you want.

To edit your text, simply click it in Design or Code view and click the Edit button in the Properties panel. Test your text link and color change by using the Play button in Design view.

FlashPaper

Macromedia FlashPaper is a stand-alone product that converts files into Flash or PDF documents. To use the FlashPaper media type, you need to have both the Flash program and the FlashPaper program. After you have created FlashPaper files, you can use the FlashPaper media button in Dreamweaver to insert them into your page.

To add FlashPaper files to your page:

1. Click in your page where you want to place the FlashPaper. This can be in either Design or Code view.

2. Locate the Media button, shown in Figure 13.1, on the Common toolbar. Click it and then choose the FlashPaper menu option. The Insert FlashPaper dialog box opens, shown in Figure 13.8.

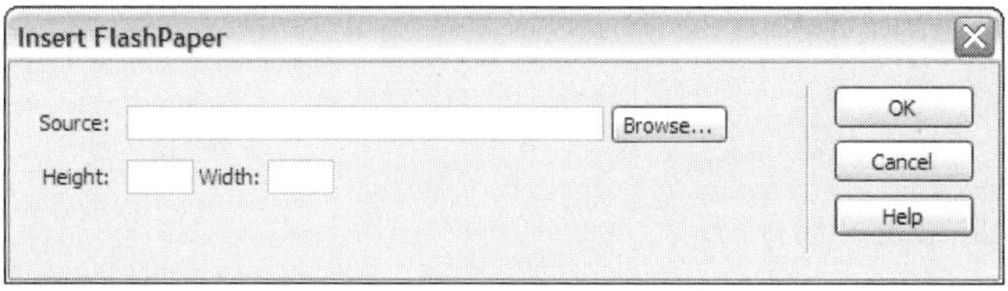

Figure 13.8. The Insert FlashPaper dialog box

3. Browse and select the Source of the FlashPaper file.

4. If desired, enter Height and Width settings. Click OK.

You can preview your FlashPaper by using the Play button on the Properties panel in Design view.

Flash video

Flash video is a type of progressive or streaming video file you can create in Flash. It can be easily embedded in your page with custom controls using the Flash Video button.

To add progressive Flash video to your page:

1. Click in your page where you want to place the Flash video. This can be in either Design or Code view.

2. Locate the Media button, shown in Figure 13.1, on the Common toolbar. Click it and then choose the Flash Video menu option. The Insert Flash Video dialog box opens, shown in Figure 13.9.

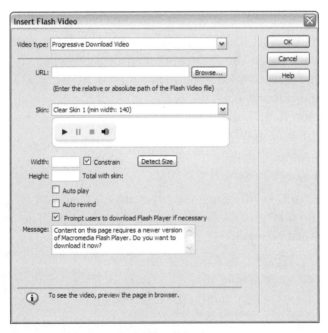

Figure 13.9. The Insert Flash Video dialog box

3. Choose Progressive Download Video for Video type.

4. Enter the path to your FLV Flash video file in the URL text box.

Inside Scoop

Streaming Flash video adds an additional layer of complexity because it requires a streaming server. As a result, I only discuss progressive Flash video here. You can get more information about streaming Flash video at the Macromedia Web site: www.macromedia.com.

5. Choose a skin from the Skin list. If your movie is especially narrow, pay attention to the minimum widths of each.

6. Enter the actual Width and Height of your movie. If you don't know them, use the Detect Size button. The Constrain check box keeps you from being able to skew your movie by changing the aspect ratio.

7. Check Auto play and Auto rewind to enable these if desired.

8. If users don't have the correct version of Flash, you can tell them to get it with the Prompt check box and the Message text box underneath. You can customize the message if you wish. Click OK.

You can't preview your movie in Design view; you must instead open your page in an external browser.

Shockwave

A Shockwave movie is any application that you create in the Macromedia Director environment. You have a DCR file, and you must put code in your page to call the file.

Here's how to insert your Shockwave file in your page:

1. Click in your page where you want to place the Shockwave file. This can be in either Design or Code view.

2. Locate the Media button, shown in Figure 13.1, on the Common toolbar. Click it and then choose the Shockwave menu option.

3. You see a Select File dialog box. Locate the DCR file you wish to insert in your page.

4. Your Shockwave file is inserted in your page. In Code view there is a block of code surrounded by <OBJECT> tags. In Design view, you see a gray rectangle with the Shockwave logo in the middle of it.

5. The Properties panel allows you to change the height and width, the V space and H space, the alignment, and the background color. You can also use the Play button in Design view.

Applet

An applet is an executable application that you create in the Java environment. You have a CLASS file, and you must put code in your page to call the file.

Here's how to insert your applet in your page:

1. Click in your page where you want to place the applet. This can be in either Design or Code view.

2. Locate the Media button, shown in Figure 13.1, on the Common toolbar. Click it and then choose the Applet menu option.

3. You see a Select File dialog box. Locate the CLASS file you wish to insert in your page.

4. Your applet is inserted in your page. In Code view there is a block of code surrounded by <APPLET> tags. In Design view, you see a gray rectangle with the Java coffee cup logo in the middle of it.

5. The Properties panel allows you to change the height and width, the base, the V space and H space, the alignment, and the background color. To preview your applet, open in a browser window.

Parameter

Most of the media types mentioned in this chapter can be communicated within the Web page using parameters. The Parameter media type gives you the opportunity of adding a parameter that you know is needed for your media without having to remove the media and start over again. Here's an example of the code for a Flash movie in a page. Notice the <PARAM> tags in the middle of it:

```
<object classid="clsid:D27CDB6E-AE6D-11cf-
96B8-444553540000"
codebase="http://download.macromedia.com/pub/
shockwave/cabs/flash/swflash.cab#version=5,0,0,0"
width="220" height="62">
 <param name="movie" value="text1.swf" />
 <param name="quality" value="high" />
 <embed src="text1.swf" quality="high"
pluginspage="http://www.macromedia.com/shockwave/down-
load/index.cgi?P1_Prod_Version=ShockwaveFlash"
```

```
type="application/x-shockwave-flash" width="220"
height="62" ></embed>
 </object>
```

To avoid having to recreate this code if you wanted to add another <PARAM> tag, you would use the Parameter button.

To insert a parameter:

1. Select a point inside the code of the media type you need to change. For example, if you are adding a parameter to a Flash movie in your page, choose a point between the close angle brace of one tag and the opening of another. This should be after the <OBJECT> and <EMBED> tags have been opened.

2. Locate the Media button, shown in Figure 13.1, on the Common toolbar. Click it and then choose the Param menu option. The Tag Editor – param dialog box opens, shown in Figure 13.10.

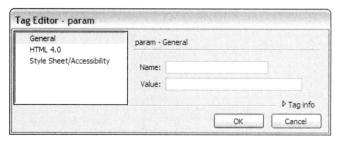

Figure 13.10. The Tag Editor – param dialog box

3. Choose the type of parameter you want to enter. If you know exactly the name and value you want, enter them under the General category. Click OK.

Your parameter should now appear in the media code.

ActiveX

An ActiveX control is an application very much like a Java applet, but with greater control over a Windows operating system. It does not run on any other type of operating system or any browser other than IE. It has fallen somewhat into disuse, primarily because of the security risks it poses to users.

Here's how to insert your ActiveX control in your page:

1. Click in your page where you want to place the ActiveX control. This can be in either Design or Code view.

2. Locate the Media button, shown in Figure 13.1, on the Common toolbar. Click it and then choose the ActiveX menu option.

3. A space holder for your ActiveX control is inserted in your page. In Code view there is a block of code surrounded by <OBJECT> tags. In Design view, you see a gray rectangle with the ActiveX logo in the middle of it.

4. To finish putting your control in the page, you need to set some properties in the Properties panel. At a minimum, you need to know the correct ClassID to use for your ActiveX control.

Other plug-ins

You can insert other Netscape Navigator plug-ins in your page with the Plug-in Media button. Using this button first prompts you for a filename. This is a file that can be read by the desired plug-in. Select your file and click OK. Dreamweaver inserts an <EMBED> tag in your page, like so:

```
<embed src="testing.xxxx" width="32"
height="32"></embed>
```

Any browser that recognizes the xxxx file type for a particular plug-in then opens that file in the browser window using the plug-in.

Just the facts

■ Dreamweaver allows you to add Flash files easily to your pages, and if you have the Flash program, you can edit source files seamlessly.

■ You can create Flash buttons and Flash text without having the Flash program.

■ In Dreamweaver and without Flash, you can create a Flash photo slide show using your own JPG files.

■ You can easily insert a variety of other media types in your pages, including Shockwave, Java applets, and Flash Video.

All About Placement

Chapter 14

The layout of your page matters. Where you put images, where you put text, how everything flows across the page — these things can make the difference between a fantastic Web site and a user interface nightmare.

Macromedia Dreamweaver offers you a number of tools to help you. With Dreamweaver, you can create your HTML tables visually, by clicking and dragging the borders in Design view in layout mode. You can also place rulers on the top and left of your page while designing it to see precisely where on the page your content will appear. Dreamweaver also gives you the option of using grids and guidelines, normally found in image editing programs. With all these tools at your disposal, you should find placing your content on your page exactly where you want it relatively easy.

Laying out your pages

An important consideration when you are creating your page is the likely screen size that your audience has. Many years ago the most common screen size was 640 by 480. As people have upgraded to larger monitors, faster computers, and broadband, the screen size has gotten larger. You have a few options. You can just design for 800 by 600, a very common screen size, or you can go larger and give yourself more freedom to design, while at the same time running the risk of disenfranchising your users. Think

Hack

You can generally keep users from being able to change the font size of your pages if you use CSS to specify your font sizes.

carefully about your audience. Do they upgrade to the latest larger monitors frequently? Or do they use older equipment? You might want to create two designs: one for smaller screen sizes and one for larger.

You also need to decide how you want your page to behave when the size you've designed is much larger or much smaller than the user's screen size. What will happen when your page is stretched out to 1024 if you've designed with 800 pixels in mind?

To complicate matters further, users sometimes override the font sizes you have set in your pages with a browser setting. In IE, for example, users can easily choose View ⇨ Text Size and choose from five different settings.

The next few subsections mention sometimes-overlooked layout concepts to keep in mind while you design your pages.

Page balance and symmetry

When I speak of the balance of your page, I am referring to how all the elements on your page work together, or don't work together. Take a look at Figure 14.1 to see an example of an extremely unbalanced page layout.

Although they may seem very modern, disturbing layouts may not be appreciated by your visitors.

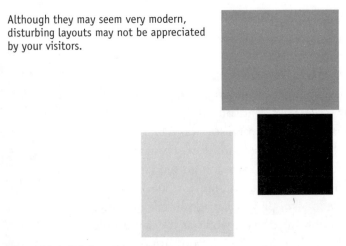

Figure 14.1. Unbalanced layout

With a well-balanced design, the page becomes unified. It's rather like having the perfect blend of flavors in a dish. Not too much salt, not too much spice, nothing overpowers it. All the elements on your page work together harmoniously. You need to think about balancing the page, and not making any piece of your design overpower any other piece—unless, of course, you intentionally want it to. An unbalanced design can make the viewer uneasy and look as though it were not intentional, but just hastily designed without any real thought given to the design.

One easy way to balance your page is to create a symmetrical layout, such as the one shown in Figure 14.2. Each side is a mirror image of the other.

Figure 14.2. Symmetrical layout

Creating a symmetrical layout is relatively simple. The result is a very formal and appealing appearance. Just as people perceive a symmetrical face as more attractive than an unbalanced one, a symmetrical design is more pleasing to the eye than an unbalanced one. Unfortunately, symmetry isn't particularly exciting and can lack energy. You must be careful to avoid creating a boring site with no focal points.

To achieve balance without a strictly symmetrical layout, you can use asymmetry. Asymmetry is achieved by balancing one element on the page with another, but not mirroring it, as in symmetry. Figure 14.3 shows an example of an asymmetrical page layout.

Figure 14.3. Asymmetrical layout

Page fold

When you first visit a Web page, if you are like most people, your monitor presents you with a rectangular area that is somewhat wider than it is tall. To see the bottom part of most Web pages, you have to click and scroll. The imaginary line between the visible part of the page and the bottom part you have to scroll down to see is known as the page fold.

You can use this information to your advantage. The area of your page that is visible without having to scroll down is by far more likely to be viewed than the part that the visitor has to scroll down to see. If you want to capture the attention of your visitors, consider the top part of your page above the fold as prime real estate. By this, I don't mean that you should neglect the bottom half, but put the attention-grabbing bits of your page in the top portion and save the bottom for exposition, or less interesting but still important sections.

Margins

Whether they are Web pages or printed pages, most pages you look at have margins. A margin is the empty space between the edge of the page and the beginning of the content. A margin works as a mat to your content and gives you a visual cue as to where the content begins. Consider the two text blocks shown in Figure 14.4, one with a margin and the other without.

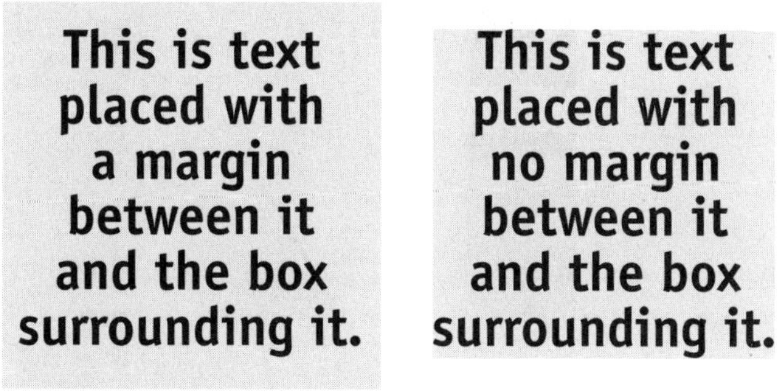

This is text placed with a margin between it and the box surrounding it.	This is text placed with no margin between it and the box surrounding it.

Figure 14.4. Two text blocks

The text block with the margin is easier to read and more appealing. That's not to say that you should always use a margin, but generally your visitors have become used to them and find their absence unsettling.

In IE and Netscape, you can control the size of your margins in your HTML page. By default, your page has a margin. To get rid of the margin or make it larger, you can modify the <BODY> tag of your HTML page. This <BODY> tag would set your top and left margins to 0 in both browsers:

```
<body leftmargin="0" topmargin="0" marginwidth="0"
marginheight="0">
```

Leftmargin and topmargin are used by IE, and marginwidth and marginheight are used by Netscape. To make your page consistent across both browsers, you need to set both sets of values.

To set these values without having to type out the tags, you can use the Macromedia Dreamweaver Page Properties dialog box. Open it by choosing Modify ⇨ Page Properties.

Inside Scoop

If you decide to change the page margins, you won't see the change reflected in Design view. You must preview your page in a browser. You can do this by choosing File ⇨ Preview in Browser or clicking the Preview in browser button on the title bar of your open file in Dreamweaver.

Using rulers and grids

In Design view, Dreamweaver offers you both rulers and grids, much like common graphic editing programs. You can't use them exactly as you would in a graphics program, because layout in HTML pages is not precisely free form. You can approximate it with layers, and to a lesser degree with tables, both discussed later in this chapter.

Rulers

Rulers in Dreamweaver are literally that, rulers. They are visual aids that you can use in Design view to help you with your page layout. Figure 14.5 shows the rulers present in Design view.

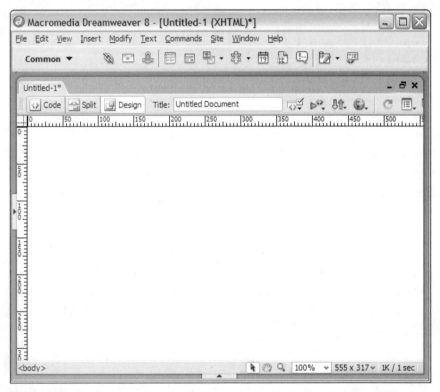

Figure 14.5. Rulers

Notice that they are along the top and left side of your view. They are very helpful if you have an idea of the page size you are designing for. Using rulers, you can accurately place images and text for your target page. In

Figure 14.5, the units of the rulers are pixels, although you can change that to inches or centimeters. If you are designing strictly for the Web, you will probably stick with pixels, but if you are creating a Web page that your users might print, you may want to use inches or centimeters for your units.

To make rulers visible in Design view, choose View ⇨ Rulers ⇨ Show. To change the units to inches or centimeters, choose View ⇨ Rulers ⇨ Inches or Centimeters. The ruler origin — that is, the 0,0 intersection of the ruler — is by default located at the upper left-hand corner of your document. If for some reason you want to change the origin, you can click and drag the origin icon on the upper left-hand corner where the two rulers meet, as shown in Figure 14.6.

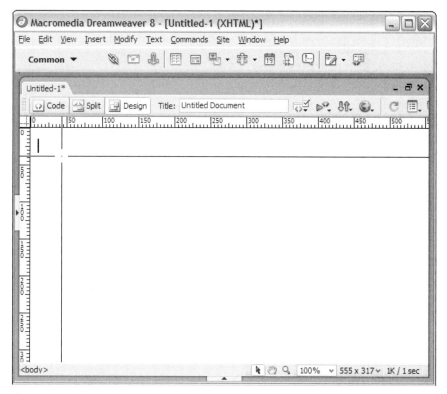

Figure 14.6. Change ruler origin

As you drag the origin, two black lines show you where on the page and on the ruler you are. Releasing then sets the new origin at that spot. To reset it back to the upper left-hand corner, choose View ⇨ Rulers ⇨ Reset Origin.

Guides

Guides are horizontal and vertical lines that you can place in your Design view to help you with your layout and with designing your page with a particular page size in mind. They are only present in Design view, and do not appear on the final Web page in a browser. When designing with layers, you can use the Snap to Guide option to precisely position them on the page. You can lock the guides in place to keep from accidentally moving them. Finally, when you save the page with guides present, Dreamweaver saves information on the location of the guides in a notes file associated with your file. Every time the file is opened in Dreamweaver, the guides are present.

The Guides menu under the View menu is shown in Figure 14.7. I will discuss the various options available to you in this menu.

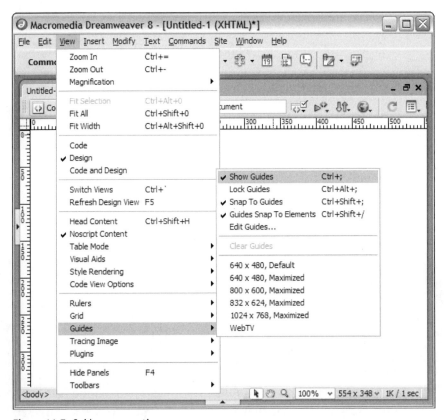

Figure 14.7. Guides menu options

To create guides:

1. Open or create a new page in Design view.

2. If necessary, make rulers visible by choosing View ⇨ Rulers ⇨ Show.

3. Create a horizontal guide by clicking anywhere in the ruler at the top of your document and dragging into the page. Vertical guides can be created by dragging from the ruler on the left.

4. You see green guidelines on your page.

5. To edit guide locations, simply move your mouse cursor over the guide until it changes to two small lines. Click and drag your guide to the new location.

To delete guides:

1. Move your mouse cursor to the guide you want to delete.

2. When the cursor changes to two small lines, click and drag the guide back in to the ruler.

3. To delete all guides at once, choose View ⇨ Guides ⇨ Clear Guides.

Here are a few more things you should know about guides:

■ You can see the distance between two guides with distance lines. These become visible if you Control-click (PC) or Command-click (Mac) anywhere between pairs of horizontal or vertical guides.

■ To see the actual location of a guide, simply move your mouse over it as though you were going to edit it. The pixel location pops up next to your cursor.

■ You can move a guide to a specific position without having to drag it around. Simply double-click the guide, enter the location you want in the Move Guide dialog box, and press OK.

■ Guides can be added to a template and are included on any page derived from that template. Users can move these guides, but each time the page template is updated the guides revert to the location in the template. See Chapter 10 for more information on using templates.

■ Under the View ⇨ Guides menu are a number of preset coordinates. Choosing these add guides to your page to represent the viewable area of your page that a browser in that resolution would see.

Inside Scoop

If the guides are important to keep on your page for future edits, but you don't want to see them, you can hide them from view. Uncheck the menu option View ➪ Guides ➪ Show Guides. They are still there, you just can't see them. Check Show Guides when you are ready to see them again.

To edit the appearance and behavior of your guides, choose View ➪ Guides ➪ Edit Guides. This opens the Guides dialog box, shown in Figure 14.8.

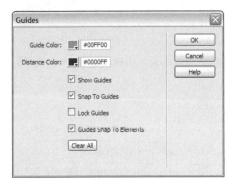

Figure 14.8. The Guides dialog box

Here are the guide options:

- **Guide Color:** This is the color of the guides. You may need to change it if you are working with a background color that is similar enough to a color that the guidelines aren't very visible.

- **Distance Color:** This is the color of the distance indicator lines.

- **Show Guides:** This check box shows guides, and is the same as choosing View ➪ Guides ➪ Show Guides.

- **Snap to Guides:** This check box makes layers snap to any guide close to where you move them, and is exactly the same as choosing View ➪ Guides ➪ Snap to Guides.

- **Lock Guides:** This option locks your guides in place so they can't be moved, and is the same as choosing View ➪ Guides ➪ Lock Guides.

- **Guides Snap to Elements:** This check box makes guides snap to any nearby layers as you move them, and is exactly the same as choosing View ➪ Guides ➪ Guides Snap to Elements.

▪ **Clear All:** This button clears all the guides from your page, and is the same as choosing View ⇨ Guides ⇨ Clear Guides.

Grids

Somewhat similar to guides, displaying the grid places regularly spaced horizontal and vertical lines in your Design view. As with guides, they are only present in Design view, and do not appear on the final Web page in a browser. When designing with layers, you can use the Snap to Grid option to make your layers position themselves at a grid line. You can specify the spacing of the grid lines. The grid does differ from guide lines in that it is not saved with the file even if you change the spacing of the grid lines.

To make your grid visible, choose View ⇨ Grid ⇨ Show Grid. Your grid appears as brown lines, 50 pixels apart. To hide the grid, uncheck Show Grid. You can also choose View ⇨ Show Grid ⇨ Snap to Grid. This option makes layers snap to any grid lines close to where you move your layer.

To edit the appearance and behavior of your grid, choose View ⇨ Grid ⇨ Edit Grid. This opens the Grid Settings dialog box, shown in Figure 14.9.

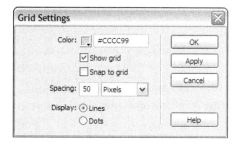

Figure 14.9. The Grid Settings dialog box

Here are the grid options:

▪ **Color:** This is the color of the grid lines. You may need to change it if you are working with a background color that is similar enough to a color that the grid lines aren't very visible.

▪ **Show grid:** This check box shows the grid, and is the same as choosing View ⇨ Grid ⇨ Show Grid.

■ **Snap to grid:** This check box makes layers snap to any grid lines close to where you move them, and is exactly the same as choosing View ⇨ Grid ⇨ Snap to Grid.

■ **Spacing:** Use this to set the distance between grid lines. You can use pixels, inches, or centimeters.

■ **Display:** Your grid can appear as either solid lines or dots.

■ **Apply:** Click the Apply button if you would like to preview the settings in Design view before committing yourself to them.

Creating layers

A layer is a rectangular container on your page, created by using the <DIV> or <SPAN> tag. A layer can contain anything that the body of an HTML page can contain. In terms of layout, layers are invaluable because a certain type of layer can be precisely placed on your page using pixel coordinates. You can use as many layers as you want and they can overlap or nest within each other. Layers only work with version 4+ browsers. In this section I'll show you how Dreamweaver allows you to precisely lay out your page using layers. For more information about layers, see Chapter 15.

Drawing a layer anywhere you want on your page is quite simple. Figure 14.10 shows the Layout toolbar.

Click the Draw Layer button on this toolbar. Now click and drag anywhere in Design view where you want to place your layer. You can use grids and guides to help you precisely place your layer. Notice that in Figure 14.10 there is a layer already drawn in Design view. The little tab on the upper left-hand corner of it can be used to drag the layer if you need to reposition it. You can also use the small handles along the corners and edges that appear when the layer is selected to resize or reshape the layer.

Layer visual aids

Here are a few other things that can help you lay out your page with layers in Design view:

■ Choose View ⇨ Visual Aids ⇨ CSS Layout Backgrounds. This option randomly colors your layers and hides any background images or colors.

- Choose View ⇨ Visual Aids ⇨ CSS Layout Box Model. This shows you the margins and padding of the selected layer.

- Choose View ⇨ Visual Aids ⇨ CSS Layout Outlines. This shows you the outlines of all layers on the page.

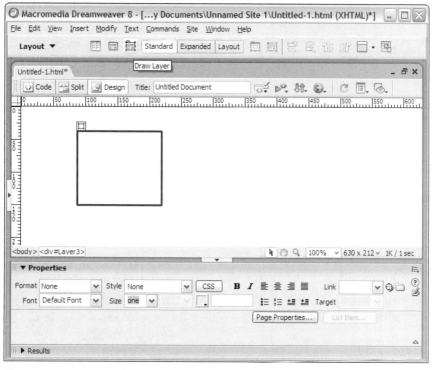

Figure 14.10. Draw Layer button on the Layout toolbar

Convert layers to tables

At some point, you may need to convert your layers into tables to support older browsers. Dreamweaver can convert them for you; however, it converts every layer on the page. You cannot use Dreamweaver to convert layers selectively. To convert from layers to tables, choose ⇨ Modify ⇨ Convert ⇨ Layers to Table. This opens the Convert Layers to Table dialog box, shown in Figure 14.11.

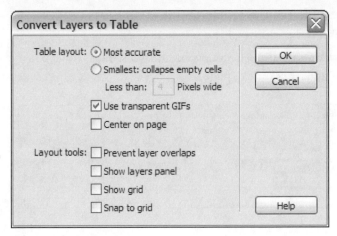

Figure 14.11. The Convert Layers to Table dialog box

Here is an explanation of the Table layout options in this dialog box:

- **Most accurate:** Creates the most complex tables with each layer being converted into its own cell and cells created for the spaces between the layers.

- **Smallest Collapse empty cells:** Consolidates any cells less than the width specified by the Pixels wide text box. This gives you a less complicated table, but it may not look like the original layout.

- **Use transparent GIFs:** Adds invisible GIF images into the table to help make it match the original layers. You won't be able to click and drag the table borders to change the size of cells in your table if you have selected this check box.

- **Center on page:** Places the new table in the center of the page if this box is checked. Otherwise, the table begins on the left side of the page.

- **Layout tools:** These check boxes specify the appearance of Design view after you have converted your file.

- **Prevent layer overlaps:** Prevents you from creating layers that overlap each other.

- **Show layers panel:** Automatically opens the Layers panel if it is closed.

- **Show grid:** Displays the grid.

- **Snap to grid:** Causes page elements to snap to the grid when moved near a grid line.

Watch Out!

Tables were never designed to be precise layout tools. Layers are so much more precise that when you convert your layers to tables, you may end up with extremely complex tables. These tables can be nearly impossible to edit by hand, so if you really do need tables, it is probably best to create your page using tables in the first place.

Modifying tables with the Properties panel

Prior to CSS, using a table on your page was the best way to place and format information if you needed to display anything more than a simple text page. However, because not all browsers support CSS layers, and often tables are the easiest way to accomplish simple layout tasks, tables are still quite important. Tables can have a number of attributes, including a border, padding between cells, spacing inside cells, vertical and horizontal alignment, and background colors and images. Tables can be used to create quite complex layouts.

Table visual aids

Here are a few other things that can help you lay out your page with tables in Design view:

- Choose View ⇨ Visual Aids ⇨ Table Widths. This displays the widths of your table and columns.

- Choose View ⇨ Visual Aids ⇨ Table Borders. If you have created a table with the border set to 0, this gives you a border while you work on the table in Design view. The border will not appear in the published page.

Table Layout modes

To create a table in Design view, you have three modes from which to choose:

- Standard mode allows you to create a table and do basic resizing operations on the table.

- Expanded mode can be used to add spaces temporarily in all the cells in a table to allow you to click more easily inside the cells to add content.

- Layout mode allows you to draw layout cells and tables and then move and adjust cells as content is added to them.

Standard mode

If you need a simple table to present information, using standard mode is the easiest way to create it. Figure 14.12 shows the Standard mode button selected in Design view.

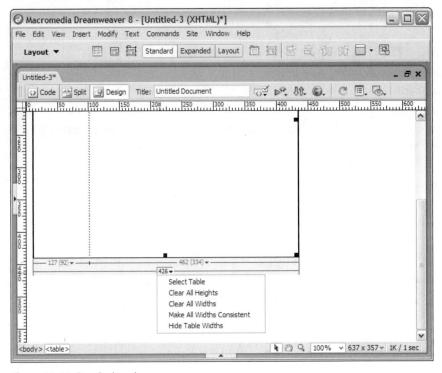

Figure 14.12. Standard mode

To create and manipulate a table in standard mode:

1. In Design view, open the Layout toolbar, shown in Figure 14.12. Click the Standard mode button.

2. Insert a table by clicking the Table button on the Layout toolbar or choosing Insert ⇨ Table.

3. The Table dialog box opens. Create a table with any settings you want, then click OK.

4. Your table should now appear in Design view. You can use the small black handles on the bottom and along the right side and the bottom right corner to resize your table.

Inside Scoop

Your table and column widths can be set to percentages instead of pixel values. The percentage represents the width of the viewer's browser. A 100 percent table width would stretch all the way across; 50 percent would go only halfway across.

Notice that the pixel width of the table appears in green along the bottom of the table. Next to it and under each column are green arrows that allow you to further control the dimensions of your table.

Here are the options from the green arrow menus:

▪ **Select Column:** This selects the current column. Use this if you need to delete a column. Select it and then choose Modify ⇨ Table ⇨ Delete Column.

▪ **Clear Column Width:** If your column has a specific width set in any of the <TD> tags, this removes it.

▪ **Insert Column Left, Insert Column Right:** Use this to add new columns to your table.

▪ **Select Table:** This selects the entire table.

▪ **Clear All Heights, Clear All Widths:** If the table has any HEIGHT or WIDTH tags set, this removes them.

▪ **Make All Widths Consistent:** You may see two width numbers for a column. This means that the actual content in the column is wider than the value set for the column's width. Use this option to make the value match the actual width of the content.

▪ **Hide All Widths:** This hides the green lines and width numbers. To make them visible, choose View ⇨ Visual Aids ⇨ Table Widths.

Expanded mode

Expanded mode is useful when you've placed content in your table but need to click in a tight table space; for example, between a table border and an image that fills up an entire cell. Figure 14.13 shows a table in expanded mode.

To manipulate a table in expanded mode, simply click the Expanded mode button on the Layout toolbar. You can perform exactly the same actions on your table that you can in Standard mode (see previous section).

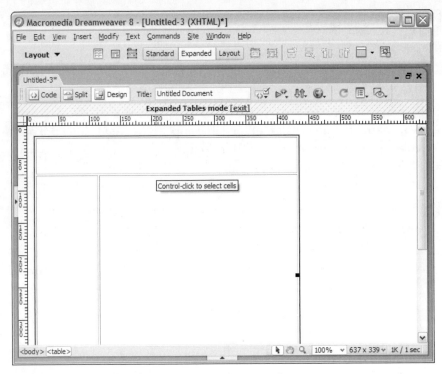

Figure 14.13. Expanded mode

Layout mode

Using layout mode, you can easily create complicated tables. Figure 14.14 shows a table in layout mode.

To create and manipulate a table in layout mode:

1. In Design view, open the Layout toolbar, shown in Figure 14.14. Click the Layout mode button, located to the right of the Standard and Expanded buttons.

2. Draw the outline of your table by clicking and dragging in the Design view window.

3. Click the Draw Layout Cell button. This is used to create all the interior areas where you can add editable content.

4. Draw your layout cells and insert any content you want.

5. To edit a layout cell, click its blue border to select the cell, then use the handles along the sides to stretch it.

Bright Idea

You can use layout mode to modify an existing table. This is useful for creating areas in your table that can span multiple rows or columns.

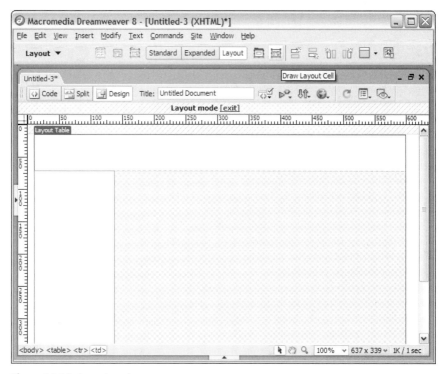

Figure 14.14. Layout mode

Convert tables to layers

You may want to convert your tables to layers. Dreamweaver can convert them for you, although it converts every table on the page and can't be used to convert tables selectively. To convert from tables to layers, make sure you are in Standard or Expanded table mode. Choose ⇨ Modify ⇨ Convert ⇨ Tables to Layers. The Convert Tables to Layers dialog box opens.

Here is an explanation of the options in this dialog box:

▪ **Prevent layer overlaps** prevents you from creating layers that overlap each other.

- **Show layers panel** automatically opens the Layers panel if it is closed.
- **Show grid** displays the grid.
- **Snap to grid** causes page elements to snap to the grid when moved near a grid line.

Just the facts

- Get as much information as possible about what screen size your visitors typically use so that you can design for it.
- Use graphic design concepts such as balance, symmetry, and asymmetry to make your page appealing.
- Rulers and guidelines help you build your page and preview what it will look like in different screen sizes.
- Grid lines can be used to help you line up your layers.
- Absolute layers can be placed anywhere on your page.
- Layers can be converted to tables, and tables to layers.
- Use the three-table design modes — standard, expanded, and layout — to help you easily create and edit complicated tables.

GET THE SCOOP ON...

Using timeline animation ▪ Adding objects to timelines ▪
How to create animation ▪ Modifying animation ▪
Working with multiple timelines

Adding Motion with Dreamweaver Timelines

T he Macromedia Dreamweaver Timelines panel is a special tool, quite unlike anything else in the Dreamweaver interface. This panel is used to create animated layers. You can perform such tricks as moving, hiding, resizing, and restacking any content you have placed in a layer. The timeline allows you to create all these effects without ever typing any code.

When you create an animation in a timeline, Dreamweaver inserts JavaScript code. This code is able to tell a layer or image in your page to perform the specified actions. For the curious, we will take a quick peek at the code, and I'll give you a summary of how it actually works. I'll show you what the timeline allows you to do, and describe the Timelines panel.

Using timelines to animate layers

The earliest type of animation used in Web pages was the animated GIF. This was simply multiple frames in a single image file. Because it was an image, and because downloading was a bit slower, they were generally used sparingly. You still see them today — cartoon dogs, hula girls, or dancing hamsters.

Inside Scoop

Timeline-created animations are generally viewable by most browsers. No Java applets or plug-ins are required. The browser needs to be version 4 or later, and it needs JavaScript viewing capabilities.

Then Macromedia Flash came along and changed everything. Now you could, in a relatively small file, have all sorts of creatures jumping, fireworks exploding, and text warping.

A type of animation that evolved around the same time was created using JavaScript functions. Around the time of the version 4 browsers, Dynamic HTML, or DHTML, began appearing. DHTML is simply the combination of JavaScript and named HTML elements. By naming the elements, the JavaScript code is able to reference them and change their properties, including location on the page, style, and size. This is what Dreamweaver is using behind the scenes. This animation is less limited than an animated GIF, but much more limited than a Flash movie. Still, it definitely can be worth knowing how to create these DHTML effects using the Dreamweaver timeline for just the right purpose.

What can you do with it?

Dreamweaver can move, resize, change the visibility of, and change the contents of layers over time.

Here are some specific tasks the timeline can help you with and possible uses for them:

- **Move a Layer:** You can define a path for your layer to move on your page. It can move anywhere on the page, and can be made to float above all the content, or below some other layers. This could be used to create a fluid display effect for your images, possibly a virtual art show.

- **Create a Slide Show:** You can use the timeline to change the image displayed in a layer after a period of time you specify. You can easily make a slide show using this.

- **Change Layer Content:** You can use a timeline to change any of the contents of your layer. For example, you could create virtual flashcards or tell parts of a story.

- **Hide or Show a Layer:** You can make a layer gradually appear or disappear. Perhaps you could fade out an image so the content underneath it on the page becomes readable.

- **Change Layer Size:** You can change the size and shape of your layer. You could make it appear to zoom in or out with this effect.

- **Change Stacking Order:** Every layer on your page has a stacking order, called a z-index. With your timeline, you can change this value, rather like shuffling a deck of cards.

The Timelines panel

Before we can start creating all these nifty animated effects, I need to show you the Timelines panel and explain how it works. Figure 15.1 shows the Timelines panel. To open the Timelines panel, choose Window ⇨ Timelines.

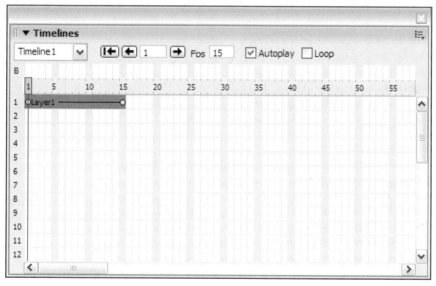

Figure 15.1. Timelines panel

Here are the controls on this window:

- **Timeline drop-down menu:** This drop-down box allows you to choose which timeline you want to work with. You can add new timelines by clicking the context menu in the upper right corner of the panel and choosing Add Timeline.

Inside Scoop

If you find that your animation seems choppy and not as smooth as you wish, change the frames per second to a higher number. If that doesn't help, the test machine you are using may not be capable of processing the frames more quickly.

- **Rewind button:** Clicking this button returns the currently selected frame-to-frame 1.

- **Back button:** Clicking this button moves the selected frame back one frame.

- **Frame number text box:** This box contains the frame number of the currently selected frame. You can type a frame number in the box to move the selected frame to that frame.

- **Forward button:** Clicking this button moves the selected frame forward one frame.

- **Frames per second:** This box contains the frames-per-second rate. This specifies how quickly or slowly your animation will play.

- **Autoplay:** Selecting this check box inserts the code in your page to make your animation start playing as soon as the page is loaded.

- **Loop:** Selecting this check box makes your animation play in a loop. When it reaches the final frame of animation, it will return to frame 1. If you decide to loop, you should make sure that the last frame and the first frame of your animation are the same. Otherwise, your animation will seem to jump each time it replays.

- **B Channel:** Macromedia refers to the lists of frames in the Timelines panel as channels. This channel is located across the top of the panel and is labeled with the letter "B." It is used to define layer behavior changes, changes to the layer including such things as visibility, border style, background color, and even the content inside the layer. Even though there is only one B channel, you can add as many behaviors as you wish to as many layers as you have in your timeline. This will be clearer when we actually create some animations in the next section.

- **Frame numbers:** This is a list of frame numbers between the B timeline and the numbered timelines. The currently selected frame is shaded in red.

▪ **Main Channels:** These numbered channels take up the entire bottom of the panel. They are used to display the frames of the actual layers to be animated. You use them to animate changes in location. Figure 15.2 shows three layer objects in the main channels.

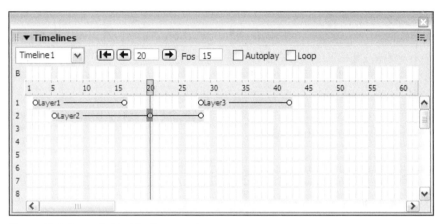

Figure 15.2. Layers in the Timelines panel

The gray shaded areas in the main channels are the frames defined for each layer. The round circles are called keyframes and are the points at which the location of the layer can be changed for animation.

Adding objects to timelines

Timelines can interact with only two HTML element types in your page: layers and images. In this section, I will show you how to create layers and images and add them to the timeline to be animated.

For much of the rest of this chapter, I will be working with a page for my Complete Traveler Web site. This page will consist of text about a recent fictional trip. The animations will consist of changing text in layers and images that drift on the screen and then disappear.

Create the layers

To begin, we need to create a page with the layers and images we will be using. I will have four layers. One will contain the text and the other three will contain images.

To create the layers:

1. In Design view, open the Layout toolbar.

Inside Scoop

While you can insert an image into your timeline, you can't do much with it. The only change you can make to an image is to change the source. In other words, your image can change to another image, but nothing else. To do anything else it needs to be in a layer.

2. Make sure you are in Standard mode, then click the Layer button and draw a layer on the screen. This will be the layer with the text in it. In the Properties panel, rename the Layer something distinctive, such as "TravelText," as shown in Figure 15.3.

The name text box on the Properties panel is on the upper left, just under the words "Layer ID."

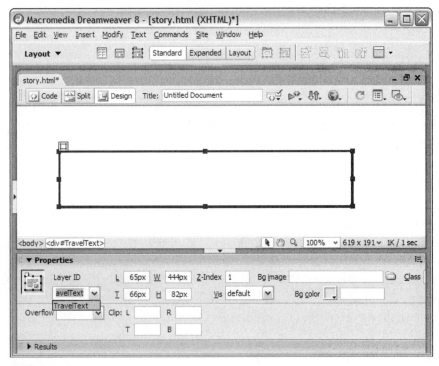

Figure 15.3. Layer Properties panel

3. Create three more layers and place a different image in each. Give them each an identifying name. I have used Image1, Image2, and Image3.

4. Insert images in each of the three image layers.

5. Enter some text in the TravelText layer that describes the image in the Image1 layer.

6. Modify the layer colors, margins, and borders as desired. In Figure 15.4, you can see the four layers. Notice the different color, padding, border color, and border width of the text layer. You can select the layer and use the CSS panel to modify this layer.

Figure 15.4. Four layers

Inside Scoop

Look at your Timelines panel. Notice the keyframes — the small round circles in the first and last frames of the layers — you have dragged into it. You can click or drag these frames to make the animation longer and to resize your layer.

Add layers to timeline

Now that the four layers are created, we can add them to the timeline. Because the text layer will always be present, it will be added first and will have frames for the entire length of the animation. The other three will appear in turn.

To add layers to the timeline:

1. You should still have the Design view open with the four layers present.

2. Open the Timelines panel by choosing Window ⇨ Timelines.

3. Click the handle on the upper left corner of the TravelText layer and drag it into the number 1 channel of the Timelines panel. You can also simply select the layer to insert and click the context menu in the upper right-hand corner of the Timelines panel and select Add Object. Don't worry about which frame you add it to, you will be able to change it whenever you like.

4. Drag the other layers, Image1, Image2, and Image3, into the next three channels, number 2, number 3, and number 4. Again, you will be able to move these, so don't worry about which frames they are on for now.

5. Your Timelines panel should look something like the one shown in Figure 15.5.

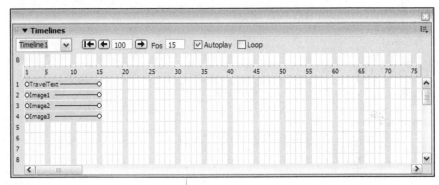

Figure 15.5. Four layers inserted in Timelines panel

Hack

There is another way to change the text without using the Change Property dialog box. When you click the plus (+) button (see previous step 3), choose the option Set Text ⇨ Set Text of Layer. Then enter the new text in that dialog box.

Change the text in a layer

The text in the text layer is different for each of the three images. In the following steps, we will increase the length of the TravelText layer in channel 1, add two more keyframes, and change the text content in those two keyframes.

To change the text in a layer:

1. Begin by lengthening the TravelText layer in the Timelines panel. If the beginning of the layer isn't at frame 1, drag it there now by clicking the small circle on the left of the layer in channel 1 and dragging it to the left. Then drag the small circle on the right of the layer to frame 120.

2. To change the text in the layer, we need the Behaviors panel. Choose Windows ⇨ Behaviors.

3. Click frame 60 of the B channel. With it selected, click the plus (+) button on the Behaviors panel to add a behavior.

4. From the menu, choose Change Property.

5. The Change Property dialog box opens, shown in Figure 15.6. For Type of object, choose DIV. For Named object, choose div "TravelText." For Property, choose Select innerText. In the New value text box, type the new text you want to appear in the TravelText layer. This should correspond to the second image you will be displaying.

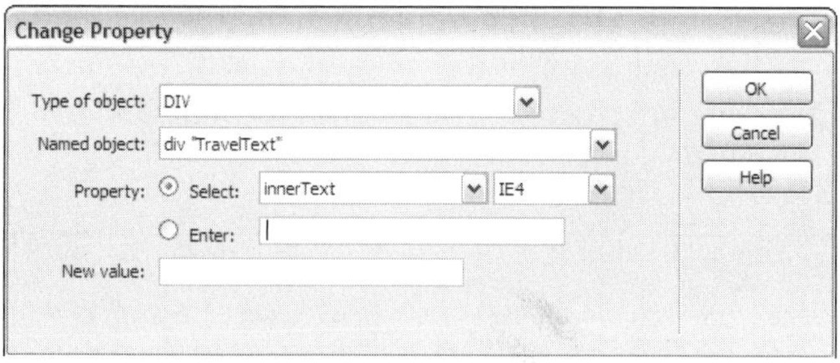

Figure 15.6. The Change Property dialog box

Inside Scoop

Creating animated movement is quite simple. Just click the first frame of your layer in the channel and then move the layer wherever you want it. Click the last frame of your layer in the channel and then move the layer where you want it. A black line in Design view indicates the path along which your layer moves.

6. Repeat the last step for the behavior frame at 120.

7. Make sure the Autoplay check box is checked on the Timelines panel. Now save your page and choose File ⇨ Preview in Browser. You should see the text change in your text layer after about four seconds, and then again after eight seconds.

Creating animation

We now need to move the three images in channels 2, 3, and 4 to the correct locations on the timeline. The actual layers will then be moved to their starting positions offscreen, and then animated moving onscreen. Finally, we will hide the image layers.

Create an animation path

In the following steps, I will take you through the animation of a single layer, the Image1 layer:

1. Move the Image1 frames in channel 2 to begin at keyframe 1 and end at keyframe 60.

2. Create the animation path for Image1 to follow. You will need the Properties panel, Timelines panel, and Design view visible. Click the first keyframe of Image1 in the Timelines panel, shown in Figure 15.7.

3. With keyframe 1 of Image1 selected, change its location in the Properties panel. We want it to come from off-screen, so make the L (left) a negative value that moves it from Design view. Press Enter. The layer should now be offscreen, so you will not see it in Design view.

Bright Idea

A simple way to know what value to use to move your layer outside your page is to use the layer's width and make it a negative value. For example, if your image is 200 pixels wide, set the L value in the Properties panel to -200.

4. Click the last keyframe of Image1, located at frame 60. Drag the layer to the right of the TravelText layer.

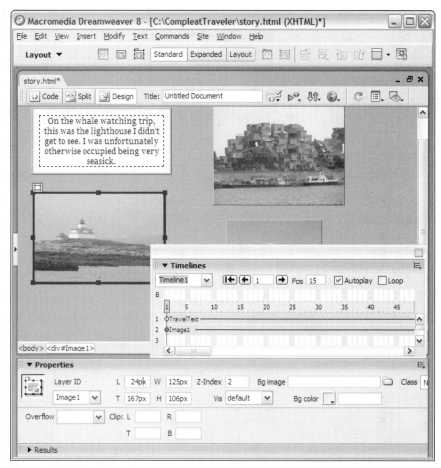

Figure 15.7. Animating a layer

Curve the animation path

The black line you see is the path your image will take as it travels across the screen. As it stands right now, it may cut across your TravelText layer. We can make it curve underneath. Click frame 30 of Image1.

To curve an animation path:

1. Right-click (Ctrl-click on a Mac) the context menu of the Timelines panel and choose Add Keyframe. You can also choose Modify ⇨ Timeline ⇨ Add Keyframe.

2. Click the new keyframe and then drag the layer beneath the TravelText layer, as shown in Figure 15.8. Notice how the line now curves.

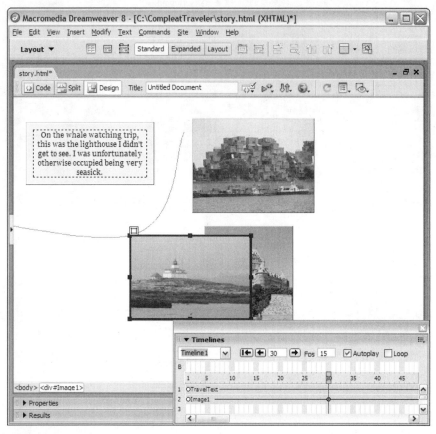

Figure 15.8. Curving the animation path

Hide a layer

The last step for this page is to make Image1 disappear. Simply deleting the layer from Design view after frame 60 will not work. Instead, click the B channel at frame 61. In the Behaviors panel, click the plus (+) button and choose Show-Hide layers. The Show-Hide dialog box appears. Choose Image1 and click the Hide button, then click OK. From frame 61 on, Image1 is hidden. Look at your page in a browser to check the results.

Inside Scoop

If you are testing your work on your local machine and not using a Web server, you may see the IE Security Bar warning you about a potential security risk. This warning will not appear when your site is viewed from a Web server.

Create a start button

You don't have to start your animation automatically with the Autoplay check box. You can also create something on your page to trigger the animation.

Here's how to create a button to start your animation playing:

1. Insert a button in your page. To use a Flash button, choose Insert ⇨ Media ⇨ Flash Button, or choose a Flash button from the Media menu on the Common toolbar.

2. This opens the Insert Flash Button dialog box. Figure 15.9 shows the Control-Play button selected. You don't need to change any other settings in this dialog box. Click OK.

Figure 15.9. Inserting a Control button

Inside Scoop

You are not limited to using a Flash button to control the playing of your timeline. Any object on your page to which you can attach behaviors can be used. You can also stop and go to a frame in your animation in much the same way.

3. Open the Behaviors panel by choosing Window ⇨ Behaviors. Click the button you just created and then click the left side of the first entry in the Behaviors panel. Choose "On Focus."

4. Click the plus (+) button and choose Timeline ⇨ Play Timeline.

The animation begins when the Flash button is clicked.

Behaviors you can add

There are quite a few style and behavior changes you can make to a layer using the B channel and the Behaviors panel.

Here's a summary of the options in the plus (+) button of the Behaviors panel.

- **Call JavaScript:** You can call a JavaScript function at any point in your timeline.

- **Change Property:** This opens the Change Property dialog box and offers you a number of options for changing your layer. Some of the more important ones are z-index, height, width, colors, visibility, font styles and colors, innerHTML, and innertext.

- **Check Browser:** This handy option can be used to redirect users with browsers not capable of viewing the current page to another page.

- **Check Plugin:** This can be used to redirect users with browsers lacking a specific plug-in on the current page to another page.

- **Go to URL:** This sends all browsers to another URL you specify when this point in the timeline is reached.

- **Open Browser Window:** Another window containing the Web page you specify opens at this point.

- **Play Sound:** This plays the sound file you choose at this frame.

- **Popup Message:** This opens a JavaScript alert box.

- **Preload Images:** If you have large images you will display at a later point in your timeline, you can begin sending them to the visitors' browsers at this point, making the download occur more gradually.

The images won't be visible until you actually use them in your page in some way.

■ **Set Text:** Use these options to change the text in your layers or the status bar.

■ **Show-Hide Layers:** This allows you to hide or show layers at this point in the timeline.

■ **Swap Image, Swap Image Restore:** You can change images in a layer at a specific frame on the timeline and then replace them at another frame.

■ **Timeline:** The options in this submenu allow you to jump around your timeline and play sections repeatedly or stop playing the timeline.

Changes to layers in timeline channels

You can add keyframes anywhere between the first and last keyframes in your current layer by clicking the context menu and choosing Add Keyframe. You can also choose Modify ➪ Timeline ➪ Add Keyframe.

Here are a few changes you can make to your layers in the channels with keyframes selected:

■ **Change location:** Select the keyframe you wish to change. Use the Properties panel and modify the L (left) and T (top) values. Alternatively, simply drag the layer to the desired location. This modifies the animation path.

■ **Change height and width:** Select the keyframe you wish to change. Use the Properties panel and modify the H (height) and W (width) values. Alternatively, simply click the layer and use the small square resize handles on the corners and sides to change the shape. This animates the change in shape.

■ **Change visibility:** Select the keyframe you wish to change. Use the Properties panel and click the Vis drop-down box to select inherit, visible, or hidden. If you hide the layer, it simply disappears at that frame rather than fading out.

■ **Change source file:** To change the source file of an image in a layer at a particular keyframe, select the image at that keyframe and change the source in the Properties panel.

Bright Idea

Instead of changing the source file, just create two layers and use the Show-Hide behavior. When you change the source, the new image has to be downloaded and can cause the animation to slow down.

- **Change z-index:** If your layers overlap during animation, you may wish to change which one is on top at a specific frame. To do this, select a keyframe in the layer you wish to be on top and change the z-index value in the Properties panel. The higher values are on top, the lower ones underneath.

Modifying animation

After you have created an animation, you can easily change anything about it, including the timeline, the layers, the behaviors, the name, the frame rate, and the length.

Here are some things you can change in an animation:

- **Change behaviors:** Simply click the B channel frame where you previously inserted behaviors. You see them listed in the Behaviors panel, where you can modify, add, or delete them.

- **Move entire animation on timeline:** Click between any two keyframes on the layer in the timeline. The entire set of frames is selected and can be clicked and dragged to the new location.

- **Change location of keyframes:** You can click and drag any keyframe to any location you wish.

- **Change length of timeline:** Use the first and last keyframes to click and drag to increase the length of your timeline.

- **Loop timeline:** Click the Loop button.

- **Autoplay timeline:** Click the Autoplay button.

- **Rename timeline:** You can change the name of the timeline to something more descriptive by clicking the context menu in the upper right corner of the Timelines panel and choosing Rename Timeline. Enter the new name and click OK. If you have created any objects that referenced the old timeline name — for example, a button that tells Timeline1 to play — you will need to edit them and enter the new name.

- **Duplicate animation:** Click between any two keyframes on the layer in the timeline. Choose Copy from the context menu in the upper right corner of the Timelines panel, then choose Paste. The new copy is directly behind the original. Click between any two keyframes and drag it to its new location.

- **Change object:** You can apply an already created animation to a different layer. Simply duplicate the animation as above. Select the animation and choose Change Object from the context menu in the Timelines panel. Then choose the new layer or image to use.

Working with multiple timelines

Although you can insert up to 32 individual channels in one timeline, you can also create separate timelines. This can be useful if you are using animations and behaviors for different parts of a page. For example, if you have three buttons, each controlling a different animation, you can create three timelines to help you keep your animations organized.

Create a new timeline by choosing Modify ⇨ Timeline ⇨ Add Timeline. It is a good idea to give each timeline a descriptive name. Choose Rename Timeline from the context menu in the Timelines panel. To switch between timelines, you can select from the drop-down menu on the top left of the Timelines panel.

Just the facts

- Use the Dreamweaver Timelines panel to create animations and trigger behaviors at specific points in time.

- Layers can be animated to move across the page, change size, change z-index, and change visibility.

- Layers can also have behaviors attached to them at certain frames in the timeline.

- Use Autoplay to make the animation play when the page is loaded.

- You can create buttons to start, stop, and loop the playing of your timeline.

- Apply your animation to multiple layers by copying the animation and choosing Change Object from the context menu in the Timelines panel.

- Create multiple timelines if you have several animated sections of the page that serve different functions.

GET THE SCOOP ON...
The Text Properties panel in depth ■ Image alignment ■
HTML text styles ■ CSS text styles ■ Creating a uniform
style for your site

Controlling Text Appearance

T ext may be the single most important part of any Web page. I think it actually is the single most important part of a page. I take my text very seriously, and so should you!

This chapter is all about how to control the style, alignment, color, and fonts on a page and across an entire site. Basic text appearance can be controlled with HTML and CSS. Both have advantages and disadvantages. Macromedia Dreamweaver can help you format your text with one or both and save you time as you create your text layout.

Setting text styles with the Properties panel

In Chapter 8, I discussed the Properties panel for text. In this chapter, I will go into more detail, and show you the options available to you for controlling your text.

HTML or CSS?

The Properties panel for text can format text with either CSS or HTML options. The choice is yours. By default, Dreamweaver creates CSS rules when you change text with the Properties panel. To force it to use HTML tags, open the Preferences Panel, shown in Figure 16.1. Choose Edit ⇨ Preferences and click the General category on the left. Uncheck the Use CSS instead of HTML tags check box.

Chapter 16

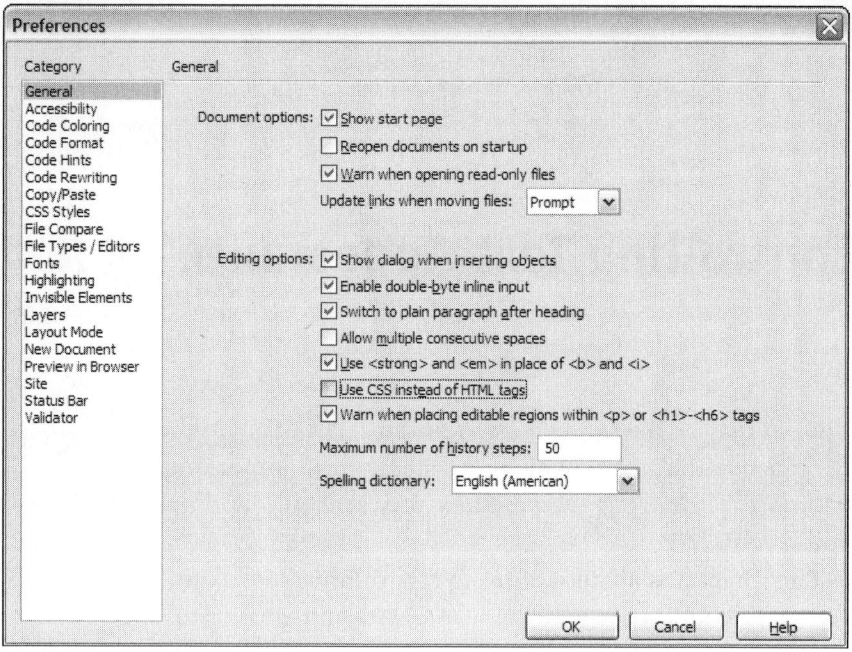

Figure 16.1. The Preferences dialog box

Text Properties panel

Figure 16.2 shows the Text Properties panel.

The Text Properties panel appears any time you have any non-HTML text selected between the <BODY> tags. It also appears when you are between tags inside the <BODY>.

The options you can set are:

- **Format:** Select a standard HTML heading or paragraph format to apply to your text. The available formats are:

- **None:** No formatting tags are applied.

- **Paragraph:** The text is surrounded by an HTML paragraph tag.

  ```
  <P>Here is the HTML for text with paragraph tag.</P>
  ```

- **Heading 1-6:** These tags vary in size and boldness. They range from 1 as the biggest to 6 as the smallest.

  ```
  <H1>Here is the HTML for text with a heading 1
  tag.</H1>
  ```

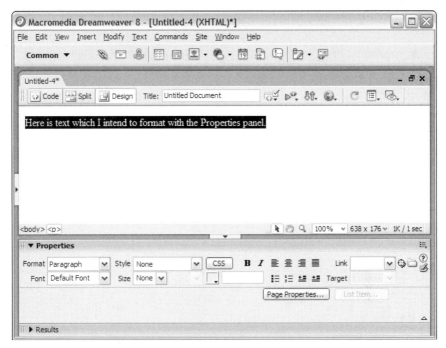

Figure 16.2. Text Properties panel

- **Preformatted:** If you surround your text with a <PRE> tag, extra spaces and carriage returns will not be ignored, as is normally the case in HTML text.

  ```
  <PRE>Here is the HTML for text with the preformatted
  tag.</PRE>
  ```

  These formatting styles are shown in Figure 16.3.

- **Style:** Any named CSS styles available in this page or an associated CSS file appear here. You can select one to apply to the text.

- **CSS Button:** This populates the CSS panel with editable information about the current style.

Inside Scoop

Earlier iterations of the HTML specifications used the <B> tag and the <I> tag for boldface and italics, respectively. Current specs suggest the <STRONG> and <EM> tags. Browsers will interpret any of them correctly.

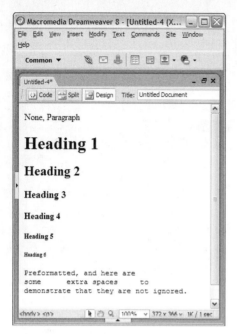

Figure 16.3. Text formats

- **Bold:** Make your text boldface with this button.

  ```
  <STRONG>Here is HTML for boldfaced text.</STRONG>
  ```

- **Italic:** Make your text italicized with this button.

  ```
  <EM>Here is HTML for italicized text.</EM>
  ```

- **Align Left:** This aligns the selected text to the left side of the page or table cell or other container the text is in.

  ```
  <P align="left">Here is HTML to left align text.</P>
  ```

- **Align Center:** This aligns the selected text to the center of the page or table cell or other container the text is in.

  ```
  <P align="left">Here is HTML to center align text.</P>
  ```

- **Align Right:** This aligns the selected text to the right side of the page or table cell or other container the text is in.

  ```
  <P align="left">Here is HTML to right align text.</P>
  ```

- **Justify:** This aligns the selected text so that it is justified in the page or table cell or other container the text is in. Justified text often

resembles left aligned text, but the right side is also aligned whenever possible.

```
<P align="left">Here is HTML to justify text.</P>
```

Figure 16.4 shows these options applied to text on a page.

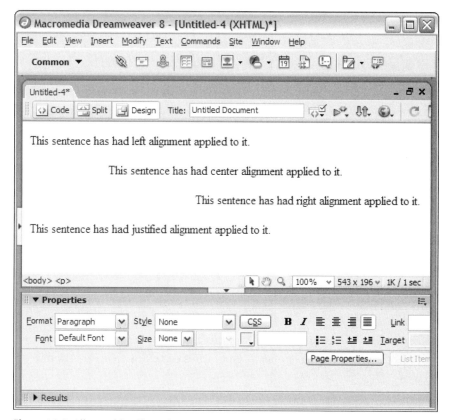

Figure 16.4. Align and justify options

- **Link:** Type a Web address or anchor name in this text box to turn
  the selected text into an HTML link.

- **Font:** Set the font of the selected text. Displayed are common font
  families. You also have the option of adding a font to the list from the
  fonts installed on your computer. In the following HTML text, notice
  that there are three font assignments being made with the same face
  tag. The browser viewing your page displays the text in the first font
  face it comes to that is installed on the browser's machine.

Watch Out!

Although the Font box in the Properties panel lets you add any font installed on your machine, if the browsers visiting your site don't have that font installed on their machine, they won't see it. It's generally best to stick to the fonts in the font list and not add your own unless you know for certain your audience has the other font installed.

```
<FONT face="Arial, Helvetica, sans-serif">This text
is assigned a set of fonts.</FONT>
```

- **Size:** Set the size of your font. The sizes with the plus and minus signs in front of them are relative sizes and make your font larger and smaller, respectively. A font with no size information is assumed to be the same as the "3" font size. The numbers in the list with no plus or minus are specific sizes. The smallest numbers are the smaller sizes and the largest are the biggest.

```
<FONT size="+2">This text is being assigned a rela-
tive size of +2.</FONT>
```

- **Color:** Set the color of your text here. You can type in the hex value or use the color chooser to pick a color and Dreamweaver adds the hex value for you.

```
<FONT color="#FF0000">This text color is red.</FONT>
```

- **Bulleted or Unordered List:** Use this button to begin a bulleted (or unordered) list. You can also select lines of text to convert them to a list.

```
<UL>

<LI>Item in bulleted list</LI>

<LI>Item in bulleted list</LI>

</UL>
```

Inside Scoop

Notice that the attributes face, size, and color are all inside the <FONT> tag. These can be combined in the same <FONT> tag. The result would look something like this:

```
<FONT color="#FF0000" size="+2" face="Arial, Helvetica,
sans-serif">Example text</FONT>
```

- **Numbered List:** Use this button to begin or create a numbered list (or ordered) list.

```
<OL>

<LI>Item in numbered list</LI>

<LI>Item in numbered list</LI>

</OL>
```

Figure 16.5 shows a bulleted list, also known as an unordered list. Also shown is a numbered list, also known as an ordered list, and indented text.

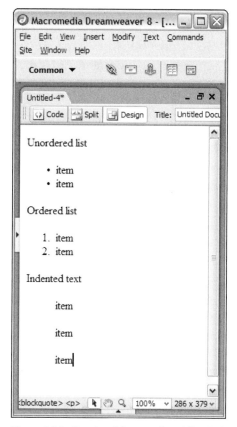

Figure 16.5. Unordered list, numbered list, indented text

- **Indent, Un-indent:** Use these buttons to indent or un-indent selected text. Un-indenting is also referred to as outdenting.

```
<BLOCKQUOTE>

Indented text<P>

Indented text

</BLOCKQUOTE>
```

- **Target:** If you have defined a link, this button lets you choose the target window for that URL.

- **Page Properties Button:** This button opens the Page Properties dialog box.

Text alignment

I've already mentioned the main text alignment settings in the previous section. These are left, right, center, and justify. But when you have an image on your page and text around it, the image alignment can affect the text. Here is a list of the possible image tag alignment options and how they change text alignment:

- **Default, baseline, and bottom:** Text on either side of the image is aligned to the bottom of the image. The bottom of the text is considered the text line.

- **Top and text top:** Text on either side of the image is aligned to the top of the image.

- **Middle:** Text on either side of the image is aligned to the middle of the image. The bottom of the line of text lines up with the middle of the image.

- **Absolute middle:** Text on either side of the image is aligned to the middle of the image. Slightly different from middle, the center of the line of text lines up with the middle of the image.

- **Absolute bottom:** Text on either side of the image is aligned to the bottom of the image. The bottom of the text is considered the lowest character that hangs below the text line.

- **Left:** The image is left justified, and all text on either side of the image is placed on the right.

- **Right:** The image is right justified, and all text on either side of the image is placed on the left.

Figure 16.6 shows some images with different alignments chosen and text on either side of each image.

Figure 16.6. Image alignments

Setting text styles in HTML

The Dreamweaver interface has a Text menu with a number of HTML formatting options for text. Here are the options from the menu, along with a brief explanation of what each does. Because these options are all present in the Text Properties panel as well as in this menu, these explanations are brief. For more information, look in the earlier section, "Setting text styles with the Properties panel."

- **Indent:** Choose this menu option to begin creating an indented block of text or to modify existing text.
- **Outdent:** Use this to remove the indent on your text.
- **Paragraph format:**
  None: No format is applied.

Paragraph: A <P> paragraph tag is added.

Heading 1-6: These are shown in Figure 16.3 and vary in size.

Preformatted: Text that is preformatted ignores any text tags outside of the <PRE> tag. Extra spaces and carriage returns appear in the page.

- **Align:** Choose left, center, right, or justify.
- **List:** Create a bulleted or numbered list.
- **Font:** Set the font of the text.
- **Style:** The Style menu option has a few choices that are not found in the Text Properties panel. Examples of each are shown in Figure 16.7.

```
<B>Bold</B>
<EM>Italic</EM>
<U>Underline</U>
<S>Strikethrough</S>
<TT>Teletype</TT>
<EM>Emphasis</EM>
<STRONG>Strong</STRONG>
<CODE>Code</CODE>
<VAR>Variable</VAR>
<SAMP>Sample</SAMP>
<KBD>Keyboard</KBD>
<CITE>Citation</CITE>
<DFN>Definition</DFN>
<DEL>Deleted</DEL>
<INS>Inserted</INS>
```

- **Size:** Changes the text size.
- **Size Change:** Changes the text size relative to the current font size tag around the text.
- **Color:** Opens the color chooser to allow you to set the font color.

Figure 16.7. Text styles from Style menu

Setting text styles with CSS

CSS text styles can be set with both the CSS Styles panel and the Text Properties panel. To use the Text Properties panel to create CSS code, make sure the Use CSS instead of HTML tags check box in the Properties dialog box is checked. To get to this check box, choose Edit ⇨ Preferences and click the General category on the left.

CSS text styles

To see the available CSS text styles, open the CSS Styles panel by choosing Window ⇨ CSS Styles. Figure 16.8 shows a text style in both the CSS Styles and Properties panels.

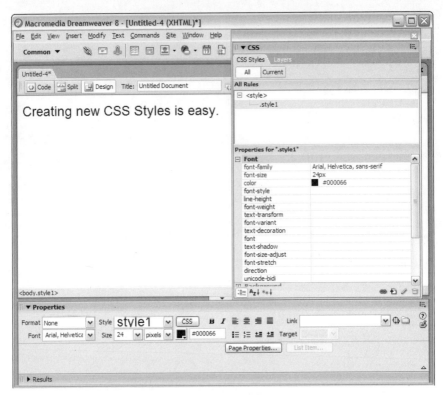

Figure 16.8. Text style in CSS panel and Text Properties panel

Here are the CSS styles, their options, and the CSS code Dreamweaver uses to create them. All the CSS tags mentioned in this section are inside another tag, the <STYLE> tag. The syntax looks like this:

```
<style type="text/css">
<!—
.style1 {
      font-family: Arial, Helvetica, sans-serif;
}
--!>
</style>
```

- **Font-family:** The pre-set font families available in Dreamweaver using CSS are the same as the HTML font families. The primary difference is how they are set in the <STYLE> tag. HTML fonts use the <FONT> tag, CSS fonts use the *font-family* tag within the CSS style definition. Example: *font-family: Arial, Helvetica, sans-serif;*

- **Font-size:** You have a number of options with font size in CSS that you do not have with the HTML font-size tag:

  Actual pixel size: You can use font sizes much as you would find them in a word processor. A 10px font is much like a 10-point font in a document, depending on the monitor resolution.

  Predefined sizes: These are named sizes you can select. They are xx-small, x-small, small, medium, large, x-large, xx-large, smaller, and larger.

  Inherit: The font takes on the size of any parent font-size tags surrounding it. Example code: *font-size: 24px;*

- **Color:** Color values are exactly the same hex values as the HTML color values. Example code: *color: #000066;*

- **Font-style:**

  Normal: No style is applied.

  Italic: Font is italicized.

  Oblique: Most browsers treat oblique style the same as italic.

  Inherit: The font takes on the style of any parent font-style tags surrounding it. Example code: *font-style: normal;*

- **Line-height:** This defines the space between lines. You can use a variety of different values. Units include numbers, pixels, inches, and percents. You can also set it to inherit. Example code: *line-height: normal;*

- **Font-weight:** This defines the boldness of the font.

  100-900: These values define the boldness, with 900 being the boldest and 100 being the least bold. A normal weight is 400.

  Predefined weights: These are named weights you can select. These values are normal, bold, bolder, and lighter.

  Inherit: The font takes on the font weight of any parent font-weight tags surrounding it. Example code: *font-weight: normal;*

- **Text-transform:** This option changes your text style in a variety of ways:

  Capitalize: All first letters of words that are lowercase in the text string are capitalized.

  Uppercase: All letters in the text are capitalized.

Lowercase: All the letters in the text are made lowercase.

None: No changes are made.

Inherit: The font takes on the style of any parent text-transform tags surrounding it. Example code: *text-transform: none;*

- **Font-variant:** This style can take only three values: normal, small-caps, or inherit. Small-caps converts all the lowercase letters to uppercase, but all the letters in the font have a smaller font size compared to the rest of the text. Example code: *font-variant: normal;*

- **Text-Decoration:** This option changes your text style in a variety of ways:

  Underline: Text is underlined.

  Overline: A line appears above the text.

  Line through: A line crosses through the text.

  Blink: This makes the text blink, but is generally ignored by most browsers.

  None: No changes are made.

  Inherit: The font takes on the style of any parent text-decoration tags surrounding it. Example code: *text-decoration: none;*

- **Font-Stretch:** This style condenses or expands the width of the font. Example code: font-stretch: wider;

There are a few more CSS font styles, but they are more obscure and you will seldom use them. For more information on such styles as direction, text-shadow, font-size-adjust, and unicode-bidi, check out the built-in CSS reference in the Dreamweaver program.

Creating your own style

The simplest way to create a style is to use the Properties panel to first automatically generate a style. Then you can use the CSS Styles panel to refine it.

To create your own style:

1. Make sure the Use CSS instead of HTML tags check box in the General category of the Properties dialog box is checked.

2. Open Design view and the Properties panel. Type two lines of text, as shown in Figure 16.9.

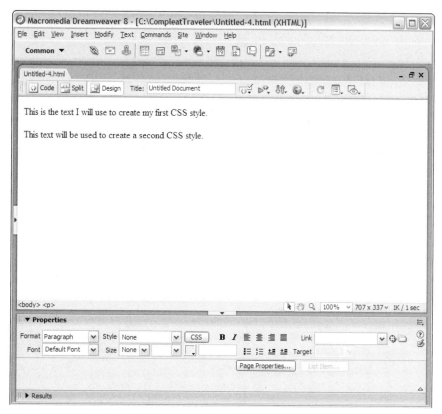

Figure 16.9. Design view with text

3. Select the first line of text.

4. Change the size to 16. As soon as you do that, notice that the text "style1" appears in the Style list on the Properties panel. This means that the CSS code for this new style, style1, has been automatically inserted into your page. The new style also appears in the Text ⇨ CSS Styles menu.

5. Open the CSS Styles panel by choosing Window ⇨ CSS Styles. Click anywhere in your first line of text.

Inside Scoop

To take a peek at the CSS code, change to Code view and scroll up to the top of your page. You will see the <STYLE> tag, and a block of CSS code that begins with ".style1."

6. You can see and change information about the current style using either the All or Current button. See Figure 16.10 for the Current button with style1 selected.

To change any property, simply click the right side of the panel next to that property.

7. Now select the second line of text in Design view. This time, change the font color in the Properties panel.

8. Notice that a new style appears in the Styles box, "style2." Also notice that the Styles box gives you a preview of what that style looks like. Whatever color you changed your text to is shown in that box.

9. To make changes to either style without having to select the text in Design view, click the All button on the CSS Styles panel. You will see in the top section of the panel the styles defined in your page.

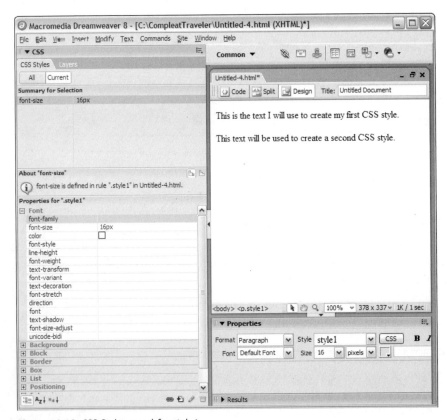

Figure 16.10. CSS Styles panel for style1

Inside Scoop
You may see a plus sign and <STYLE> instead of your styles. Simply click the plus sign to expand this listing.

Creating a uniform style for your site

CSS styles in Dreamweaver are really powerful. You can create styles, modify them, and then apply them to any text in your page by simply selecting it and then choosing the style you want to use from the Properties panel.

But to really get the most out of CSS styles, you should create a separate file to store them in. That way, every page in your site can call that same file and have access to all the same styles. Dreamweaver makes this ridiculously easy for you. First, you can easily export your styles. Then you can attach the newly created CSS file without having to type a line of code. Finally, once you have attached the CSS file, you can see all of the styles in that external file showing up in the Style box on the Properties panel, just waiting for you to select text and use them.

Rename styles

Before you create a CSS file, you should make sure your styles have meaningful names. Typically, these names have something to do with where you intend to use the style on your page.

To change the name of a style:

1. Locate your style in the CSS Styles panel.

2. Select your style and click the CSS Styles panel context menu. This is located on the upper right corner of the panel.

3. Choose Rename from the menu. Enter a new name for your CSS style in this box, then click OK.

4. The Results panel opens, as shown in Figure 16.11.

   Dreamweaver automatically searches for any references in your code to the old style and renames it for you. The Results panel shows you where it was found in your code. In Figure 16.11, ".style1" has been renamed ".my_header."

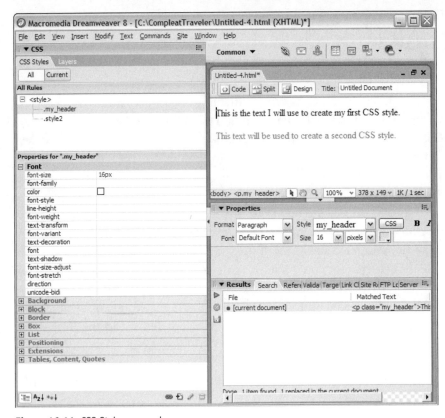

Figure 16.11. CSS Style renamed

Export styles

After you've named your styles in a way that helps you keep track of them, you are ready to export them.

To export styles:

1. Locate the CSS Styles panel and click the context menu.

2. Choose Export Styles. The Export Styles as CSS File dialog box opens.

3. Give your new CSS file a name and click Save.

If you were to open that file, you would see that it simply contains all the code that is inside the <STYLE> tag in your current file.

Attach styles

Exporting the styles does not remove them from your current page. You need to attach the new CSS file to your page and then delete the old styles.

To attach styles:

1. Click Text ⇨ CSS Styles ⇨ Attach Style Sheet.

2. Use the Attach Style Sheet dialog box to locate the CSS file you created when you exported your styles. Click OK.

3. The new style sheet has been attached. If you look at your code, you will see the old styles, followed by a new line of code, the <LINK> tag:

```
<style type="text/css">
<!--
.my_header {font-size: 16px}
.style2 {color: #993399}
-->
</style>
<link href="my_styles.css" rel="stylesheet"
type="text/css" />
```

4. You should delete the <STYLE> tag and everything in it. Keep the <LINK> tag.

At this point, all you have to do is select the text you want to apply a style to and choose that style from the Properties panel. You can also choose Text ⇨ CSS Styles, which displays a list of all the styles in the attached CSS file.

Just the facts

- The Properties panel can create either HTML font tags or CSS font tags, depending on the Properties dialog box.
- The alignment setting of images can affect the layout of the text around it.
- The Text menu contains a number of options for modifying the text in your page.
- Use the CSS Styles panel to apply CSS formatting to text.
- Give your CSS styles meaningful names.
- Use the CSS Styles panel to export your styles so other pages in your site can use the same styles.
- Attach CSS files to your page to easily access defined styles in the Properties panel Style list.

Code View

GET THE SCOOP ON...
Code view options ∎ Basic HTML coding ∎ Modifying page
properties ∎ Adding hyperlinks, e-mail links, and named
anchors ∎ Creating tables ∎ Making lists ∎ Adding forms ∎
Using code snippets

PART IV

HTML Basics

This chapter is all about creating HTML code in the Code view, rather than relying on Macromedia Dreamweaver's Design view code creation. Dreamweaver does a good job of automatically creating code, but there are times when you need to get in to the code and make your changes in Code view.

Even though you can create web pages in design view without ever looking at the code side of things, there are a few HTML basics you should be familiar with. Even the most basic Web page will have at its heart the same basic tags as the most complicated page you've ever seen. You should know how to write HTML links, images, tables, lists, and forms without the aid of a visual layout tool. They are not difficult to learn, and once you know them, you can look at any page and get a clear idea of how it was put together.

Activating Code view options

In Chapter 11, I gave you an overview of the Code view buttons. These are the 15 buttons along the left side of the Code view window. In the same chapter, I also discussed the Browser check, Validate markup, and other buttons at the top of the Code view window. In this section, I'll mention a few more Code view options you should be aware of to help you create your own HTML code. All of these are accessible from the View options button on the top right of the Code view title bar. You can also get to these options by choosing View ⇨ Code View Options, as shown in Figure 17.1.

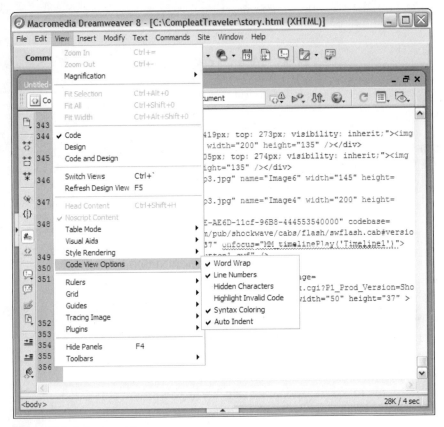

Figure 17.1. Code view options

Word wrap

You can have some very long lines of HTML or code in your page. The Word Wrap setting allows you to see the entire line without having to scroll to the right. The line instead wraps to the next line for viewing. As you stretch the Dreamweaver interface wider, the wrapped lines also extend. Word wrap does not put any extra spaces or line breaks in your code; it is strictly in the Code view.

To turn on word wrap, click the View Options button on the title bar and check the Word Wrap setting.

Line numbers

When you turn on line numbers, you see numbers in the left-hand gutter of the Code view window. These numbers can be helpful when you are debugging your code or looking for a specific line from the Results panel.

Line numbers are also good to use when you have word wrap turned on. Figure 17.2 shows both word wrap and line numbers selected.

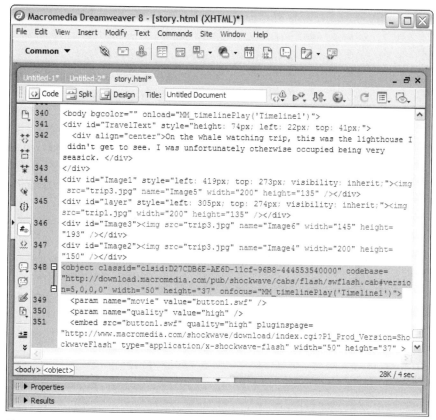

Figure 17.2. Line numbers and word wrap

Notice that the line numbers on the left are not continuous. The spaces between them let you know that the line you are on is wrapped. This can be very helpful when working on your code.

Hidden characters

When you view hidden characters, you see symbols representing white-space characters, such as line return, tab, and space. Spaces in the code are represented by dot characters, ·, and tabs are shown with two right arrow characters, ». A paragraph symbol, ¶, is used for line returns. If you have word wrap on, you will not see a paragraph symbol on lines where they wrap since there is no actual line return there.

Highlight invalid code

Any HTML code that is not valid is highlighted in yellow when you select this option. To fix the invalid code, you can click it to view information about the tag in the Properties panel. See Figure 17.3 for an example of an <IMG> tag missing a quote on the source parameter.

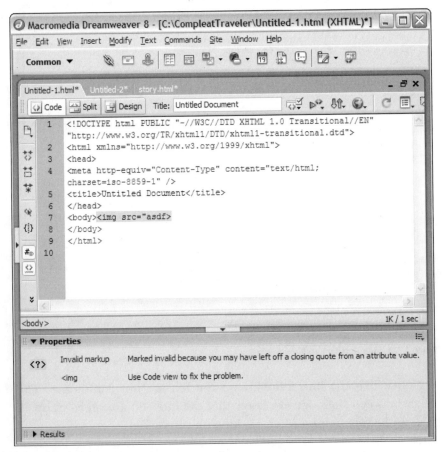

Figure 17.3. Invalid code detection in Properties panel

Bright Idea

Depending on what your page is used for, you can use code coloring to make certain elements in your page really stand out so you have an easier time editing them in Code view. For example, if you are creating a page with lots of images, you might want to make the <IMG> tags stand out by making them boldface with a yellow background to make them appear highlighted.

Syntax coloring

Dreamweaver comes with a default set of code coloring schemes, which you see in Code view when you select this option. You can customize your Code view display colors by choosing Edit ⇨ Preferences and clicking the Code Coloring category. You can then select a document type from the right and edit that particular code coloring scheme. Click the Edit Coloring Scheme button. The dialog box that opens contains a list of all the tags or keywords for that document type and lets you change the color, font style, and even background color of just that type of tag or keyword, as well as the background color for the entire document.

The syntax color has no effect on the actual code saved in the page; it is strictly used by Code view.

Auto indent

When you are creating any kind of nested structure, be it a JavaScript function or an HTML table, you may want to indent the inner code to make it easier to view. With auto indent selected, each time you type and indent a line of code or structure and press Enter, Dreamweaver inserts an indent on the next line automatically. This keeps you from having to manually indent each line when you are inside a code block.

Creating a page from scratch

When you create a Web page in Dreamweaver, you don't need to worry about inserting the basic framework tags for a Web page. It is still good to know what they are and why you need them. At times I have inadvertently removed an important HTML tag and couldn't figure out for some time why my page wasn't displaying properly or at all. This section is a rundown of the most important HTML tags and what they do. These are workhorses that you see again and again.

A simple page

When you create a new HTML page in Dreamweaver, you see this in the Code view:

```
<!DOCTYPE html PUBLIC "-//W3C//DTD XHTML 1.0
Transitional//EN"
"http://www.w3.org/TR/xhtml1/DTD/xhtml1-
transitional.dtd">
<html xmlns="http://www.w3.org/1999/xhtml">
<head>
<meta http-equiv="Content-Type" content="text/html;
charset=iso-8859-1" />
<title>Untitled Document</title>
</head>
<body>
</body>
</html>
```

DOCTYPE

The <DOCTYPE> tag is the very first line in the Dreamweaver-generated code. This tag tells the browser exactly what type of HTML or XHTML specification the document is using. It is unlikely you will need to change this tag, since Dreamweaver manages it for you. It is determined by the options you choose on the New Document dialog box.

HTML

This tag exists simply to tell the browser that an HTML document is being processed. It stands alone and has only one attribute added. Dreamweaver includes an xmlns attribute that makes the HTML page adhere to XHTML specifications.

Inside Scoop

Notice that most tags occur in pairs. There is an open tag, for example <BODY>, and then a close tag with a slash in front of it, such as </BODY>. Make sure you close your tags. Even though some browsers can figure out what should happen if a closing tag is missing, some can't, and your page will not display correctly.

HEAD

The <HEAD> tag indicates to the browser that certain page information is forthcoming. The head section contains any <META> tags and the <TITLE> tag. It has no attributes.

META

<META> tags are used for a variety of purposes. You can use <META> tags to store keywords about and descriptions of your site for search engines to find when their indexing programs visit your Web site. <META> tags have some other uses, including redirecting users to another site after a specified amount of time.

TITLE

The <TITLE> tag simply sets the title of your page. Without it, your browser displays "Untitled Document" in the title bar — not particularly appealing when someone sees your page listed in a search on Google.

You can easily set the title of your page by entering it at the top of the Code view window.

BODY

The <BODY> tag tells the browser that the page content is about to begin. It is located just after the closing <HEAD> tag, </HEAD>. The <BODY> tag has a number of attributes you can set. These are all settings used in displaying the page. They are:

- **BACKGROUND = "image source":** This sets a background image for the page.
- **BGCOLOR** = **"color":** This sets the background color for the page. By default it is white.
- **TEXT = "color":** This sets the text color. By default it is black.
- **LINK = "color":** This sets the link color. By default it is blue.

Inside Scoop

If you use a background image, you will not see your background color unless the image is a transparent GIF.

- **ALINK = "color":** This sets the active link color. By default it is red.

- **VLINK = "color":** This sets the visited link color. By default it is purple.

These settings can easily be made and modified in Dreamweaver by choosing Modify ➪ Page Properties.

IMG

The <IMG> tag displays a GIF, JPG, or PNG picture on a page. The primary settings used by this tag are:

- **SRC = "image source":** This sets the location of the image.

- **ALT = "text describing the image":** This is text that displays while the image is loading and when the mouse cursor is moved over the image. It can also be accessed by certain browsers for users who may have difficulty viewing the image.

- **WIDTH = "pixel value":** This sets the width of the image. It is optional, although recommended.

- **HEIGHT = "pixel value":** This sets the height of the image. It is optional, although recommended.

When you insert an image using the Image button on the Insert toolbar or by choosing Insert ➪ Image, the image SRC value is filled out for you. Dreamweaver also automatically enters the width and height values when the image is inserted.

FONT

The <FONT> tag specifies the appearance of the text surrounded by this tag in your page. The primary settings are:

- **COLOR = "color":** This sets the font color. By default it is black.

- **SIZE = "value":** This sets the size of the text.

- **FACE = "list of fonts":** This sets the font to use.

When you type text on your page, no <FONT> tag is automatically applied. To customize your font, select the text and use the Properties panel. By default Dreamweaver creates CSS font styles, not HTML <FONT> tags. To force Dreamweaver to use <FONT> tags, choose Edit ➪ Preferences and click the General category on the left. Uncheck the Use CSS instead of HTML tags check box.

Modifying page properties

The `<BODY>` tag is used to change a few of the page properties. The page margins can also be set in the `<BODY>` tag. To easily change the `<BODY>` tag without having to type in the code, choose Modify ⇨ Page Properties. The Page Properties dialog box opens, shown in Figure 17.4.

Page Properties		
Category	**Appearance**	

Figure 17.4. The Page Properties dialog box

In the Page Properties dialog box you can change all the body settings. These are background image, background color, text color, link color, visited link color, and active link color. You can also set margin values here. These values tell browsers how much white space to set around the edge of your page.

Here is an example of a `<BODY>` tag in HTML with all the attributes set:

```
<body bgcolor="#999999" background="my_placeholder.gif"
text="#0033FF" link="#CC9900" vlink="#996600"
alink="#0033CC" leftmargin="5" topmargin="5" margin-
width="5" marginheight="5">
```

Watch Out!

If your Page Properties dialog box has quite a few more options on it than this one, your Dreamweaver preferences are still set to produce CSS code. You need to change your preferences and uncheck the Use CSS instead of HTML tags check box.

Adding the three types of links

Dreamweaver creates three types of links from the Insert menu. These are hyperlinks, e-mail links, and named anchors. Here is a description of what each does and the HTML code used to create it.

Hyperlink

A hyperlink is simply what we refer to as a link. Links are usually underlined and when clicked, change the browser page to a specified URL. They may also open a page in a separate browser window.

To create a hyperlink, type and select the text that will be linked. Choose Insert ⇨ Hyperlink. This opens the Hyperlink dialog box, shown in Figure 17.5.

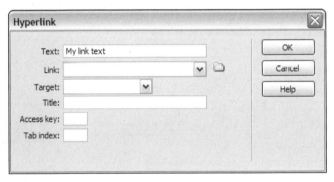

Figure 17.5. The Hyperlink dialog box

These are the link options:

- **Text:** The text you selected appears in this text box.
- **Link:** This is the URL or filename of the Web page to link to.
- **Target:** This drop-down box contains a list of targets where the link page should open. The box lists standard target names.

  _blank loads the link URL into a new browser window.

  _parent loads the link URL into the parent frame.

  _self loads the link URL into the current page.

  _top loads the link URL into the top level page. If the current page is in a frame, the URL loads into the top level and the frameset is gone.

- **Access key:** This is an accessibility option. Enter a single keyboard key to select the link in the browser.

- **Tab index:** This number is used to determine the tab order for selecting links on a page. When a user visits a page and presses the tab key, a link on the page is selected with each tab press. The default order is from the top left to the bottom right. Entering a tab index value changes the order.

- **Title:** Entering a value here acts like the alt attribute in an <IMG> tag. When the mouse is moved over the link, the Title text appears. You can use this to provide more information about the link.

The code that Dreamweaver creates in HTML looks something like this:

```
<a href="http://www.compleattraveler.com" title="Click
me to follow my link." target="_blank">Here is my
link!</a>
```

E-mail link

An e-mail link is a hyperlink that contains an e-mail address instead of a URL. Clicking an e-mail link opens whatever e-mail program the user has associated with e-mail addresses. The link has only an e-mail address in the HTML tag and looks like this:

```
<a href="mailto:mynamehere@somewebsite.com">Send me an
email</a>
```

Named anchor

A named anchor is similar to a hyperlink, but instead of linking to another URL, it links to a point on the current page. It's useful if you have a very long page with multiple sections and want to create some sort of table of contents or index.

There are two parts to creating an anchor. You have to insert an anchor at the point you want to jump to, then you have to create a link to call that anchor. That sounds more complicated than it is. The easiest way to explain it is to show you the two pieces of code.

Anchor code:

```
<a name="myanchorpoint" id="myanchorpoint"></a>
```

Link code to reference my anchor:

```
<a href="#myanchorpoint">Link to my anchor</a>
```

Creating tables

Dreamweaver makes it so simple to create tables in Design view that you may be tempted to never look at them in Code view. And I can't blame you; tables, especially complicated ones, can be difficult to decipher. You can't quickly locate a table cell under another one since table cells are coded left to right.

What follows is a very basic introduction to creating tables in HTML. Ready?

A basic table

Here's the HTML code for a very simple table. This table has two rows and two columns and looks like Figure 17.6 on a Web page.

Figure 17.6. Simple table

```
<table border="1">
<tr>
<td>First Row, Cell 1</td>
<td>First Row, Cell 2</td>
</tr>
<tr>
<td>Second Row, Cell 1</td>
<td>Second Row, Cell 2</td>
</tr>
</table>
```

Not too scary. Now what do those tags mean?

Inside Scoop

If you decide to create a table by typing it in Code view, if you use correct HTML syntax, it is always editable in Design view.

Table tags

- **TABLE:** This tag begins the table. Most of the table properties are defined here. In the previous example, the table border property is set to 1.

- **TR:** This defines a row in your table. Each row contains cells with the actual content.

- **TD:** This is a table cell tag. All content in your table goes between <TD></TD> tags.

  Here are a few more facts you should know about tables:

- Every set of <TR></TR> tags in a table need to have the same number of <TD></TD> cells in it, although you can use the colspan setting in your <TD> tag to make it take up more than one cell.

- Use cellspacing and cellpadding in the <TABLE> tag to pad your table.

- The border attribute in the <TABLE> tag should be set to 0 if you want a borderless table.

- The <TABLE> tag and <TD> tags can be assigned colors and background images.

Making lists

There are two types of HTML lists: unordered and ordered. Ordered lists are numbered lists of items, while unordered lists are bulleted lists. Figure 17.7 shows an ordered list in Split view.

The only difference between the HTML code for an ordered list and an unordered list is the outside tag. Use <OL> for ordered and <UL> for unordered lists.

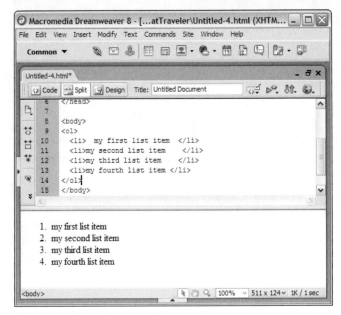

Figure 17.7. Ordered list in Split view

Adding forms

This is a brief introduction to the HTML code Dreamweaver generates to create forms and form elements. Chapter 21 discusses forms creation with Dreamweaver in more detail. For now, I will go over a few of the common HTML form tags.

First, take a look at the form in Design view in Figure 17.8.

Here is the code that creates that form:

```
<form action="process.php" method="get">
```

Enter your name:

```
<input name="fname" type="text" value="" size="20"
maxlength="20" /> <p>
```

Text block:

```
<textarea name="textarea"></textarea><p>
<input type="checkbox" name="checkbox" value="checkbox"
/>
Check this<p>
<input type="radio" name="RadioGroup1" value="radio" />
```

```
Select me<br />
<input type="radio" name="RadioGroup1" value="radio" />
Or select me</label><p>
<input type="submit" name="Submit" value="Submit" />
</form>
```

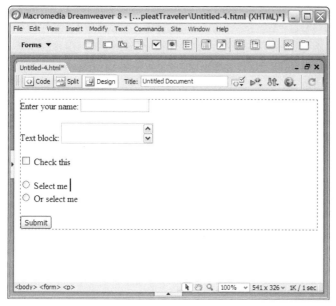

Figure 17.8. Form in Design view

Here are the tags used in this sample and a brief explanation of what they do:

- **FORM:** This tag signals the beginning of a form within an HTML document. This tag also specifies the code to use to process the form in the action setting of the tag, as well as the format to send the information in the setting.

- **INPUT type ="text":** This creates a text entry field. It is the default type of <INPUT> tag.

- **INPUT type ="checkbox":** This creates a single toggle check box.

- **INPUT type ="radio":** This creates a single radio button; however, more radio buttons with the same name can be grouped together so that only one can be selected at a time.

- **INPUT type ="submit":** This is the button on the form that causes the current form contents to be sent to the processing code specified in the FORM action setting.

- **TEXTAREA:** This tag can be used to create a multi-line text entry field.

Using code snippets to save time

In Chapter 9, I discussed the basics of the Snippets panel. In this section, I am going to revisit that panel to mention a few very useful snippets to save you time when you are creating HTML code.

Choose Window ⇨ Snippets to open the panel shown in Figure 17.9.

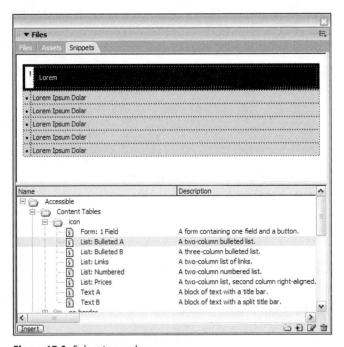

Figure 17.9. Snippets panel

Snippets are reusable lines of code that you can save and reuse. You can create your own, but Dreamweaver already has a number of snippets created. Here are a few of my favorites:

Inside Scoop

To add a snippet to your page, click at the location you wish to insert the item in your document and then click the Insert button on the bottom of the panel. You can also drag the item to the page or double-click it.

Accessible ⇨ Footers

This opens a list of five footers. They are all attractive and can give your site a professional feel. I especially appreciate the copyright text on some of them that helps remind me to put that on corporate sites I am working on.

Here's an example of the code produced by one of the simpler ones, the Title and Hanging List:

```
<table    width="100%"    border="0"    cellspacing="0"
cellpadding="2" style="background-color: #cccccc;">
<tbody><tr>
<td style="vertical-align: top;">Lorem:</td>
<td width="100%"><a href="#">Lorum</a> | <a
href="#">Ipsum</a> | <a href="#">Dolar</a>
| <a href="#">Sic Amet</a> | <a
href="#">Consectetur</a> | <a href="#">Lorum</a>
| <a href="#">Ipsum</a> | <a href="#">Dolar</a> | <a
href="#">Sic Amet</a>
| <a href="#">Consectetur</a> </td>
</tr></tbody>
</table>
```

The table is created and formatted for you; the links are already in place. All you need to do is fill in the link URLs and change the text for the links.

Headers

This opens a list of five headers. Much like the footers, the code is ready to be customized for your own use. Here is the code from the Basic: Image on Left snippet:

```
<table  width="100%"  border="0"  cellspacing="0"  cell-
padding="4">
<tbody><tr>
```

```
<td style="background-color: #999999;"><a href="#"><img
src="" name="Logo" alt="logo name" width="150"
height="70" border="0" style="background-color:
#cccc99;"></a></td>
<td style="text-align: right;background-color:
#999999;"><a href="#">Lorem</a> &#149; <a
href="#">Ipsum</a> </td>
</tr></tbody>
</table>
```

Unlike the footer code example, this snippet needs to have the
<IMG> src tag filled out as well as the width and height tags changed to
reflect your image's dimensions. This is important because using the preset image height and width may lead to your image being skewed or
stretched.

Navigation

There are many good navigation snippets in the folders under here.
Some of them match the styles in the footer and header sections I mentioned previously, which can be a good first step to creating a consistent
site design.

Form Elements ⇨ Dropdown Menus

These can save you a huge amount of time when you are creating forms.
For example, if you have a form that asks for a month of the year in a
drop-down box, to create it by hand you would have to enter each
month. The snippets in this section are drop-down form boxes already
populated with various ranges of values. It's a shame there isn't a list of
states in one of these snippets. Fortunately, if you ever do create one, you
can turn that code into your own snippet.

Just the facts

■ Use word wrapping to see entire lines of code in Code view.

■ The basic parts of an HTML page are created automatically by
Dreamweaver when you create a new HTML page.

■ There are three types of links: hyperlinks, e-mail links, and named
anchors.

- Simple tables can be created in Code view and modified in Design view.

- Dreamweaver page properties differ between HTML and CSS.

- Snippets can add correctly formatted HTML code. Some Dreamweaver snippets contain headers, footers, and navigation elements for your page.

GET THE SCOOP ON...
CSS syntax ▪ Controlling page layout ▪ CSS page properties ▪ Setting styles ▪ Positioning objects ▪ Options for
boxes and borders

CSS Basics

Macromedia Dreamweaver integrates Cascading Style Sheets, or CSS, seamlessly as it creates code for your pages. The main focus of CSS is separating Web site content from the formatting of the HTML elements in it. CSS allows you to avoid repeating the same formatting code again and again. With Dreamweaver, you can create the code a single time and call it from multiple pages.

This chapter is all about using Dreamweaver to create CSS content to control your page and all the pages on your site in a consistent manner.

CSS overview

Before diving into the world of Dreamweaver-created CSS, I will begin with a basic explanation of what CSS actually is and how it works with your HTML tags.

What is CSS?

CSS can be thought of as an extension to HTML. CSS can be used to extend the formatting and layout of HTML elements. CSS allows more control over the HTML elements in a page than traditional HTML formatting options. CSS can be placed anywhere in an HTML page. It can also be placed in an external file and referenced by multiple pages.

Here is the basic structure of a CSS rule:

```
selector {
      property: value
}
```

The selector is usually the HTML tag to which you wish to apply a style. The property refers to the particular property you wish to change. This might be the color, border, or size. The value refers to the value you wish the property to have. Here is an example of a CSS rule to change the color of text:

```
font {
      color: #0099FF;
}
```

CSS rules also allow you to set multiple rules at once:

```
font {
      color: #0099FF;
      font-style: italic;
}
```

With this rule set, every time the <FONT> tag is used, the CSS rules change the text on the page to the color #0099FF and italic style.

This may not be ideal. You may want to have a number of different styles and instead of modifying the font tag, add these and other rules where you want them. In the next section, I'll show you how to create a CSS rule that can be applied to text or other items on your page when you wish.

CSS and HTML tags

You can assign CSS rules to most HTML tags. The ones most commonly used are the <P> (paragraph) tag, the <DIV> tag, and the <SPAN> tag.

 Inside Scoop

Applying styles to the <FONT> tag is probably not that useful. However, you may wish to apply a style to some specific HTML tag you use repeatedly; for example, the <TD> tag in every table on your site may need the same background color to maintain consistency.

You aren't limited to creating rules for existing HTML tags. You can also create classes. Here is an example of code to create a class:

```
.myclass{
font-family: verdana,arial,helvetica,sans-serif;
color: #000000;
font-size: 10pt;
font-weight: 500
}
```

To actually use my class in my HTML, I can create a <DIV>, <SPAN>, or <P> tag and set an attribute in it to class=myclass.

All the text within that HTML tag will have the styles specified in .myclass.

The CSS code within an HTML file has to be enclosed in the <STYLE> tag inside the head section of your page. Here is the code of an HTML page with the .myclass rule included:

```
<html>
<head>
<title>CSS Example</title>
<style type="text/css">
<!--
.myclass{
font-family: verdana,arial,helvetica,sans-serif;
color: #000000;
font-size: 10pt;
font-weight: 500
}
-->
</style>
</head>
<body>
<span class="myclass">Using the SPAN tag</span>
<p class="myclass">Using the P tag</p>
<div class="myclass">Using the DIV tag</div>
</body>
</html>
```

Figure 18.1 shows the Design view of this page.

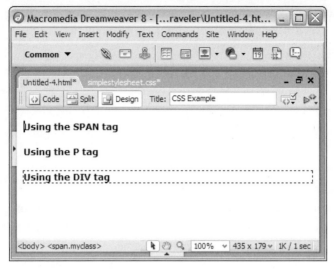

Figure 18.1. Design view of simple CSS rule

Adding CSS rules to the page you are working in tends to make it extremely long, as shown in the previous code. It makes more sense to put all your CSS rules in a single file and call them from your pages.

CSS file

The most efficient way to handle your CSS rules is to create a separate CSS file to hold all that information. A CSS file looks exactly like a list of rules, but does not include the <STYLE> tag you see when you place CSS rules in your HTML page.

Here's what might be in a basic CSS file:

```
.myclass{
font-family: verdana,arial,helvetica,sans-serif;
color: #000000;
font-size: 10pt;
font-weight: 500
}
```

That's it. If you create a file and use a .css file extension, you have created an external style sheet. To link your new CSS file to your current page, you need only include this line of code in the head portion of your page:

```
<link href="my_styles.css" rel="stylesheet"
type="text/css">
```

You can choose Text ⇨ CSS Styles ⇨ Attach Style sheet to locate your CSS file and attach it to the current page. Chapter 16 discusses in detail how to create a new style, rename that style, export styles, and then attach styles to your page.

Controlling layout

In the previous chapter, the emphasis was on using HTML to control the appearance of your page. There are good reasons for using HTML; some older browsers can't process CSS at all, and some newer browsers vary in the way they interpret it. And yet it's a powerful way to control your pages. If you know your audience uses primarily newer browsers that can support it, there is no reason not to use it.

To make Dreamweaver create CSS rules to control your page appearance, you must make a change to the preferences. To force Dreamweaver to use CSS tags, choose Edit ⇨ Preferences and click the General category on the left. Check the Use CSS instead of HTML tags check box.

CSS page properties

Also in the previous chapter, we changed the page properties using HTML settings. With Dreamweaver's Use CSS check box checked, you have quite a few more page properties available to you. To work with these properties, open the Page Properties dialog box by choosing Modify ⇨ Page Properties. The Page Properties dialog box opens.

Here are the options available in the Appearance category of the Page Properties dialog box, shown in Figure 18.2.

- **Font:** This is the font family to use in the current page.

- **Size:** This sets the default font size to use in the current page.

- **Text Color:** This sets the default font color to use on the current page.

- **Background Color:** This sets the background color to use on the current page.

- **Background Image:** This sets the background image to use on the current page. This differs from setting a background image in the HTML <BODY> tag, because you can apply the following options in the Repeat drop-down menu to control how it displays in the current page:

No-repeat: Displays the background image once at the upper left part of the page.

Repeat: Tiles the background image over the page.

Repeat-x: Tiles background image across the top of the page.

Repeat-y: Tiles the background image down the left side of the page.

- **Left, Right, Top, and Bottom Margin:** These specify how many pixels to use for the margins around the current page.

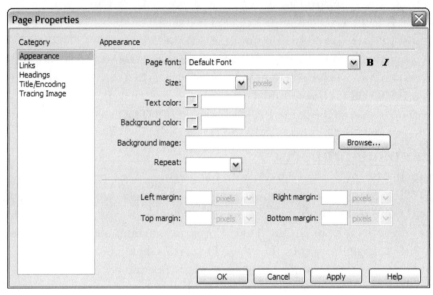

Figure 18.2. Appearance category of the Page Properties dialog box

Here are the options available on the Links category of the Page Properties dialog box, shown in Figure 18.3.

- **Font:** This is the font family to use for links in the current page.
- **Size:** This sets the default font size to use for links in the current page.
- **Link Color:** This sets the font color to use for links in the current page.
- **Visited Links:** This sets the font color to use for visited links in the current page.

- **Mouseover Links:** This sets the font color to use for links in the current page when the mouse cursor moves over them.

- **Active Links:** This sets the font color to use for links in the current page when they are clicked.

- **Underline Style:** This sets the way the link underline should behave. The options are:

  Always underline: The link is underlined. This is the default behavior of a link.

  Never underline: The link is not underlined.

  Show underline only on rollover: The underline on the link appears only when the mouse cursor moves over it.

  Hide underline on rollover: The underline on the link is hidden when the mouse cursor moves over it.

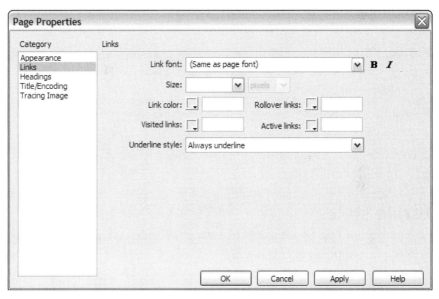

Figure 18.3. Links category of the Page Properties dialog box

Here are the options available on the Headings category of the Page Properties dialog box, shown in Figure 18.4.

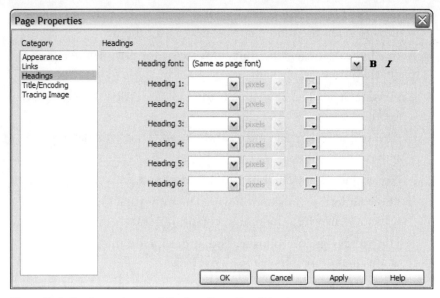

Figure 18.4. Headings category of the Page Properties dialog box

- **Font:** This is the font family to use for any header tags in the current page. You can also use the bold and italic buttons. This setting applies to all heading tags on the page.

- **Heading 1 through Heading 6:** These boxes allow you to choose a font size and color for a specific heading tag.

The Title/Encoding and Tracing Image categories are not CSS-specific and were discussed in Chapter 8.

Setting styles

You can use the CSS Styles panel to create CSS rules for current tags, or styles you can apply to HTML tags.

Create CSS rule for existing tag

To apply a CSS rule to an HTML tag, begin by opening the CSS Styles panel, shown in Figure 18.5.

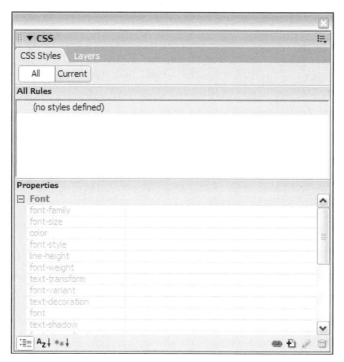

Figure 18.5. CSS Styles panel

When you first open the panel with no styles yet set, the bottom settings on the panel are grayed out as shown in the figure. To add a style to an existing tag:

1. Click the New CSS Rule button on the lower right corner of the panel. It looks like a white paper with a black plus sign on it.

2. The New CSS Rule dialog box opens. For Selector Type, choose Tag.

3. The Tag menu is now populated with every standard HTML tag. Choose one. For this example, I choose the <TD> tag.

4. Use the Define In setting to choose where this rule should go. You can write it to a new CSS file by choosing New Style Sheet File. You can add it to an existing file currently attached to the page you have open. These files appear in the list. Or you can put it in the <HEAD> tag of the current page open in the Dreamweaver editor by choosing This document only. For this example, let's create a new CSS file to put it in. Choose New Style Sheet File, then click OK.

5. The Save Style Sheet File As dialog box opens. Here you can create a new file with a .css file extension. Your new rule is saved here. Click Save.

6. The CSS Rule Definition dialog box opens. Use this dialog box to specify any styles you want the `<TD>` tag to have. Jump down to the section titled "The CSS Rule Definition dialog box" for more information on this box.

Create a new CSS rule

To create a new CSS rule, begin by opening the CSS Styles panel, shown in Figure 18.5. Let's create a new style:

1. Click the New CSS Rule button on the lower right corner of the panel. It looks like a white paper with a black plus sign on it.

2. The New CSS Rule dialog box opens. For Selector Type, choose Class.

3. Enter a name for your new class. Your name must begin with a period; for example, ".my_new_class." (Dreamweaver adds a period if you forget.)

4. Use the Define In setting to choose where this rule should go. This time, the CSS file we created above should appear in the list. Choose that file and click OK.

5. The CSS Rule Definition dialog box opens. See the following section for more information on this box.

The CSS Rule Definition dialog box

There are so many options in this dialog box that two of the categories are discussed later in this chapter. For the Position category, go to the "Positioning objects" section. For the Border category, go to the "Changing boxes and borders" section.

Inside Scoop

You can edit already created styles in the CSS Rule Definition dialog box at any time. Simply click the Edit button on the bottom right of the CSS Styles panel with the current style loaded. You can also edit styles directly in the CSS Styles panel.

Here is an overview of the options you can change under the Type category, shown in Figure 18.6. Most of these are covered in more detail in Chapter 16.

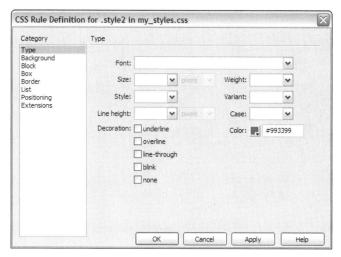

Figure 18.6. Type category of the CSS Rule Definition dialog box

- **Font:** This sets the font for the current rule.
- **Size:** This sets the size of the font for the current rule.
- **Style:** You can select from the style options normal, italic, or oblique to apply it to the current rule.
- **Line Height:** This sets the line height for the text.
- **Decoration:** You can select from the decoration options underline, overline, strikethrough, blink, or none. Blink is not supported by IE.
- **Weight:** This controls how bold the text is.
- **Variant:** This sets the text in the current rule to small caps.
- **Case:** Choose capitalize, uppercase, lowercase, or none to change the case of the text in the rule.
- **Color:** This sets the color of the text in the rule. The color attribute is supported by both browsers.

Here are the options you can change under the Background category, shown in Figure 18.7.

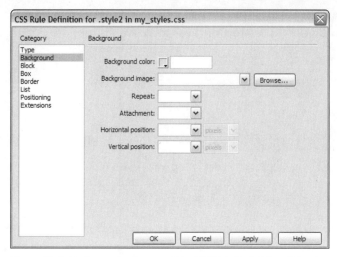

Figure 18.7. Background category of the CSS Rule Definition dialog box

- **Background Color:** This sets the background color for elements using this rule.

- **Background Image:** This sets the background image for elements using this rule.

- **Repeat:** This drop-down menu controls how the background image displays in elements using this rule:

    No-repeat: Displays the background image once at the upper left part of the element.

    Repeat: Tiles the background image over the element.

    Repeat-x: Tiles the background image across the top of the element.

    Repeat-y: Tiles the background image down the left side of the element.

- **Attachment:** This controls the behavior of the background image if the content in the element can scroll.

- **Horizontal Position, Vertical Position:** These control the position of the background image, which can be aligned on the center of the page both vertically and horizontally.

Here are the options you can change under the Block category, shown in Figure 18.8.

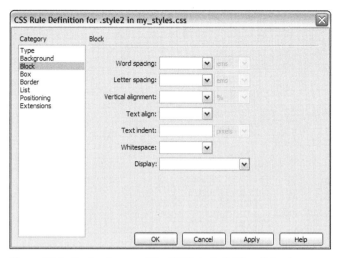

Figure 18.8. Block category of the CSS Rule Definition dialog box

- **Word Spacing:** This controls the spacing between words.

- **Letter Spacing:** This controls the spacing between characters.

- **Vertical Alignment:** This controls the vertical alignment of page elements using this rule.

- **Text Align:** This sets the text alignment. Choose left, right, center, or justify.

- **Text Indent:** This specifies how much to indent text.

- **Whitespace:** Choose normal, pre, or nowrap for handling white space in HTML. Normal ignores extra white space, pre displays it, and nowrap forces text in the browser to not break at the edge of the browser window.

- **Display:** This menu lists a number of HTML tag types and displays the element in the option chosen.

Positioning objects

To position objects, open the current style sheet in the CSS Rule Definition dialog box and change to the Positioning category.

Here are the options you can change under the Positioning category, shown in Figure 18.9.

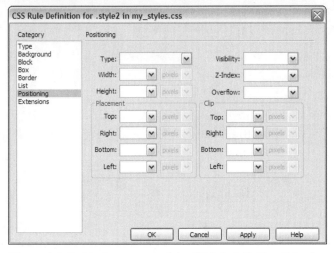

Figure 18.9. Positioning category of the CSS Rule Definition dialog box

■ **Type:** Use this to control how a layer is positioned. The options are:

  Absolute: The element is removed from the normal flow of the page and positioned with respect to its containing block. This means that no matter where it is in your HTML code, it will appear at the location set in the CSS coordinates inside its parent layer. Unless your layer is nested in another layer, your layer is placed with respect to the top left corner of the browser window.

  Fixed: This layer stays in the page where it was placed, even when the page scrolls.

  Relative: The layer is moved from its current position in the page to a new position by the location offset specified.

  Static: The element is placed in the page as though it were any HTML element and is part of the page; that is, it does not float over other page elements.

■ **Visibility:** Choose whether your layer will be visible or hidden.

■ **Z-Index:** This option controls the stacking order of the layer.

■ **Overflow:** If the content of a layer is bigger than the layer size, this option controls what the layer should do. The options are:

  Visible: The layer size stretches to display all the content.

  Hidden: The content is only displayed inside the layer. Anything too large for the layer is not visible.

Scroll: The layer stays the same size, but has scroll bars to make all the content accessible. If the contents of the layer fit, the scroll bars are still visible.

Auto: The layer has scroll bars when the layer's contents are too big. If the contents fit, the scroll bars are not visible.

■ **Placement:** These values control the size and location of the layer. If the layer type is absolute, the location will be from the upper left corner of the browser. If the layer type is relative, it will be placed relative to its actual position in the HTML page.

■ **Clip:** These values control which part of the layer is visible.

Changing boxes and borders

Open the current style sheet in the CSS Rule Definition dialog box and change to the Box page.

Here are the options you can change under the Box category, shown in Figure 18.10.

■ **Width, Height:** This controls the width and height of the box element.

■ **Float:** This controls to which side other page elements float around this box.

■ **Clear:** This controls which sides of the box will not allow layers around this element.

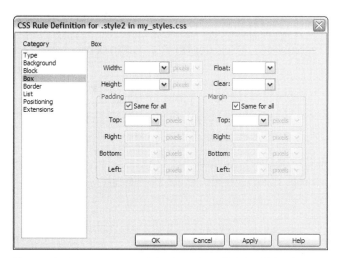

Figure 18.10. Box category of the CSS Rule Definition dialog box

- **Same For All:** This makes all padding attributes uniform for all sides of the box.

- **Margin:** This controls how much padding exists between the border or padding of the box and other elements.

- **Same For All:** This makes all margin attributes uniform for all sides of the element.

Here are the options you can change under the Border category, shown in Figure 18.11.

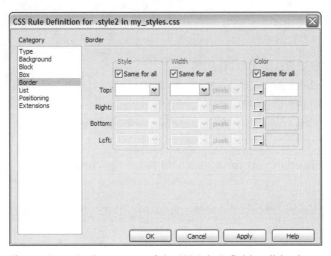

Figure 18.11. Border category of the CSS Rule Definition dialog box

- **Style:** Use this to choose the border style. Options include solid, dashed, dotted, grooved, and ridged. Dreamweaver does not display border styles in Design view; to see the border you have to preview it in a browser.

- **Same For All:** This sets all sides to the same border style.

- **Width:** This controls how wide the border should be.

- **Same For All:** This sets all sides to the same border width.

- **Color:** This specifies the color of the border.

- **Same For All:** This sets all sides to the same border color.

Just the facts

- CSS rules consist of a selector, a property, and a value, or sets of properties and values grouped under one selector.

- A selector can be an existing tag or a user-defined class.

- Use the <LINK> tag to connect a CSS file to a Web page. Dreamweaver automatically fills the Properties panel Style box with the styles in the linked file.

- CSS rules can be created using the New CSS Rule button on the CSS Styles panel.

- Existing CSS rules can be edited in the CSS Styles panel or by clicking the Edit Style button on the panel.

GET THE SCOOP ON...
The Document Object Model, or DOM ▪ Changing
text styles dynamically ▪ Hiding and showing layers ▪
Moving layers ▪ Dragging layers ▪ Changing the content
of layers dynamically

DHTML Basics

Dynamic HTML, or DHTML, is simply HTML that has been programmed to change style or content after a page has been loaded in a browser. Back in Chapter 15, the timeline animations and events you created are considered DHTML. At the heart of DHTML is the Document Object Model.

The Document Object Model, or DOM, is the hierarchy of the objects in your HTML page, their properties and events, and the language that lets you reference them. It is this language to describe each object and each property on your page that allows you to create code to change the style of text or the location of a layer after the HTML page is loaded in a browser.

Not only does the DOM allow you to change parts of your page, you can make changes in response to certain standard page events. Events like a link being clicked, the mouse cursor moving over a section of the screen, or simply the page being loaded can all be used to change the properties of objects on your page.

The Document Object Model

With Macromedia Dreamweaver, you don't need to know the name of the DOM object you are trying to change. Dreamweaver never refers to the properties and events you can control as part of the DOM; instead, they are simply properties or events. The good news is that instead of having to remember how to reference a specific element on your page so you can change it, Dreamweaver keeps track of the names of everything and a list of properties. Dreamweaver also creates the JavaScript code that makes the changes happen. You can simply point and click your way into DHTML.

Changing text styles

In this section, you will create a text layer and then add a button and a link to change the text styles in the layer.

1. Begin by creating a new HTML page.

2. Open the Layout toolbar. In Design view, draw a layer on the page.

3. Open the Properties panel. Select your layer by clicking the handle on the upper left. Give your layer a descriptive name such as **TextChange**. The Name box on the Layer Properties panel is located on the left, just under the label Layer ID.

4. Click in the layer and type some text in it. Your page should look something like Figure 19.1.

   Notice the layer name, TextChange, in the Properties panel. Now you need to create a link. This link changes the style of the text in the TextChange layer when it is clicked.

5. On the page outside of the layer you just created, type the text **Change the Layer Text**. Select it.

6. In the Properties panel, make it a link by typing the character # in the Link box on the right.

   Take a peek at the Code view of the current page. So far it's pretty simple, nothing you couldn't have typed yourself:

```
<div id="TextChange">I just entered this text in
this layer. This text is nothing special. It doesn't
say much and is just using the default page font.
This text has no style! </div>
<p><a href="#">Change the Layer Text </a></p>
```

Inside Scoop

By typing a pound sign (#) for the link, you are telling the browser to make this text a link, but not to leave the current page when the link is clicked.

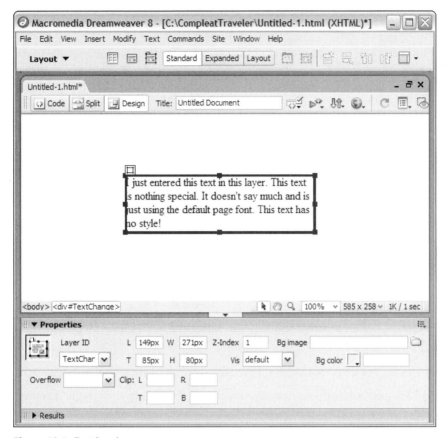

Figure 19.1. Text in a layer

7. Tie the link and the layer together. Change back to Design view and open the Behaviors panel.

8. Click your link and then on the plus (+) button in the Behaviors panel. Choose Change Property. The Change Property dialog box opens, as shown in Figure 19.2.

9. Change the settings in this dialog box to match those in Figure 19.2. Set Type of object to DIV. For Named object choose div "TextChange." Click the Select radio button and choose style.color from the list. For New value, enter the hex code for red, **#FF0000**. Most browsers also recognize the word red if you prefer using that. Click OK.

Figure 19.2. The Change Property dialog box

10. Repeat steps 8 and 9, but this time choose a different property, style.fontWeight. Enter **900** in the New value box. Click OK.

You now see the onClick events in the Behaviors panel whenever you select the link. You can repeat steps 8 and 9 and change other properties for the text in the TextChange layer. You might want to try changing the font and font size. Now all that remains is to open this page in a browser, click the link, and watch your text change!

But maybe you want your text to change back to black. Add a button to do this.

1. Click outside of your layer. Choose Insert ⇨ Form ⇨ Button.

2. A button, surrounded by a form, should be visible in Design view. See Figure 19.3.

3. You need to change some button properties. Open the Properties panel and select the button. Change the properties to those shown in Figure 19.3. Change the Button Value to "Change Text." Change the Action to None.

4. Now you need to add the behavior to your button to change the layer text to black. Click your link and then the plus (+) button in the Behaviors panel. Choose Change Property.

5. Set Type of object to DIV. For Named object choose div "TextChange." Click the Select radio button and choose style.color from the list. For New value, enter the hex code for black, **#000000**. You can enter the word black if you prefer. Click OK.

Test your page in a browser. If you take a peek at the Code view, you see the Dreamweaver-generated JavaScript functions that make the changes to the text occur. What a lot of code for such a small change!

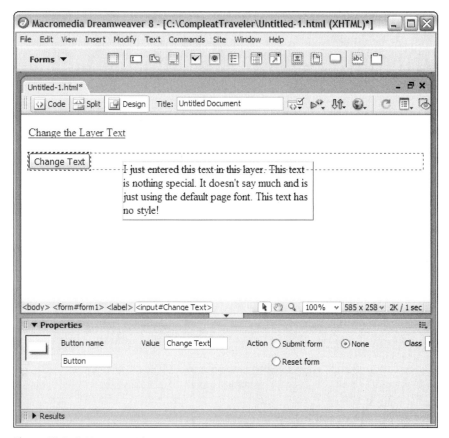

Figure 19.3. Button properties

Hiding and showing objects

In Chapter 15, you saw how to use a timeline to hide or show a layer at a particular point in time. In this section, you will add content to a layer and then add a button and a link to show and hide the layer.

1. Begin by creating a new HTML page.

2. Open the Layout toolbar. In Design view, draw a layer on the page.

3. Open the Properties panel. Select your layer by clicking the handle on the upper left. Give your layer a descriptive name such as **VisLayer**. The Name box on the Layer Properties panel is located on the left, just under the label Layer ID.

Inside Scoop

You can add any HTML element you wish inside a layer. This means that you can make anything on your Web page appear or disappear with this technique.

4. Click in the layer and choose Insert ⇨ Image. Locate an image. You can also add text to the layer under the image.

Your page should look something like Figure 19.4.

Notice the layer name, VisLayer, in the Properties panel. Now you need to create a link. This link hides the contents of the VisLayer when it is clicked.

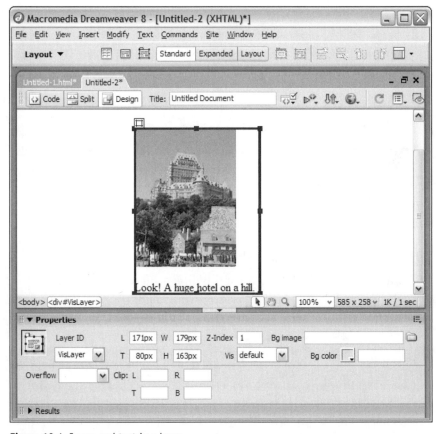

Figure 19.4. Image and text in a layer

5. On the page outside of the layer you just created, type the text **Hide the Layer**. Select it.

6. In the Properties panel, make it a link by typing the character # in the Link box on the right.

7. Open the Behaviors panel.

8. Click your link and then on the plus (+) button in the Behaviors panel. Choose Show-Hide Layers. The Show-Hide Layers dialog box opens, as shown in Figure 19.5.

Figure 19.5. The Show-Hide Layers dialog box

9. Click your layer, VisLayer. Click the Hide button. Notice that the layer now has (hide) next to it. Click OK.

You now see the onClick event in the Behaviors panel whenever you select the link.

Now take a look at this page in a browser, click the link, and watch the layer vanish. So you've hidden the layer, but now you want it back? Add a button to make it visible again.

1. Click outside of your layer. Choose Insert ⇨ Form ⇨ Button.

2. A button, surrounded by a form, should be visible in Design view. See Figure 19.6.

3. You need to change some button properties. Open the Properties panel and select the button. Change the properties to those shown in Figure 19.6. Change the Button Value to "Show Layer." Change the Action to None.

Inside Scoop

The visibility of your layer is actually a property, just like the font color was in the previous section. Dreamweaver just isolates it into its own menu option since showing and hiding layers is used so frequently.

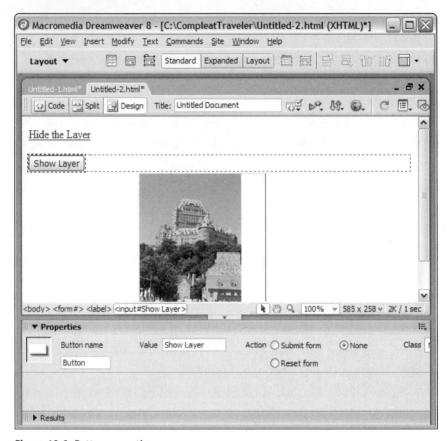

Figure 19.6. Button properties

4. You need to add the behavior to your button to bring your hidden layer back. This time, just to show you that you can, I won't use Show-Hide Layers; instead, I'll choose to change a property.

   Click your link and then the plus (+) button in the Behaviors panel. Choose Change Property.

5. See Figure 19.7 for the settings to use. Set Type of object to DIV. For Named object, choose div "VisLayer." Click the Enter radio button and type **style.visibility**. For New value, type **visible**. Click OK.

   Test your page in a browser. Click the link to hide the layer and the button to bring it back. You can also attach additional behavior changes to the Button; for example, you could change the text size.

Figure 19.7. The Change Property dialog box

Moving objects

In Chapter 15, the timeline was used to set an animation path to move layers. In this section, you will move a layer from one location on the screen to another when the mouse cursor moves over a link on the screen, and back to the original location when the layer is double-clicked.

1. Begin by creating a new HTML page.

2. Open the Layout toolbar. In Design view, draw a layer on the page.

3. Open the Properties panel. Select your layer by clicking the handle on the upper left. Give your layer a descriptive name such as **MoveLayer**. The Name box on the Layer Properties panel is located on the left, just under the label Layer ID.

4. This time, place your layer at a specific spot on the page and make it a specific size. Figure 19.8 shows the Properties panel.

   Notice the L (left), T (top), W (width), and H (height) in the Properties panel. In your panel, set L to **100px**, T to **50px**, W to **200px**, and H to **150px**.

5. Click in the layer and add some text. I used the text "This layer will move if your mouse cursor touches the Move Layer link."

6. On the page outside of the layer you just created, type the text **Move Layer**. Select it. In the Properties panel, make it a link by typing the character # in the Link box on the right.

7. Open the Behaviors panel. So far you have only onClick method for triggering behaviors. This time you will use the onMouseOver method. Click the Move Layer link. Now click the left column of the Behaviors panel, as shown in Figure 19.9, and select the onMouseOver method from the list.

8. Click the plus (+) button in the Behaviors panel. Choose Change
   Property. The Change Property dialog box opens.

9. Change the settings in this dialog box. This time, set Type of object
   to Layer. For Named object, choose layer "MoveLayer." Click the
   Select radio button and choose style.left from the list. For New value,
   enter **200px**. The layer was originally located 100 pixels from the
   left side of the browser; this moves it to 200 pixels away. Click OK.

10. Repeat steps 7, 8, and 9, but this time change the style.top property
    to a value of your choice. Click OK.

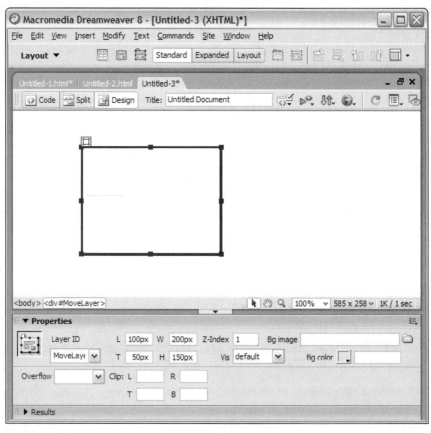

Figure 19.8. Properties panel

Watch Out!

Don't forget to put the px after your values. If you don't, the values won't be recognized and your code won't work.

Figure 19.9. Behaviors panel

Add an action to your layer itself. When the layer is double-clicked, it should return to the original location.

1. Click your layer to select it.

2. Click the left column of the Behaviors panel, as shown in Figure 19.9, and select the onDblClick method from the list.

3. Now you need to add the behavior to your layer. Click your link and then on the plus (+) button in the Behaviors panel. Choose Change Property.

4. Set Type of object to Layer. For Named object, choose layer "MoveLayer." Click the Select radio button and choose style.left from the list. For New value, enter **100px**. Click OK.

Test your page in a browser. When you move your mouse over the link, the layer shifts right. When you double-click inside the layer, it moves left.

Inside Scoop

You can actually use negative values for style.left and style.top. These move the layer off the page to the left, or on top of the visible page. Your layer still exists if you do this; it just won't be viewable in a browser window.

You've been making your layer jump around, but what if you want the user to be able to click and drag it?

1. Create a new HTML page and place two layers on it in Design view. Use the Properties panel to make one with a gray background and one with a black background, as shown in Figure 19.10.

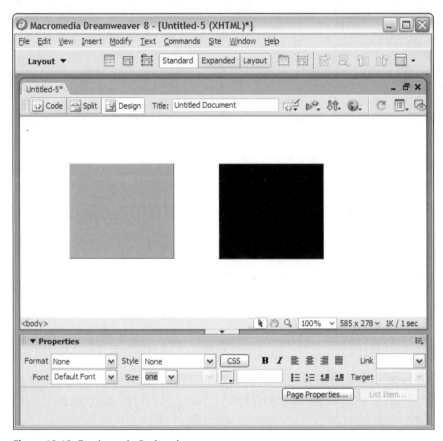

Figure 19.10. Two layers in Design view

2. Name the two layers GrayLayer and BlackLayer.

3. Click anywhere outside of the two layers. Click the plus (+) button in the Behaviors panel. Choose Drag Layer.

4. The Drag Layer dialog box opens. This dialog box has quite a few options, which I'll go over at the end of this section. For now, choose layer "GrayLayer," Movement Unconstrained, and leave the rest of the dialog box as is. Click OK.

5. Now for the black layer. Click the plus (+) button in the Behaviors panel and choose Drag Layer again. This time, choose layer "BlackLayer" and change Movement to Constrained. Enter a value of **100** for Down and **100** for right. Click OK.

Here's the fun part. Open the page in a browser. Click and drag the two layers around the page and notice the behaviors. The black layer can be moved 100 pixels to the right or down from its starting position because of the constrained values you gave it.

Here's an overview of the Drag Layer dialog box options, beginning with the Basic tab, shown in Figure 19.11.

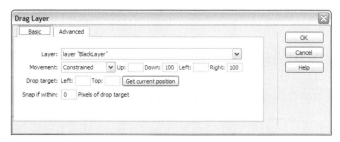

Figure 19.11. Basic tab of the Drag Layer dialog box

- **Layer:** Use this list menu to choose the name of the layer you wish to add the drag behavior to.

- **Movement:** You have two choices, Constrained or Unconstrained:

    Constrained movement restricts the layer from being dragged past a specified distance from its starting point. You can enter values for left, right, up, and down. Entering a value of 150 in the left box would mean that the layer can only be dragged 150 pixels to the left of its original location. Leaving the value blank allows the layer to be dragged without constraint in that particular direction. Finally, if you enter 0, the layer can't be dragged in that direction at all. The values must be positive integers.

    Unconstrained movement allows the layer to be dragged in any direction as far as desired. The Web page grows to accommodate a layer dragged offscreen to the right or down.

- **Drop target:** A drop target is a location on the page where the layer should be dragged and then is not draggable any more. Enter values in the left and top boxes. When the layer's top and left corner touches that point on the page, the layer stops there. An example of a use for this would be to build puzzles, made up of layers with partial images in them. When the user drags the layer to the correct place, it can't be dragged any more.

- **Get current position:** This sets the left and top boxes to the layer's current position on the page. You can then move it away in Design view. This can help you place all your layers where they belong and then mix them up after you finish setting the drag behavior.

- **Snap if within:** If the layer is within this many pixels of the drop target, it snaps to the target and locks.

Here are the options available on the Advanced tab, shown in Figure 19.12.

Figure 19.12. Advanced tab of the Drag Layer dialog box

- **Drag handle:** By default, you can click anywhere on a layer to drag it. If you choose Area within layer, you can define a specific rectangular region within the layer that has to be clicked to be dragged.

- **While dragging:** With these options, you can choose to bring the drag layer to the top while it is being dragged. You can drag it underneath other layers with higher z-indexes. You can make it the new top layer after it has been dragged if you check Bring layer to front and choose Leave on top.

- **Call JavaScript:** You can enter a function call to JavaScript code you wish to execute while dragging occurs.

- **When dropped:** You can enter a function call to JavaScript code you wish to execute when the layer is no longer being dragged. The Only if snapped check box executes the code only if the layer has reached the drop target.

Changing the content of objects

The final DHTML layer trick you will perform is an extremely powerful one. With this trick you can change the actual HTML objects within a layer to entirely different ones. You will start by strictly changing the text in a layer, and then you'll change other types of content.

First, you use the Set Text behavior when a button is pressed.

1. Begin by creating a new HTML page.

2. Open the Layout toolbar. In Design view, draw a layer on the page.

3. Open the Properties panel. Select your layer by clicking the handle on the upper left. Give your layer a descriptive name such as **TextLayer**.

4. Click in the layer and type some text in it. I used "Click on the button to change this text."

5. Now you need to create a button to trigger the text change. Click outside of your layer. Choose Insert ⇨ Form ⇨ Button. A button, surrounded by a form, should be visible in Design view.

6. Open the Properties panel and select the button. Change the Button Value to "Change Text." Change the Action to None.

7. Now you need to add the behavior to your button to change the text. Click the button and then the plus (+) button of the Behaviors panel. Choose Set Text ⇨ Set Text of Layer. The Set Text of Layer dialog box opens, shown in Figure 19.13.

Figure 19.13. The Set Text of Layer dialog box

8. Enter new text in the dialog box. I entered "You clicked the button. Good job!." Click OK. Notice that I entered HTML code in the box!

9. Make sure that the event on the left of the behavior is set to onClick.

Check out this page in a browser. You will see your text change when the button is clicked. Notice that the <EM> tags I used are being interpreted in the layer.

The fact that this Set Text of Layer dialog box does allow you to enter HTML code directly opens up a wide range of possibilities. This behavior acts like the innerHTML property you may be familiar with. Like innerHTML, all the HTML code inside the layer is replaced with what you enter in the box.

Now try putting an image and a table in the layer when a button is clicked.

1. Use the same page you worked on previously. Begin by clicking next to the first Change Text button and choose Insert ⇨ Form ⇨ Button.

2. Use the Property settings for the new button, shown in Figure 19.14. Change the Button Value to Insert Image. Change the Action to None.

3. Click the button and then the plus (+) button of the Behaviors panel. Choose Set Text ⇨ Set Text of Layer. The Set Text of Layer dialog box opens.

4. Enter some HTML code in this dialog box and click OK. I used some basic table code with an image inside:

```
<table border="0" cellpadding="5" cellspacing="0"
bgcolor="#FF0000">
<tr>
<td><img src="stonehenge.jpg" width="344"
height="370" /></td>
</tr>
</table>
```

5. Make sure that the event on the left is onClick. Now look at your page in a browser and see your layer change!

Bright Idea

Before inserting the new behavior, build the code you want to put in the layer in another page. Then copy the Code view into another simple text processing application, such as Notepad. That way, you can simply cut and paste correct code rather than typing it on the fly and potentially making typos. It also gives you the chance to preview what the layer will look like.

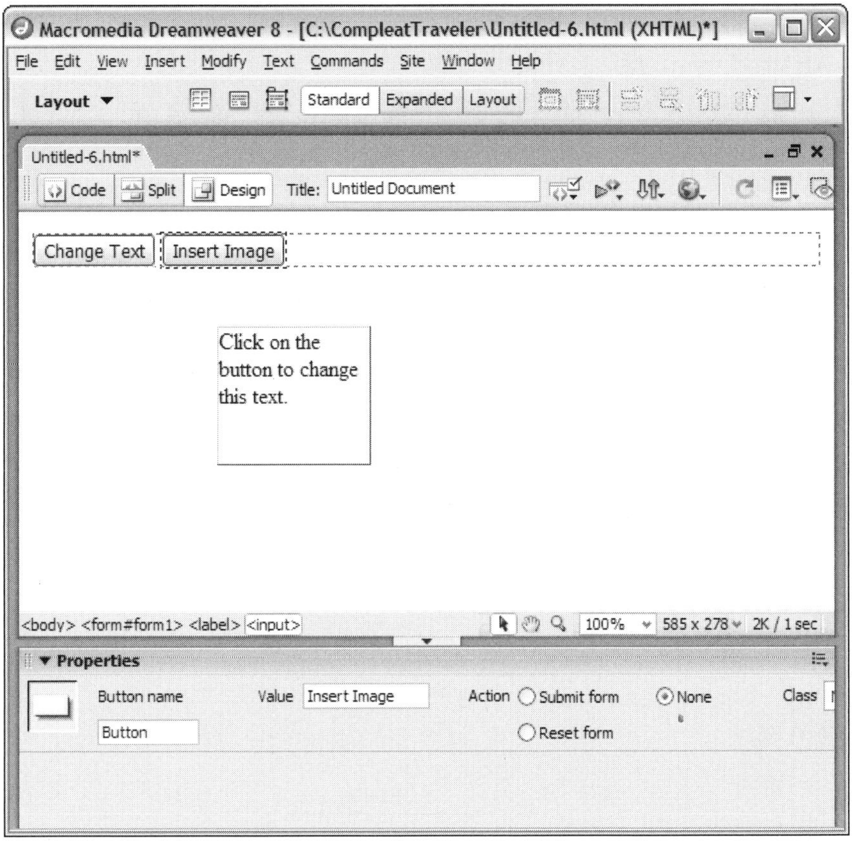

Figure 19.14. Button properties

Just the facts

■ DHTML is basically changing the content of a Web page after the page has already loaded.

■ Dreamweaver lets you use events to trigger changes to anything on your Web page.

■ Use Behaviors to dynamically change the text style in a layer.

■ The Drag Layer behavior allows users to click and drag content around the page.

■ You can completely change the content in a layer using the Set Text of Layer behavior.

GET THE SCOOP ON...
Understanding how frames work ▪ Creating framesets ▪
Nested framesets ▪ Choosing frame styles ▪ Tips for
frame navigation

Frame Basics

I seldom use frames because they have some fundamen-
tal problems you have to address each time you use
them. They can be difficult to organize and work with.
They take up screen real estate. They break the correct
functioning of the back button. You won't find many fans
of frames these days; they are a bit controversial in the Web
design world.

However, Macromedia Dreamweaver makes creating
frames simple, and there are valid reasons why you might
want to use them. Frames allow you to keep important
information always visible. When one frame is scrolled, the
other remains fixed. Frames are also good for creating
tables of contents for your site. Here then is a chapter all
about creating frames with Dreamweaver!

Understanding frames

Simply stated, frames are several Web pages appearing in
the same browser window at the same time. A frameset is a
set of HTML tags that divide the browser window into sections or frames. Each frame can display a separate page.

Figure 20.1 shows you what a simple frameset looks like
in a browser.

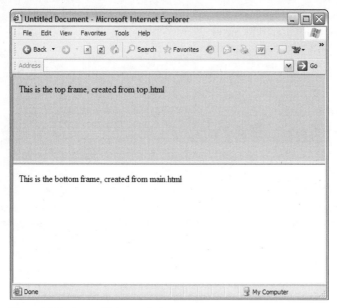

Figure 20.1. Page with frames in browser

Here is the code for this frameset:

```
<frameset rows="150,*">
<frame src="top.html">
<frame src="main.html">
</frameset>
```

What does this code mean? This frameset creates two frames. It is a two-row set featuring a frame at the top, perhaps for some navigation links, and a much larger frame on the bottom to hold content. The top frame is only 150 pixels tall. The bottom frame takes up the rest of the height of the browser.

Before we go any further, I need to explain nested framesets. The previous code example was straightforward enough. Create a page with two frames. Put top.html in the top frame, and main.html in the bottom.

But what if we want to have two frames in the bottom part of the page? Maybe we want a left_main.html to be on the left, and a right_main.html to be on the right. Our page would now have a frame across the top, and then two frames underneath, one left, one right.

Our previous frameset code can't do this by itself. We need to change our original main.html to contain a frameset of its own. It might look like this:

```
<frameset cols="50%,*">
<frame src="left_main.html">
<frame src="right_main.html">
</frameset>
```

The second frameset is considered a nested frameset because it is inside another frameset. Confused yet? Fortunately, Dreamweaver can manage all the frameset code for you. See the section "Creating subframes" for more information.

Creating framesets

Dreamweaver gives you a number of ways to create framed sites easily. In this section I'll show you how to create predefined frames and how to customize them.

Predefined framesets

There are two ways to get to Dreamweaver's already created framesets. The first is to choose File ⇨ New and click the General tab. Select the Framesets category. You can also click the Frames button menu on the Layout toolbar. Seems easy enough.

But notice that the predefined framesets don't match up. See Figure 20.2 for a comparison of the two menus.

Figure 20.2. Predefined framesets

Here is the complete list, matched up, along with descriptions. In the following list, when the name is bold, it is from the New Document dialog box. When it is italicized, it is from the Frames button menu.

- **Fixed Bottom**, *Bottom Frame:* Split horizontally with fixed-size bottom frame; 1 frameset, 2 frames.

- **Fixed Bottom**, **Nested Left**, *Bottom and Nested Left Frame:* Fixed-size bottom frame and nested left frames; 2 framesets, 3 frames.

- **Fixed Bottom**, **Nested Right**, *Bottom and Nested Right Frame:* Fixed-size bottom frame and nested right frames; 2 framesets, 3 frames.

- **Fixed Left**, *Left Frame:* Split vertically with fixed-size left frame, 1 frameset; 2 frames.

- **Fixed Left**, **Nested Bottom**, *Left and Nested Bottom Frame:* Fixed-size left frame and nested bottom frames; 2 framesets, 3 frames.

- **Fixed Left**, **Nested Top**, *Left and Nested Top Frame:* Fixed-size left frame and nested top frames; 2 framesets, 3 frames.

- **Fixed Right**, *Right Frame:* Split vertically with fixed-size right frame; 1 frameset, 2 frames.

- **Fixed Right**, **Nested Bottom**, *Right and Nested Bottom Frame:* Fixed-size right frame and nested bottom frames; 2 framesets, 3 frames.

- **Fixed Right**, **Nested Top**, *Right and Nested Top Frame:* Fixed-size right frame and nested top frames; 2 framesets, 3 frames.

- **Fixed Top**, *Top Frame:* Split horizontally with fixed-size top frame; 1 frameset, 2 frames.

- **Fixed Top**, **Fixed Bottom**, *Top and Bottom Frames:* Fixed-size top and bottom frames; 1 frameset, 3 frames.

- **Fixed Top**, **Nested Left**, *Top and Nested Left Frame:* Fixed-size top frame and nested left frames; 2 framesets, 3 frames.

Inside Scoop

The word *fixed* is short for fixed width or fixed height. Frames are known as fixed when they are created with a specific pixel width or height in the frameset. If they are created with a percentage, their width or height can vary, so they are not considered fixed.

- **Fixed Top**, **Nested Right**, *Top and Nested Right Frame:* Fixed-size top frame and nested right frames; 2 framesets, 3 frames.

- **Split Horizontal:** Split in half horizontally; 1 frameset, 2 frames.

- **Split Vertical:** Split in half vertically; 1 frameset, 2 frames.

Creating predefined framesets

In the previous list, the layouts with a single frameset and two frames are the simplest. Let's create one.

1. We are going to create a fixed left frame layout. Choose File ⇨ New. The New Document dialog box opens.

2. Click the General tab and choose the Framesets category from the left as shown in Figure 20.3.

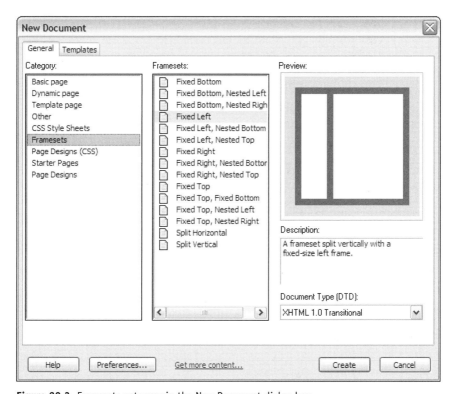

Figure 20.3. Framesets category in the New Document dialog box

Watch Out!

When you click Create, you may see a Frame Tags Accessibility Attributes dialog asking you to specify a title for your frames. You can disable this by choosing Edit ⇨ Preferences. Choose the Accessibility category on the left and uncheck the Frames checkbox.

3. Choose the Fixed Left frameset from the list on the right. You will see a preview of the layout next to it. Click Create.

4. Choose File ⇨ Save Frameset As and save this file as myframe.html.

Switch to Code view and look at the code. The code that is created consists of a frameset block, located just after the closing <HEAD> tag and before the <BODY> tag. The code looks like this:

```
<frameset   cols="80,*"   frameborder="no"   border="0"
framespacing="0">
<frame src="file:///C|/CompleatTraveler/UntitledFrame-
2" name-"leftFrame" scrolling-"No" noresize-"noresize"
id="leftFrame" title="leftFrame" />
<frame src="file:///C|/CompleatTraveler/Untitled-1"
name="mainFrame" id="mainFrame" title="mainFrame" />
</frameset>
```

Notice that there are no existing HTML files being named in the src setting of the <FRAME> tags. We need to change these <FRAME> tags and create the actual pages our frame will call. Let's do that now.

1. Create two basic HTML files. We can add content to them later. Save one as left.html and one as right.html.

2. Open the Properties panel and click the first <FRAME> tag in your code, the one named leftFrame. You should see a Properties panel like the one in Figure 20.4.

3. Change the src value to left.html in the Properties panel. Click the second <FRAME> tag and change this src value to right.html.

Inside Scoop

If you are testing your work on your local machine and not using a Web server, you may see the IE security bar warning you about a potential security risk. This warning will not appear when your site is viewed from a Web server.

4. If you were to view your frames in a browser right now you would see a blank page. The borders of the frames would not show up because our <FRAMESET> Borders setting is set to No. To change this, click the <FRAMESET> tag in your code. Change the Borders setting in the Properties panel to Yes. Choose File ⇨ Save Frameset.

5. View your newly created frameset, the file called myframe.html, in a browser. You can click the Preview/Debug in Browser button on the title bar.

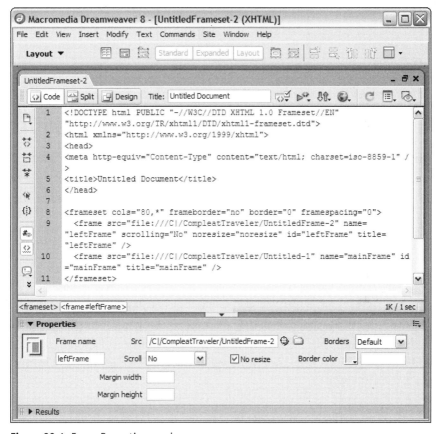

Figure 20.4. Frame Properties panel

Selecting frames in the Frames panel

We now have three files that make up our frameset. To help you navigate them, open the Frames panel by choosing Window ⇨ Frames. The Frames panel shown in Figure 20.5 opens.

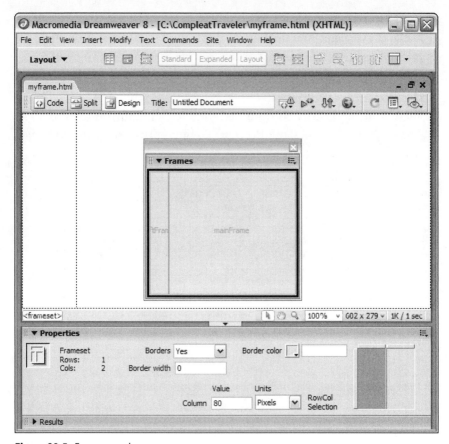

Figure 20.5. Frames panel

In Figure 20.5, you can also see the Design view of the frameset page, myframe.html. If you begin adding content to the frame on the left side of the dotted line, the Design view switches to left.html. To get back to the frameset view in myframe.html, click the outer edge of the Frames panel.

Resizing predefined frames

When we created the predefined left frame, our frameset was created with an 80-pixel left frame and a right frame that takes up the rest of the browser window to the right. Suppose we want our left frame to be 100 pixels wide. Or perhaps we want it to stretch to 50 percent of the browser size. You can modify the frameset values to make the frames take up the space you wish.

In frames, spacing is set in the <FRAMESET> tag. Here is a closer look at the tag we generated earlier:

```
<frameset cols="80,*" frameborder="yes" border="0"
framespacing="0">
```

The cols="80,*" setting is what controls the width of the left column, fixing it at 80 pixels. The asterisk represents the width of the second column, and it is telling the browser to use whatever space is left over on the page for that column. Our current page has two columns, but it could have been created with two rows instead. A setting of rows="80,*" would create a page with an 80-pixel-high top frame and a bottom frame that takes up the rest of the browser page.

The values you use don't have to be in pixels; you can also use percentages. A setting of cols="20%,*" would create a frameset with a left column taking up 20 percent of the total space on the page. You could also create exactly the same layout using cols="20%, 80%". The values should add up to 100 percent.

Setting frameset properties

The Frameset Properties panel has settings specific to the <FRAMESET> tag. In the Frameset Properties panel, you can change the overall appearance and behavior of your frames. Figure 20.6 shows the Frameset Properties panel.

To activate the Frameset Properties panel for the current frameset, you can either click the <FRAMESET> tag in Code view, or click inside the Frames panel on the outer edge of the panel. Here are the settings you can change with the Frameset panel:

- **Borders:** If you want your frames to have visible borders, select Yes. To hide borders, choose No. The Default setting lets the browser choose. Most newer browsers hide the borders by default.

- **Border width:** If you use borders, this value controls their width in pixels.

- **Border color:** If you use borders, this value controls their color. You can type in a hex value or click the color chooser button to pick one.

Inside Scoop

Borders around your frames can be unattractive. Most sites that use frames hide them, creating a more seamless interface.

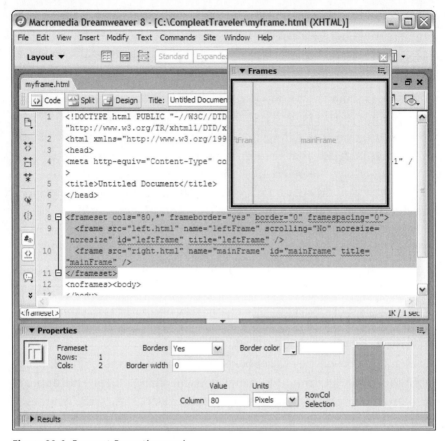

Figure 20.6. Frameset Properties panel

The diagram on the right side of the panel represents the current frames in the frameset. You can use it to set the column widths or row heights of the frames. The gray frame is the currently selected one. You can click the diagram to select the other frame or frames.

- **Value:** This box holds the value to assign to the frame height or width. Use Units to specify what kind of value it is.
- **Units:** The three choices you can select for Units are:
  - **Pixels:** This unit sets an absolute column width or row height for the selected frame.
  - **Percent:** Use percent to allow your frames to stretch larger when the browser window is widened and become smaller when it is shortened.

■ **Relative:** The relative option ignores the Value box. Relative units basically take up whatever space is left over in the window after frames set to a pixel or percent value are created. In the code, relative is represented by an asterisk.

Setting the frame properties

The Frame Properties panel has settings specific to the <FRAME> tag. In the Frame Properties panel, you can change the appearance and behavior of an individual frame. Figure 20.7 shows the Frame Properties panel.

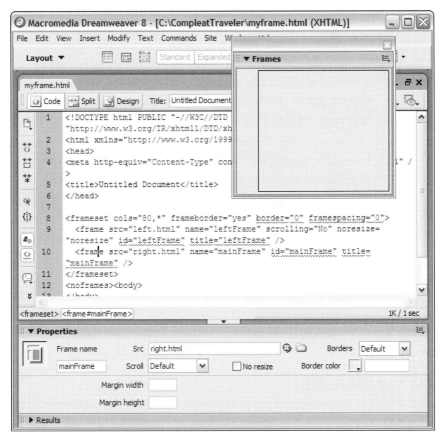

Figure 20.7. Frame Properties panel

To activate the Frame Properties panel for the current frameset, you can either click the <FRAME> tag in Code view, or click inside the Frames panel in the frame you wish to modify. Here are the settings you can change with the Frame panel:

- **Frame name:** The frame name identifies the frame and is used to identify the frame when you wish to load new pages in it.

- **Src:** This is the location and name of the HTML file in the current frame.

- **Scroll:** The scroll option is used to control how the frame behaves if the content in the page is too large for the frame when it is viewed in a browser. Yes means that scroll bars are always visible whether or not they are needed for overflowing content. No means that scroll bars never appear, not even when content overflows. Auto causes the scroll bars to appear only when the content is too large, and to not be visible when the content fits. Default allows the browser default option to decide.

- **Borders:** If you want this frame to have visible borders, select Yes. To hide borders, choose No. The Default setting lets the browser choose. Most newer browsers hide the borders by default. If you set the borders to No in the frameset, this setting overrides that one.

- **Border color:** If you use borders on your frame, this value controls their color. You can type in a hex value or click the color chooser button to pick one.

- **Margin width:** This option controls the width of the left and right margins of your frame.

- **Margin height:** This option controls the height of the top and bottom margins of your frame.

Creating subframes

Suppose you want to create a nested frameset. You want to put some kind of static content in the top frame, such as a company logo, and underneath have a navigation frame on the left and the content displayed in a frame on the right. You can use the Fixed Top, Nested Left layout from Dreamweaver to create this layout. Here's how.

Create nested frame layout

Here is how to create a fixed top with nested left frame layout:

1. Choose File ⇨ New. The New Document dialog box opens. Click the General tab and choose the Framesets category.

2. Choose the Fixed Top, Nested Left frameset from the list on the right. Click Create.

3. Choose File ⇨ Save Frameset As and save this file as nestedframes.html.

Switch to Code view and look at the code. The code that is created consists of a frameset block, as before. But this time, there is another frameset nested in the first. Here is the code:

```
<frameset    rows="80,*"    cols="*"    frameborder="no"
border="0" framespacing="0">
<frame src="UntitledFrame-10" name="topFrame"
scrolling="No" noresize="noresize" id="topFrame" />
<frameset cols="80,*" frameborder="no" border="0"
framespacing="0">
<frame src="UntitledFrame-11" name="leftFrame"
scrolling="No" noresize="noresize" id="leftFrame" />
<frame src="Untitled-5" name="mainFrame" id="mainFrame"
/>
</frameset>
</frameset>
```

We need to change these <FRAME> tags to point at our source files. Let's do that now.

1. This time, we need to create three basic HTML files. We can add content to them later. Save them as top.html, left.html, and main.html.

2. Either use the Properties panel to change each of the three <FRAME> Src values, or change them in the code. From top to bottom, the values are top.html, left.html, and main.html.

3. You can now see your new nested frameset in both the Frames panel and in Design view. Figure 20.8 shows the three frames that make up this layout.

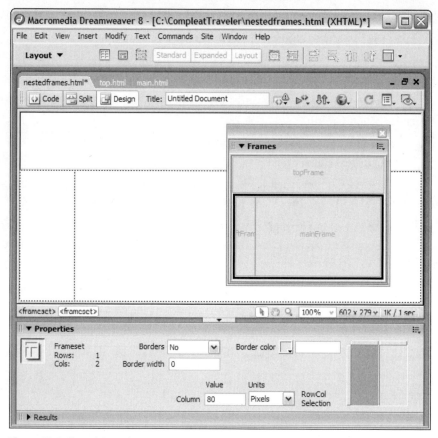

Figure 20.8. Nested frame layout

Frame styles

The Frameset and Frame Properties panels allow you control over the appearance of your frames. Here are a few suggested options you may want to select for the most attractive frames possible.

Scrolling

The two best choices for the Scroll option in a frameset are Auto and No. Auto only shows the scroll bars when the page content is too big for the frame. Selecting No ignores content that exceeds the frame size. If you can get by without scroll bars, you should. They take up a significant amount of the page space and disrupt the design of the page.

Borders

A well-designed frames site shouldn't need borders. Much like scroll bars, they disrupt the design of the page. Without borders, the page can be made to look like a single page, not frames.

Colors

Using colors on your borders tends to draw even more attention to them, when the attention should really be on the content of your site, not the layout of it.

NOFRAMES tag

The `<NOFRAMES>` tag surrounds the `<BODY>` tag in your frameset page. It causes any browsers that can't view frames to see any Web page content you put inside the body section of your page. It is always a good idea to put content in your page to accommodate those browsers without frames capability.

Frame navigation tips

One of the difficulties with frames is keeping the navigation organized. You have to know what frame you want the content to appear in, and you have to make sure that any links in that content frame reference the correct frame. If you aren't careful, you can create a big nested mess with your framed Web site showing up in a frame inside your framed Web site, rather like looking at a mirror reflection of another mirror.

Each `<FRAME>` tag in your frameset should be given a distinct name. Here is an example of how you use the name setting in a frameset:

```
<frameset rows="40,*">
<frame src="frame1.html" name="nav">
<frame src="frame2.html" name="content">
</frameset>
```

In this frameset, I have named the two frames nav and content. I want to place links in frame1.html that when clicked load in the other frame, where frame2.html is currently being displayed. To do this, I would simply create the link as normal, but add a target setting. This would be set equal to the name of the frame I want the page to load in. In this case, the link code would look like this:

```
<a href="newpage.html" target="content">See Page</a>
```

There are four reserved target values you can use that also have an impact on your frames. These are _blank, _parent, _self, and _top. There are four magic target names that can be used instead of a frame-name location:

target = "_blank": Loads the document in a new window.

target = "_parent": Loads the document in the parent frameset. This may be another frame if the frameset is nested.

target = "_self": Loads the document in the current frame.

target = "_top": Loads the specified URL in the full browser window and gets rid of the frames.

Just the facts

- Frames are created by the <FRAMESET> tag, with a <FRAME> tag inside it for each frame.
- <FRAMESET> tags can be nested.
- Frame heights or widths can be set as absolute pixel sizes or as percentages.
- If the content in a frame is too large to fit, you can add scroll bars to the frame.
- The name attribute set in the <FRAME> tag is used to target a particular frame when you wish to load a page in to it.

GET THE SCOOP ON...
Adding a form ▪ Using the Form toolbar ▪ Basic form
creation ▪ Form starter pages

Form Basics

Y ou see forms all over the Web. Forms are used to sign you up for things, let you send e-mail, get you in to sites, and sell you things online. Forms are important for how we interact with the Web. They give you a way to collect specific information from visitors to your site. Macromedia Dreamweaver makes form creation quick and easy.

Adding a form

Before you begin creating a form, you need to know two things:

- What information you want to collect.
- What you will do with the information once you have collected it.

By knowing what information you need to collect, you can design a form with the correct form elements to gather the information. Knowing what you will do with the information allows you to add the correct action to your <FORM> tag.

The FORM tag

The <FORM> tag is an HTML tag that surrounds a group of form elements. The tag tells the browser that a form is coming and when the form ends. A Web page may have multiple forms, but they can't be nested.

Figure 21.1 shows a simple form in Design view.

357

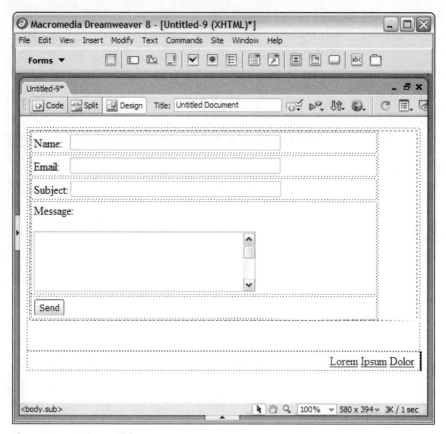

Figure 21.1. Basic e-mail form

In Design view, the <FORM> tag is represented by a box with a red dashed border. It surrounds all the form elements and tells the browser where to send the data the user has entered in it when he or she clicks the submit button.

Before you can add any elements, you need to add the open and close <FORM> tag to your page. Here's how:

1. Create a new HTML file. Click in the body section of the Code view, or anywhere on the page in Design view.

2. Add the <FORM> tag either by opening the Form toolbar and clicking the Form button or simply choosing Insert ⇨ Form.

3. You see a dotted red line in Design view that represents your form. Before we can start adding elements to our form, we need to customize it with the Form Properties panel.

Form Properties panel

We've added the <FORM> tag, now here is how to change its properties:

1. Open the Properties panel by choosing Window ⇨ Properties.

2. Select the form we created by clicking the dotted red line in Design view or the <FORM> tag in Code view.

3. The Properties panel should display the property settings for our form as shown in Figure 21.2.

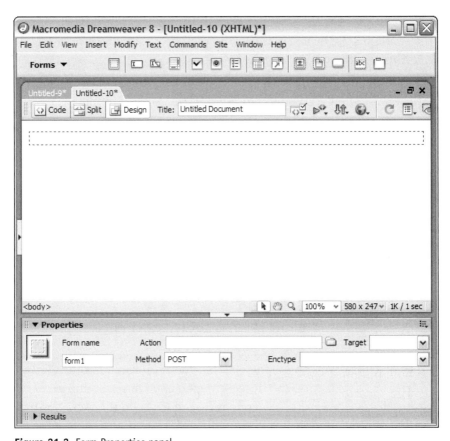

Figure 21.2. Form Properties panel

Here are the settings you can change on the Properties panel:

■ **Form name box:** Use the empty text box to give your form a distinct name. This is what JavaScript code uses to know which form to validate when you add form validation code. If you do not name your form, Dreamweaver gives it a name automatically.

Inside Scoop

The POST method is generally a better choice than GET. The GET method exposes all the data in the URL address bar of the browser, and is also limited in how much data it can send.

- **Action:** This is where you enter the file or URL of the page containing code to process the form data.

- **Method:** This tells the form how the data entered should be sent on to the form processing code specified by the Action setting:

  Default lets the browser choose the method to send information. It is usually the GET method.

  The **GET** method appends all of the information from the form to the end of the URL being requested by the Action setting.

  The **POST** method sends the information from a form immediately after the requested URL. The form data is not visible in the URL.

- **Enctype:** This controls the MIME encoding of the form data.

- **Target:** This tells the form processing page where to place the results of the form submission. If you want the results to show up in the current browser window, leave this blank. You can type in the name of a target window, or use one of the reserved targets: _blank, _parent, _self, or _top.

Overview of form fields

The best way to see the form fields that Dreamweaver can easily create is to look at the Form toolbar, shown in Figure 21.3.

- **Form:** This creates an empty form to which you can add other form elements. The form element has an open and close tag, and all other form element HTML code is placed between the tags. Nesting a form inside another form is not allowed. Here is an HTML code example:

  ```
  <form action="" method="post" name="FormName"
  id="FormName"></form>
  ```

- **Text Field:** This is the form element you would normally enter a single word in. You can set a visible length, a maximum number of characters that can be entered, and an initial value to place inside

Inside Scoop

After you have added a text field, you can select it and change its properties in the Properties Inspector. If you click the Multi line radio button in the Textfield Properties, the text field becomes a textarea.

the box. You can also make it a Password field. If you do, every character the user types in it appears in the browser as an asterisk. However, the information typed is kept by the form. This element does not have a close tag. Here is an HTML code example:

```
<input type="text" id="name" name="text1" size="50" />
```

■ **Hidden Field:** A hidden field is simply a bit of information to pass along with the form when it is submitted by the user. This element does not have a close tag. HTML code contains nothing more than the tag, a name for the field, and the value of the field:

```
<input name="myvalue" type="hidden" value="20" />
```

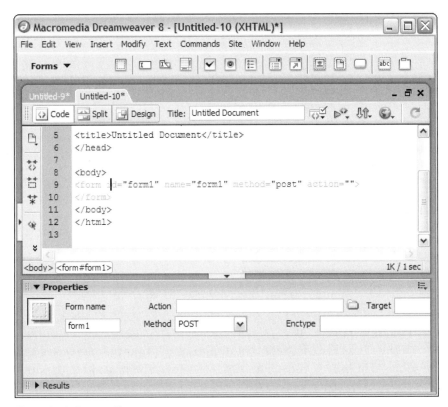

Figure 21.3. Form toolbar

■ **Textarea:** This form element allows you to enter multiple lines of text. You can set a width, the number of lines in the box. The Wrap setting lets you control whether or not the box has scroll bars. You can set an initial value to appear in the box before the user enters anything. This element has a close tag, and any text typed between the tags appears in the textarea. Here is an HTML code example:

```
<textarea id="questions" name="textfield4" rows="10"
cols="50"></textarea>
```

■ **Checkbox:** The check box lets you specify what value to send to the form processing code on submit if the box is checked. You can choose to make the box checked or unchecked initially. This element has no close tag. Here is the HTML code:

```
<input type="checkbox" name="cb1" value="checkbox" />
```

■ **Radio Button:** The radio button lets you specify what value to send to the form processing code on submit if the button is selected. You can choose to make the button checked or unchecked initially. This element has no close tag. Here is sample HTML code:

```
<input type="radio" id="option1" name="radiobutton1"
value="radiobutton" />
```

■ **Radio Group:** This is a set of radio buttons, all with the same name. Only one in the group can be selected, and the value of the selected button is sent to the form processing code when the form is submitted. All of the tags sharing type radio and name "rb" are grouped together. Here is sample HTML code:

```
<input type="radio" id="option1" name="rb" value="a" />
<input type="radio" id="option2" name="rb" value="b" />
<input type="radio" id="option3" name="rb" value="c" />
<input type="radio" id="option4" name="rb" value="d" />
```

■ **List/Menu:** This displays a list of options the user can select from. This can be either a menu element or a list element. If you choose to display a menu, you can allow the user to select multiple options by checking the Allow multiple selections box on the Properties panel. If you make this a list element, users can only select one option at a time. Use the List Values button on the Properties panel to add values to appear in the element. This element begins and ends with

<SELECT> tags. Each line in the list is surrounded by <OPTION> tags. Here is sample HTML code:

```
<select name="select">
<option value="1">crushed ice</option>
<option value="2">a poke in the eye</option>
<option value="3">sliced bread</option>
</select>
```

■ **Jump Menu:** A jump menu looks like a menu element. But instead of waiting for the submit button to be clicked, a jump menu calls a JavaScript when an item in the menu is clicked. This element does not need a submit button. This element begins and ends with <SELECT> tags. Each line in the list is surrounded by <OPTION> tags. Here is sample HTML code:

```
<select name="menu1" onchange="MM_jumpMenu
('parent',this,0)">
<option value="about.html">about</option>
<option value="contact.html">contact</option>
</select>
```

■ **Image Field:** You can select an image to be displayed and have its source sent to the form processing code when the submit button is clicked. This element has no close tag. Here is sample HTML code:

```
<input type="image" name="imgfld" src="arrow.gif" />
```

■ **File Field:** This element is a text box with a file system browse button attached. It is used to look for a specific file and send that filename along when the submit button is clicked. This element has no close tag. Here is sample HTML code:

```
<input id="file" type="file" name="file" size="30" />
```

■ **Button:** You can create a submit button to send the form contents to the form processing code specified in the action of the form. You can also create a reset button that clears out anything entered into the form. The button has no close tag. Here is sample HTML code:

```
<input type="submit" name="Sname" value="Submit" />
```

■ **Label:** This is text that can be used to describe a form element on the Web page. It has an open and close tag. The text for the label is placed between the tags. Here is sample HTML code:

```
<label>First Name</label>
```

Creating a form

At this point you know how to create a <FORM> tag and have information about the form elements you can put in your form.

Now we will create our own form, a hypothetical sign-up form for the Olsen twins' fan club.

1. Create a new HTML page.

2. Open the Form toolbar. Click the Form button to create the new form.

3. We should create a table to make the layout of the form easier. Click inside the Form box in Design view and choose Insert ⇨ Table. Use the table settings shown in Figure 21.4.

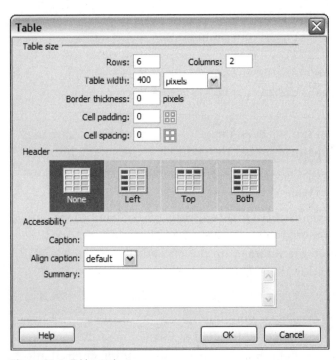

Figure 21.4. Table settings

Watch Out!

If you forget to add the <FORM> tag first, as soon as you add any other form element to a page, Dreamweaver tells you that you forgot and asks you if you want a <FORM> tag inserted.

4. On the left-hand cells of the table, we can enter the labels for the form elements. We have six rows, but the last row is for the buttons. Enter these five labels, or something like them, from top to bottom:

First Name:

Last Name:

Email Address:

Favorite Olsen:

Olsens are better than:

5. On the right side of the table, we need to insert our first text box for the First Name field. Click in the cell to the right of the First Name label and click the Text Field button on the Frame toolbar.

6. Open the Properties panel and click the text field. Rename this field **fname** on the left side of the Properties panel.

7. Repeat steps 5 and 6 for the Last Name field, and call it **lname.** Also add a text field for the Email Address. Call it **email.**

8. You should now have three text fields. Your Design view should look like Figure 21.5.

9. For the Favorite Olsen label, we are going to create a radio button group. Click in the cell to the right of this label and then click the Radio Group button.

10. In the Radio Group dialog box, change the Name to **favorite.** Change the first label in the list to say **Mary-Kate** and the first value to **m,** and change the second Label to **Ashley** and the second value to **a.**

11. For the last label, we need a list box. Click in the table cell on the right of the Olsens are better than question. Click the List/Menu button.

12. There are no values yet in this list element. Click it and then click the List Values button in the Properties panel.

13. Enter some values in the Item Label column. I will leave it to you to add what you think Olsens are better than. Be sure to give each

Hack

Use the Initially Selected box in the Properties Inspector to specify which item should appear selected by default in your list box.

Item Label a unique Value on the right. Use the plus (+) button to add more values. Click OK.

14. Finally, we will add a button to submit our form. Click in the empty cell on the bottom right and then click the Button button! In the Properties panel, the Action setting should be Submit form. Figure 21.6 shows this new form in a browser.

It needs a title, table formatting, cell spacing, and some spiffing up, which I'll leave you to do on your own.

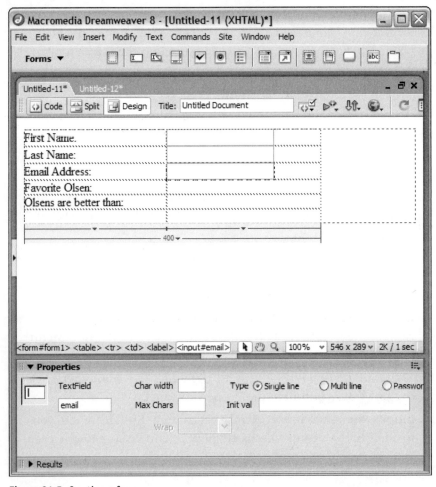

Figure 21.5. Creating a form

Figure 21.6. Completed form

Dreamweaver starter forms

Dreamweaver provides a number of starter pages containing a variety of forms. To see these, choose File ⇨ New. The New Document dialog box appears. Click the General tab, then click the Page Designs category on the left. Scroll down in the Page Designs list on the right to the UI designs. These nine designs all contain forms and are a great place to start building your own form.

Here are the nine designs and descriptions of them:

▪ **Comments Form:** This type of form is used on many corporate Web sites for customers to provide feedback. This particular version seems geared to receive feedback about a particular software product or technical problems with a Web site. As a matter of fact, Macromedia's comment form, located at www.macromedia.com/bin/webfeedback. cgi, contains a comment form similar to the one in this starter page. Figure 12.7 shows the Design view of this form.

Inside Scoop

The list boxes in the starter forms do not have values assigned. You have to add them yourself with the List Values button in the Properties panel.

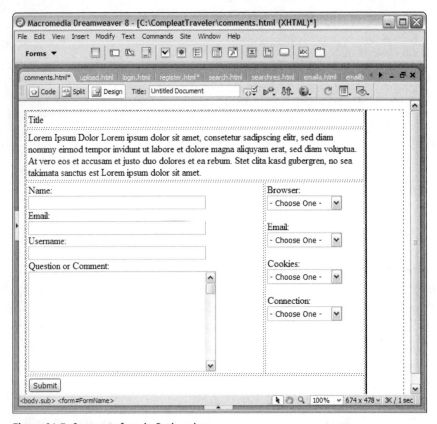

Figure 21.7. Comments form in Design view

- **File Upload:** This simple form contains a text field for a filename, a browse button, and a submit button. File upload forms might be useful for a Web-based e-mail creator, or an intranet document management system. You probably use file upload forms all the time. Yahoo mail, photo sites such as Flickr, and blog sites are good examples of where you see file upload forms.

- **Login:** Login forms are easily the most common type of form you will see on the Web. This form asks for a username and password. The password text box in this form has this HTML code:

```
<input id="password" name="password" type="password"
size="25" />
```

Because the type is set to "password," letters typed in it appear as a line of asterisks to protect prying eyes from seeing your password as you type it. A few places you can see login forms are the Web sites for The New York Times, Amazon, and Bank of America.

- **Register (Basic):** This form is shown in Design view in Figure 21.8. This form has two password fields. It also has list menus to select your birthday. However, these list menus do not contain any list values. Fortunately, Dreamweaver has some form element snippets with the list menus already populated with common ranges of values, such as months. To get to these snippets, open the Snippets panel by choosing Window ⇨ Snippets. Click the Form Elements folder and then the drop-down menus folder to find the pre-populated list elements. Simply drag your chosen snippet to the page in Design view where you need it.

- **Search:** The Search form is useful if your site has a lot of content and a large database of keywords. The form allows you to enter keywords, select an option, and choose a language. The next form, Search Results, can be made to work with this one.

- **Search Results:** The Search Results form contains sample text to display how the results from the search can be formatted. It also contains a form to carry out another search.

- **Send Email A, B:** These are two variations on an e-mail form. In many ways these are like the Comments form discussed earlier. Both gather similar information from the users, as well as comments. However, the two Send Email form fields are more geared toward fitting into standard e-mail formats. The only fields contained in these forms are those that belong in e-mail format.

Watch Out!

While having a password field protects your password from onlookers while you type it, it offers no real protection beyond that. Also remember, if the form method is set to GET, the password will appear in the URL address bar of the browser when the form is submitted.

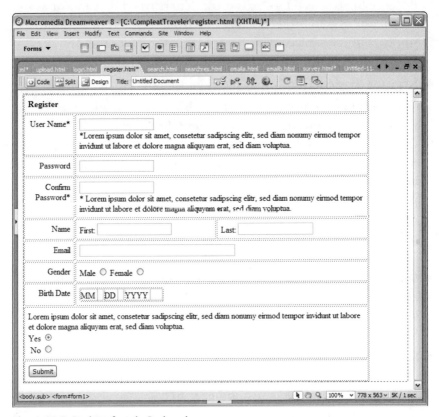

Figure 21.8. Register form in Design view

■ **Survey, Multiple Choice:** The Survey form is shown in Figure 21.9.

You will often find survey forms on news Web sites. This form differs from the rest of the forms in that it has been created from a template to allow the question and response to be changed frequently by the Web programmer, while not allowing the design of the survey to be changed. For more information on templates, see Chapter 10.

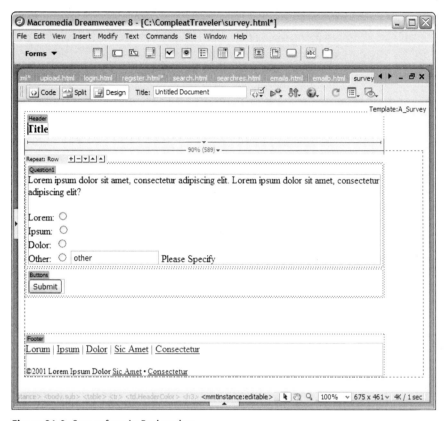

Figure 21.9. Survey form in Design view

Just the facts

- Forms are used to gather data from users and send it to another file for processing.
- The form action is used to tell the browser where to send the form when the user clicks the submit button.
- The <FORM> tag holds all the elements of a form.
- Some of the common form elements include text boxes, text areas, check boxes, and buttons.

- The two methods of sending form data after the submit button is clicked are POST and GET. POST is the preferred method, because GET displays the form data in the browser address bar.
- You can quickly create forms from scratch using the Form toolbar.
- Use the Dreamweaver starter pages to find pre-built forms and modify them as needed.

Adding Scripts, Live Data, and Multimedia

Getting the Most from JavaScript

Macromedia Dreamweaver allows you to work easily and effectively with JavaScript without actually having to type code. You can quickly insert scripts that are built into the Dreamweaver interface.

Two specific JavaScript behaviors that are included with Dreamweaver are particularly useful; these are the image swap and form validation behaviors. A JavaScript image swap allows you to replace an image on a Web page with another when the image is moused-over. It can also occur when another event triggers it, such as the user mousing over or clicking a link. Form validation code is used in conjunction with Web forms. When the user fills out a form and clicks the submit button, the JavaScript behavior is called to check the information the user has entered into that form for validity. An example of this would be making sure that only numbers are entered in a phone number field of the form. If the wrong type of data is entered, the user is alerted and given a chance to correct the data.

Choosing the right scripts

It's easy to find JavaScript code on the Web that can be inserted into your Web site. Free code is readily available. But before you just grab a script and use it, you should consider a few things:

375

- Is the script a security risk? Many JavaScripts can pose security risks to your Web site. Some scripts can allow hackers to control your Web site, and you might not even be able to tell that your site has been compromised.

- JavaScript that may work just fine on an IE/Windows browser may be broken on Netscape, or vice versa. JavaScript support differs from browser to browser. If you are going to use a script, it's crucial that you test it on as many different browsers and platforms as you can. You should also ask yourself if using the script is worth risking breaking the page.

- If you do use a JavaScript someone else has created, take a close look at it. If its creator asks to be given credit for it, do so. Also, make sure you understand what the script is doing before using it. I've seen free script that sends data out to a third party, compromising the site where it is used.

Here are a few Web sites where you can find scripts freely available:

- JavaScript Source (`http://javascript.internet.com`) has thousands of cut-and-paste JavaScripts of every description. This site also has a nice section of tutorials.

- JavaScripts.com (`www.javascripts.com`) is another huge repository of scripts. It contains a number of articles related to JavaScript as well.

- ACJavaScripts (`www.acjavascripts.com`) is more a Web forum than a script repository, but it does contain a number of scripts. It's also a good place to ask questions of experts if your script isn't functioning as expected.

- JavaScriptsearch.com (`www.javascriptsearch.com`) contains a number of free scripts.

- JavaScript Kit (`www.javascriptkit.com`) has free scripts and tutorials.

Using Dreamweaver with JavaScript

In this section you'll see how to add a script to your Web page that you have copied from a free script source. I'm going to use a simple script, but the same rules would apply for a more complicated one.

Begin by locating a script you wish to use. For this exercise, I'm picking the simplest one I can find at JavaScript Source. This script creates a button on your page that opens a JavaScript alert box when clicked. Here is the entire script:

```
<!-- ONE STEP TO INSTALL ALERT BUTTON:
1. Paste the coding into the BODY of the HTML document
-->
<!-- STEP ONE: Copy this code into the BODY of your
HTML document -->
<BODY>
<CENTER>
<FORM>
<!-- This script and many more are available free
online at -->
<!-- The JavaScript Source!! http://javascript.
internet.com -->
<INPUT TYPE="button" VALUE="Click here to be alerted"
onClick='alert("There. You have been alerted.")'>
</FORM>
</CENTER>

<p><center>
<font face="arial, helvetica" size="-2">Free
JavaScripts provided<br>
by <a href="http://javascriptsource.com">The JavaScript
Source</a></font>
</center><p>
<!-- Script Size: 0.50 KB -->
```

Analyze this script before you attempt to put it in your own page.

All the lines that begin with the characters <!-- and end with the characters --> are comments. This means that even if you were to paste them into the code of your Web page, they would not show up unless someone were to view the source of the page.

The step one instruction tells you to copy and paste the code into the <BODY> tag of your HTML page. Locate the <BODY> tag in the previous code. If this script were in your browser window, you would copy starting

with the <CENTER> tag down to the close tag, </CENTER>. The HTML
code under that tag is not necessary for the script.

After copying that code, you would paste it into your own HTML page.
The final page code would look something like this:

```
<!DOCTYPE html PUBLIC "-//W3C//DTD XHTML 1.0
Transitional//EN"
"http://www.w3.org/TR/xhtml1/DTD/xhtml1-
transitional.dtd">
<html xmlns="http://www.w3.org/1999/xhtml">
<head>
<meta http-equiv="Content-Type" content="text/html;
charset=iso-8859-1" />
<title>Untitled Document</title>
</head>
<body>
<CENTER>
<FORM>
<!-- This script and many more are available free
online at -->
<!-- The JavaScript Source!! http://javascript.
internet.com -->
<INPUT TYPE="button" VALUE="Click here to be alerted"
onClick='alert("There. You have been alerted.")'>
</FORM>
</CENTER>
</body>
</html>
```

Try viewing this page in a browser. Figure 22.1 shows what the button
looks like as well as the alert box that opens when the button is clicked.

 Inside Scoop

Notice that I've also pasted in the commented lines that give credit to the
source of the script.

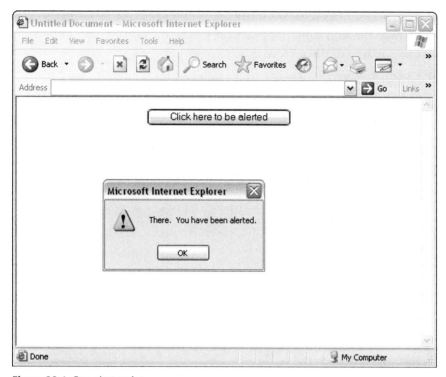

Figure 22.1. Free alert script

The Behaviors panel

As you'll recall, Dreamweaver uses the word "behaviors" to refer to JavaScript code you can easily add to your pages. In Chapter 3, I briefly discussed the Behaviors panel and some of the JavaScript codes built into Dreamweaver. Figure 22.2 shows this panel and the Behaviors menu.

Here is the complete list and a description for each:

- **Call JavaScript:** This is the most generic behavior. If you have a JavaScript anywhere in your page or in an associated JS file, you can use this to call that JavaScript code in response to a given action.

- **Change Property:** This is used for changing a property of an object on your Web page. Properties are things such as colors, locations, contents, and sizes. Objects include images, text fields in forms, and divs. An example of this would be changing the source of an image or the text inside a <DIV>. These changes would typically be triggered by an event you specify. Examples of possible events include the user double-clicking an image or moving the mouse over an area of the screen.

■ **Check Browser:** This is useful for determining which browser your visitor is using and serving up code appropriately. A good example of this is to detect older browsers and automatically send users to an alternate page without using advanced code that would break in the older browser.

■ **Check Plugin:** With Macromedia Flash used so frequently, this is a useful script for determining if the browser supports it, or a few other popular plug-ins. Again, the non-Flash user can be automatically redirected to a page with no Flash.

Figure 22.2. Behaviors menu

- **Control Shockwave or Flash:** JavaScript can tell a Flash or Shockwave movie in the page to quit playing, start playing, or go to a specific frame. This behavior allows you to control the actions of Shockwave or Flash media in your page. You can Play, Stop, Rewind, or Go To Frame.

- **Drag Layer:** Use this behavior to allow visitors to drag layers around the page. See Chapter 19 for more information on dragging layers.

- **Go To URL:** This simply tells the browser to go to a URL when an event you specify takes place.

- **Hide Pop-Up Menu:** This is used to hide the pop-up menu created with the Show Pop-Up Menu behavior mentioned a little later on in this list.

- **Jump Menu** and **Jump Menu Go:** These are used with the drop-down list found in forms. Use Jump Menu to automatically send a user to a Web page when an option from the drop-down list is selected. Jump Menu Go adds a Go button that must be clicked to send the user to the selected Web page.

- **Open Browser Window:** This is basically pop-up window code, nicely packaged for your use.

- **Play Sound:** Use this behavior to play a sound using JavaScript. Use this with caution; many users don't like sounds playing unexpectedly!

- **Popup Message:** This is the basic alert box. Like all of these behaviors, it can be triggered by an event in the Web page.

- **Preload Images:** If your Web site uses many image swaps, you may want to preload the images when the user first reaches your page. If you don't, there may be a lag between the time the mouse cursor passes over the image and when the image is swapped.

- **Set Nav Bar Image:** Use this behavior to create or modify a navigation bar image. This includes setting a different image source for when the mouse cursor is positioned over the image, and the URL to call when the image is clicked.

- **Set Text:** Use this to set the text in frames, layers, status bars, and text fields dynamically.

Hack

Use the Show Events For option under the Behaviors menu to specify your target browser platform. Only behaviors supported by that particular browser will be displayed.

- **Show Pop-Up Menu:** You can create a simple pop-up menu with this option. Dreamweaver lets you create a list of menu items, each with links that will pop up when you move your mouse over an image or layer.

- **Show-Hide Layers:** Use this behavior to change the visibility of layers.

- **Studio VII:** This is a third-party vendor behavior. It does not appear in your list unless you have gone to Dreamweaver Exchange and downloaded and installed an extension from this company. Other behaviors may appear in your list depending on what extensions you have installed.

- **Swap Image** and **Swap Image Restore:** These behaviors cause an image to swap to a different one and then return to the original. An example of using these behaviors is presented in the following section.

- **Timeline:** Use this behavior to control a Dreamweaver timeline. For more information on timelines, see Chapter 15.

- **Validate Form:** This makes the tedious chore of validating the data that users enter in your forms much easier. The last section of this chapter, "Validating forms," shows you how to use this behavior.

- **Get More Behaviors:** This menu item opens your browser to the Macromedia Dreamweaver Exchange Web site, where you can view a list of user-created scripts that can be added to your Dreamweaver interface for easy use. Some are free, some aren't.

Adding image rollovers

In this section I will show you how to create image rollovers using JavaScript with Dreamweaver behaviors. To begin, make sure you have two different images of the same height and width. Put them in the directory where you will be creating your Web page. In the following steps, I have named my images a.gif and b.gif. Figure 22.3 shows the two images, a.gif on the left and b.gif on the right.

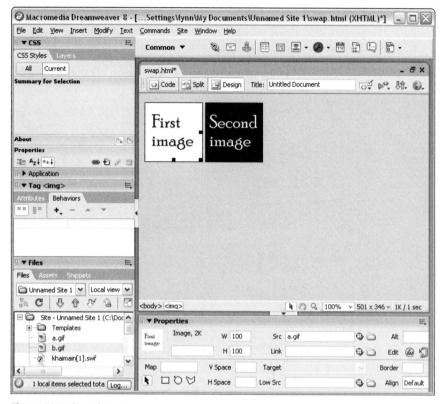

Figure 22.3. Swap images

1. Create a new blank HTML page in Dreamweaver and switch to Design view.

2. Choose Insert ⇨ Image and select your first image. In my example, I am choosing my a.gif image.

3. Your image appears in your page. Choose Window ⇨ Behaviors to open the Behaviors panel.

4. Select your image and then click the plus (+) button on the Behaviors panel. Choose Swap Image from the list. This opens the Swap Image dialog box.

Inside Scoop

Leaving Preload images checked is a good idea. This tells the Web browser to go ahead and start downloading the image even before it's needed, so that when your rollover is needed the second image will show up quickly.

5. In the Set source to field, choose the second image, the one you want to appear when the mouse cursor passes over the first image. In my case, I'm choosing b.gif, shown in Figure 22.4. Click OK.

6. You're done. You can now save and test your page in a browser.

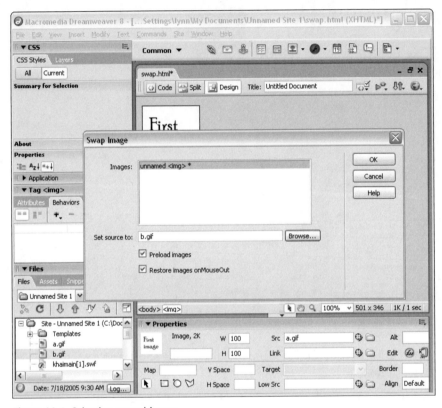

Figure 22.4. Selecting second image

Take a quick look at what using this behavior has actually done to your Web page. Change to Code view and scroll up to the top of your page. You'll see four JavaScript functions have been added to your page:

```
<script type="text/JavaScript">
<!--
function MM_preloadImages() { //v3.0
var d=document; if(d.images){ if(!d.MM_p) d.MM_p=new
Array();
var i,j=d.MM_p.length,a=MM_preloadImages.arguments;
for(i=0; i<a.length; i++)
```

```
if (a[i].indexOf("#")!=0){ d.MM_p[j]=new Image;
d.MM_p[j++].src=a[i];}}
}
function MM_swapImgRestore() { //v3.0
var i,x,a=document.MM_sr;
for(i=0;a&&i<a.length&&(x=a[i])&&x.oSrc;i++)
x.src=x.oSrc;
}
function MM_findObj(n, d) { //v4.01
var p,i,x; if(!d) d=document;
if((p=n.indexOf("?"))>0&&parent.frames.length) {
d=parent.frames[n.substring(p+1)].document; n=n.
substring(0,p);}
if(!(x=d[n])&&d.all) x=d.all[n]; for
(i=0;!x&&i<d.forms.length;i++) x=d.forms[i][n];
for(i=0;!x&&d.layers&&i<d.layers.length;i++)
x=MM_findObj(n,d.layers[i].document);
if(!x && d.getElementById) x=d.getElementById(n);
return x;
}
function MM_swapImage() { //v3.0
var i,j=0,x,a=MM_swapImage.arguments;
document.MM_sr=new Array; for(i=0;i<(a.length-2);i+=3)
if ((x=MM_findObj(a[i]))!=null){document.MM_sr[j++]=x;
if(!x.oSrc) x.oSrc=x.src; x.src=a[i+2];}
}
//-->
</script>
```

MM_findObject is used to identify the image by its location in the Web page rather than by a specific name. This allows the MM_swapImage function to be used repeatedly by a number of swap images in the page. MM_preloadImages does just what the name implies — it preloads

Inside Scoop

You can use the Swap Image behavior as often as you want on as many images as you want in the same page, and only these four functions need to be added. No further code is added.

images before they are actually called by the image swap. Finally, `MM_swapImgRestore` replaces the image to the original.

Take a look at Figure 22.5 to see what actions trigger the calls to these functions.

Notice that the onMouseOver action has been assigned to the Swap Image behavior for you automatically. The onMouseOut action is assigned to the Swap Image Restore behavior.

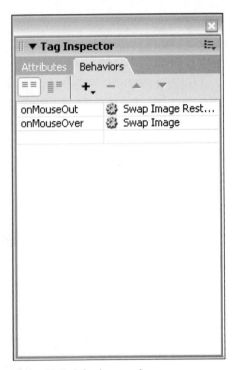

Figure 22.5. Behaviors panel

Validating forms

This section shows you basic form validation using JavaScript with Dreamweaver behaviors. The Validate behavior allows you to perform some limited validation on text elements in your form.

1. Start by choosing a pre-created form. Choose File ⇨ New. The New Document dialog box opens. Choose Page Designs from the Category list on the left, and UI: Comments Form from the Page Designs list on the right, as shown in Figure 22.6.

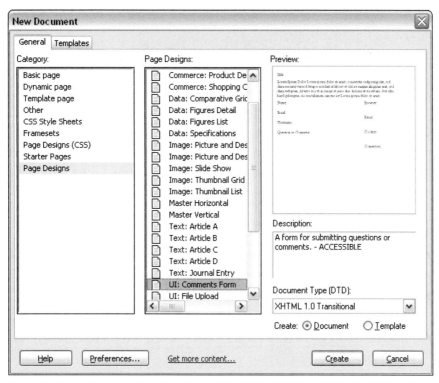

Figure 22.6. New form

2. To implement the Validate Form behavior, open the Behaviors panel if it's not open.

3. Click any text form element. Click the plus (+) button on the Behaviors panel and choose Validate Form.

4. The Validate Form dialog box opens, as shown in Figure 22.7. This reflects all the text elements in your form.

5. Click each item in the list and specify the options you wish to check for.

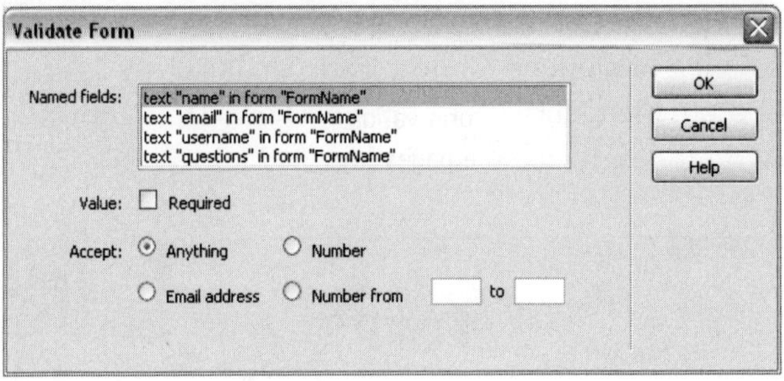

Figure 22.7. The Validate Form dialog box

You have some limited options to choose from for each text form element. Checking the Value: Required box forces the user to fill out that element before accepting the form. The Accept options allow you to accept certain types of data in the field. These are Anything, Number, Email address, and Number from...to... (any number in a range).

Just the facts

- Be careful that any JavaScript you put in your pages is safe and cross-browser compatible.

- You can easily cut and paste free JavaScripts into your Dreamweaver code.

- Make sure you give credit to the source of any scripts you use from online sources.

- Use the Behaviors panel to create image rollover effects.

- The Validate Form behavior provides you with limited form validation. Only text elements can be validated with this behavior.

GET THE SCOOP ON...
Choosing your processing language ▪ Adding action to
your forms ▪ POST or GET ▪ Adding more form validation ▪
Collecting data ▪ Better response pages

Activating Your Forms

In Chapter 21, you learned how to use Macromedia Dreamweaver to create forms. Now that you know how to make them, you need to connect them to code that works with the data the form takes. You need to make a few decisions, such as which programming language you will use to write your form processing code in, whether you'll use GET or POST, how much validation you want to add to your form, how you will gather data, and how you will respond when the form is correctly submitted.

Some of the programming languages you can use to process forms include Perl, PHP, ColdFusion, and ASP. You can write your own form processing scripts, or you can find many pre-written ones on the Web. Many form processing scripts and programs in a variety of languages are readily available on the Web, and many have clear documentation to help you get started.

Choosing your processing language

One of the factors you must consider in choosing which language you will use to process your forms is what language the Web server that will serve your pages understands. And obviously picking a language you are familiar with may be a good choice, although that shouldn't necessarily stop you from picking one you don't know.

Inside Scoop

Quite a few Web hosting companies provide pre-built form management tools that are quite simple to add to your Dreamweaver pages.

In this section I provide some Web sources to find pre-written scripts and tutorials if you'd like to write your own. You'll find both free and shareware scripts listed in the sites that follow.

PHP scripts

PHP was designed with Web page and form creation in mind. These sites offer great examples of how to create your own scripts as well as incorporate ready-to-use scripts:

- Freshmeat.net PHP Projects (`http://freshmeat.net`) contains a huge number of scripts, both commercial and open source.
- At PHP Code Exchange (`http://px.sklar.com`) you'll find many example scripts and useful functions, organized for easy searching.
- The Site Wizard (`www.thesitewizard.com`) provides you with a simple tutorial if would like to write your own form processing script in PHP.
- The PHP Resource Index (`http://php.resourceindex.com/Complete_Scripts/Form_Processing`) contains lots of PHP form scripts with user ratings.

ASP scripts

Here are a few sites offering ASP form scripts:

- Developersdex (`www.developersdex.com/asp/?p=559`) offers a number of form processing scripts.
- Hotscripts.com (`www.hotscripts.com/ASP/Tips_and_Tutorials/Form_Processing`) contains more user-submitted ASP scripts.
- Aspin (`www.aspin.com/home/components/formproc`) contains ASP form processing scripts.

ColdFusion scripts

The following sites offer tutorials for creating form processing scripts in CFML:

- Webmonkey (`http://webmonkey.com/99/17/index1a.html`) offers a CFML form processing tutorial.

- Hotscripts.com (`www.hotscripts.com/Detailed/7655.html`) has a nice ColdFusion form tutorial.

Perl scripts

The Perl language has been around for quite awhile, and a number of tried-and-true Perl form processing scripts can be found on the following sites:

- Free Perl Code (`www.freeperlcode.com/guide/Form_Processing`) offers a number of Perl form processing scripts.

- The CGI Resource Index (`http://cgi.resourceindex.com/Programs_and_Scripts/Perl/Form_Processing`) features Perl scripts with user ratings and comments.

- ScriptSearch.com (`http://scriptsearch.internet.com/Perl/Scripts_and_Programs/Form_Processing`) contains an enormous number of scripts. They also are rated by users, but do not contain user comments.

Adding action to your forms

If you have chosen the language you're going to use, you'll need to modify your form to point to the code. Begin by opening your form in Dreamweaver. For my example, I'll use one of the starter forms. To get to it, choose File ➪ New. The New Document dialog box opens. For Category, choose Page Designs, and pick the UI: Comments Form page design, as shown in Figure 23.1.

We're primarily concerned with the <FORM> tag. It's easier to get to it in Code view, so switch to that now. At the beginning of your form, you should see a line similar to this:

```
<form action="" method="post" name="FormName"
id="FormName">
```

We will be using the `action` form attribute to tell our form where the form processing code is located. An absolute or relative path to the file-name with your code is between the quotes. For example, if I wanted the form data sent to a Perl program called process.pl, my FORM command might look like:

```
<form action="process.pl" method="post" name="FormName"
id="FormName">
```

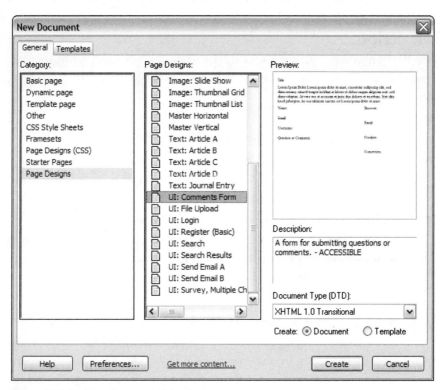

Figure 23.1. The New Document dialog box

GET versus POST

The `method` attribute of the <FORM> tag tells the browser how to send the data to the form processing code. There are two methods, GET and POST.

The GET method takes all the form field names and data in each and creates a long string out of it. This is called the query string. Your code receives all the data as this single line of text. It is in this format:
`formfield1=data&formfield2=data&formfield3=data`

If you'd like to see one for yourself,

1. Create a test form. Change your form tag to this:

   `<form action="" method="get" name="" id="">`

2. Save and upload your file to your Web server. (You don't have to do this, but it's easier to spot the query string.)

3. Look at your form in a Web browser. Enter some values and click the Submit button. Now take a look at the URL address in your browser, as shown in Figure 23.2.

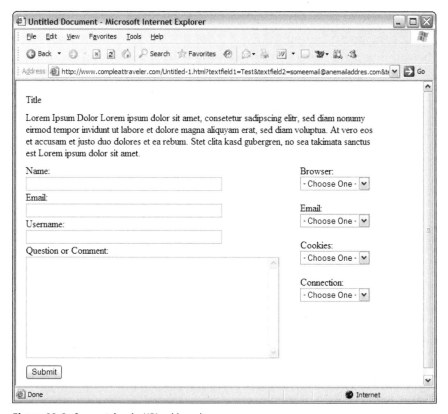

Figure 23.2. Query string in URL address bar

If you had pointed your form's action to a code file, your code would have had to parse, or break apart, all those values in the query string.

If your form is especially large or contains large text fields, GET is definitely not a good idea, because query strings are sometimes limited to 256 bytes in length on various machines. It's also never a good idea if the form contains any even slightly sensitive information. That information is clearly viewable by anyone wandering by and looking at the query string in the URL, and is usually stored on the local machine in the browser cache, easily retrievable.

POST allows you to send much more data to the server and to send that data less visibly. Form data is received by the code specified in the `action` attribute of the <FORM> tag from a source known as Standard Input. It's treated more like an array than a single string of data. Most Web programming languages make pulling out data very simple.

Generally POST is a better choice than GET. It's possible that your Web server doesn't support POST, but these days that's extremely unusual. If you are using form processing code from an outside source, you should read the documentation to find out which method it needs.

Advanced validation

When I talk about validation, I mean the act of making sure the information your user has entered into a form is of the correct type and format. For example, if you are asking for a name and someone enters numbers, a validation routine would tell the user to fix it, perhaps with a pop-up warning, before accepting the form and taking the user to the next page. In the previous chapter, you saw how to use the Dreamweaver validation behavior to perform limited validation on forms. While this validation is quick and quite easy, it's not as flexible as you might wish. For example, using the validation behavior, you couldn't check for numbers in a name field.

Take a look inside the validation routines in the Dreamweaver validation behavior. To do this, create or open a form, and then apply the validation behavior to it. Refer to Chapter 22 to see how to do this.

After you have applied it, take a look at your code. First notice the <FORM> tag:

Inside Scoop

Your code probably won't look like this. It all depends on what you told the validator to do with each text field it found.

```
<form action="" method="get" name="FormName"
id="FormName"
onsubmit="MM_validateForm('name','','R','email','','Nis
Email','username','','R','questions','','R');return
document.MM_returnValue">
```

Here's what this code is doing:

■ The `MM_validateForm` function is called when you click the Submit button; that's what the `onsubmit` action in the <FORM> tag is telling the browser to do.

■ Notice all the arguments being passed into the function (`'name','','R','email','','NisEmail','username','','R',` `'questions','','R'`). Each text box in your form is represented by three arguments. For example, the first text box on my form is just a blank asking for a name. The first set of three arguments are `'name'`, `''`, and `'R'` and are for the first text box. The R stands for required. The second set of three arguments belongs to a text box asking for an e-mail address, and is set to `'email'`, `''`, and `'NisEmail'`. Each set of three arguments is sent to the function in turn.

The point of all this is that any validation JavaScript you use will be similar to Dreamweaver's. Dreamweaver's function is rather well written, and it's a good place to start if you don't have any other scripts available to you or time to find a more thorough one.

Becoming familiar with the validation behavior should help you understand third-party code that you may wish to include. Typically, outside scripts require you to name all your text boxes in the function call,

Bright Idea!

Spend some time looking over Dreamweaver's validation function. By becoming familiar with it, you will be better able to evaluate third-party validation scripts you come across to determine whether or not they are efficiently written.

something you will have to do manually. All validation routines at the very least require that you tell the code in some way what kind of data can be taken in the text field and what the name of the text field is.

To do more thorough validation than Dreamweaver's, then, you have several choices. You can find or create a more full-featured JavaScript function and use a pop-up alert box. This is the most common way to do it. Another way is to actually code the validation into your form processing code, or find form processing code that also validates. There are a number of excellent resources offering scripts or advice about advanced form validation, including:

- The JavaScript Source (`http://javascript.internet.com/forms/basic-validation.html`)

- About.com HTML Form Validation (`www.webdesign.about.com/cs/forms/a/aaformvalid.htm`)

- WebReference.com (`www.webreference.com/js/tips/000124.html`)

- Site Experts Form Validation Techniques (`www.siteexperts.com/tips/html/ts18/page1.asp`)

Collecting data

Say you're to the point where you have valid data from a form. It's been through your validation, so you know the values are meaningful. You've sent it through some type of processing, courtesy of the file you point to with the `action` attribute of the <FORM> tag. So now you have the contents of a form. What do you do with it?

You've got several options. Often, depending on the type of form, you can change the code in your processing code to e-mail you the results of the form. If the form is informal and you only get them occasionally, perhaps a comment form, that may be sufficient.

If the data is something you need to keep track of — for example, a customer's request for a quote — you need a way to store that data. In that case you have to decide how much effort you want to make to keep up. You may be able to save the data to a text file on the local system using the current Web code you are running. Or you might find it makes sense to send this data to a database. Perl, PHP, and other Web programming languages have routines of just a few lines of code that allow you to connect to a pre-created database and run an SQL query statement, saving the data to a database. The next chapter will discuss connecting to databases using Dreamweaver to help you get started.

Responding to forms

When you fill out a form on the Web, you like to know that it's been received. Creating a form page and the code to process it isn't really enough; you need to create a page to redirect the user to once the form has been submitted. This page should indicate to users that the form has been received, and should also give users site navigation links so they can visit other pages on the site if they wish.

While any response to a form is better than none, you should try to do the best job you can. In addition to letting your visitors know their form was received, here are some things you could do in your response page:

- Thank your visitor for taking the time to fill out the form. This is especially important if you are selling something, but politeness never hurts in any situation.

- Echo the data that was submitted. Never echo sensitive or password data that might compromise your visitor if someone were to walk by as he or she is viewing the page.

- Give your visitor a way to go somewhere else. A page that just says "FORM SUBMITTED" is an unsatisfying user experience.

- A little "thank you for visiting" message might be a good idea.

- Use the response page as an advertisement for another page on your site. Definitely include your standard site navigation links here if possible.

Just the facts

- Form processing requires additional code. You'll need to write or find code in PHP, Perl, ASP, ColdFusion, or another programming language to process form data.

- The <FORM> tag's action attribute points to the code used to process your form.
- POST is generally a better method to use than GET for form submission.
- You can modify Dreamweaver's form validation or find a third-party script to use for more advanced form validation.
- Use your form response page for more than just a simple acknowledgment.

GET THE SCOOP ON...
Setting up test servers ▪ Creating recordsets ▪
Displaying data ▪ Stored procedures ▪ Inserting,
updating, and deleting records

Creating Applications

Being able to present and collect data dynamically on the Web may be the entire purpose of your site, or one of your primary goals. Macromedia Dreamweaver has done quite a bit of work to streamline the connection between your database and your Web pages. This chapter shows you how to connect to an external database and display and manipulate data stored in that database.

Before you can connect to a database, you will need a test server where you can view your pages through a Web browser. A test server is an environment exactly like the one you'll host your finished Web site on, but it is usually hidden or password protected. It allows you to work all the bugs out of your site before presenting it to visitors.

Setting up a test server

In the following example, the test server I will connect to is the Windows IIS server, although the same techniques apply to Apache and other popular servers. Once the test server is connected, I'll connect to a database. I've chosen to use MySQL because it's popular, it's free, and if you can use MySQL you can use any number of similar SQL databases. The example assumes that you have already set up a site and are adding a test server to it. If you still need to set up a site, see Chapter 7 for complete instructions.

Connect to test server

Here are the steps needed to connect to a test server:

1. Choose Site ⇨ Manage Sites. The Manage Sites dialog box opens.

2. Select your site from the list in the dialog box and click Edit. This opens the Site Definition dialog box, shown in Figure 24.1.

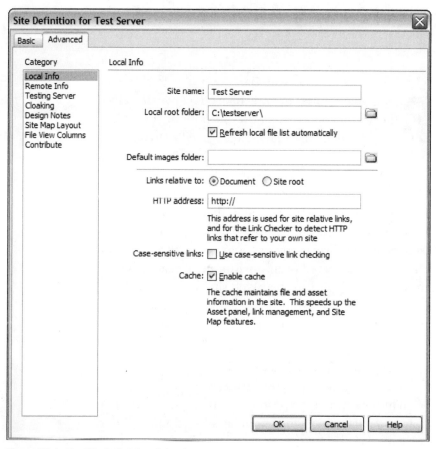

Figure 24.1. The Site Definition dialog box

3. Click Testing Server under Category on the Advanced tab to see the options presented in Figure 24.2.

4. By now, you know which programming language you'll be using to get to your data. Choose one of the options in the dialog box under Server model. I'll be using PHP MySQL.

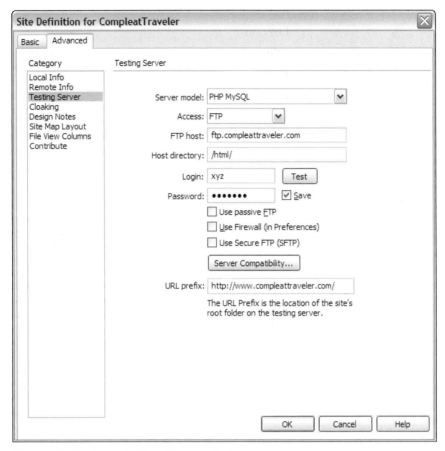

Figure 24.2. The Site Definition dialog box, Testing Server

5. Choose an Access method. The most common choices are FTP and Local/Network. My server is at a remote location, so I'll use FTP.

6. Enter a Host directory if there is one on the test server where you want your files placed.

7. You should have been provided with a Login and Password by your system administrator if your test server resides remotely. Enter those in the blanks now. To make sure they are correct, click the Test button.

8. If you are comfortable that your computer is safe and will not be used by other people, check the Save check box.

Watch Out!

Be very careful with the location of the root folder. Make sure it matches the Web address of the location of your server, not the FTP path. They may differ. For example, your FTP location might be "mydomainname.com/html/test/," but your test server might be just "mydomainname.com/test/."

9. Depending on your firewall configurations, you may need to check some of the next three options shown in the dialog box. Again, check with your system administrator if you aren't sure.

10. Finally, enter the location of the root folder on the testing server as a URL. Click OK.

Connect to database

If you haven't already, you will need to create a database on a remote system. In my case, my hosting company provides a nice Web-based user interface to the MySQL program, shown in Figure 24.3.

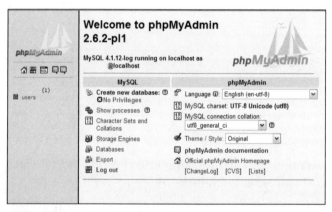

Figure 24.3. Web-based MySQL interface

You may have something similar, or you may be able to set up your database yourself. When you're done, you'll need four pieces of information to make your connection:

- **Host name:** This is the name or IP address of the computer where MySQL is installed. If your Web server is on the same machine, you can use "localhost" for this.

- **Database name:** This is the name you gave to your database when you created it.

- **Username:** This is needed if your database requires a username to connect, and it definitely should.

- **Password:** This is needed if your database requires a password to connect, and it most definitely should.

With that information, it's time to create our database connection. Open the Application panel by choosing Window ⇨ Databases. You should see four steps, as shown in Figure 24.4.

Figure 24.4. Databases panel

Steps 1, 2, and 3 should be complete and already checked. Click the plus (+) button, as mentioned in step 4. The MySQL Connection dialog box opens. In the first blank, pick a name for your connection. Fill in the remaining blanks with the four pieces of information mentioned earlier. Test your connection when you've finished to make sure it's working.

Now that you've made the connection, take a look at the Databases panel. You should see your new connection with all the tables, procedures, and views you've created visible. Figure 24.5 shows my connection.

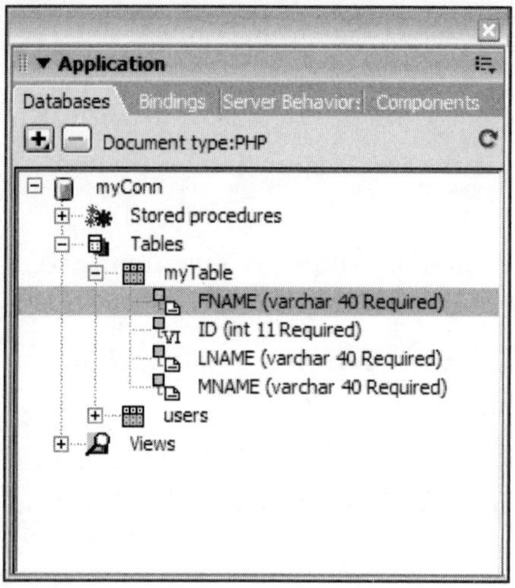
Application
Databases
Bindings
Server Behaviors
Components
Document type:PHP
myConn
Stored procedures
Tables
myTable
FNAME (varchar 40 Required)
ID (int 11 Required)
LNAME (varchar 40 Required)
MNAME (varchar 40 Required)
users
Views

Figure 24.5. MySQL connection

Linking to a recordset

Before we go on, make sure you have a table to work with in your database. Go ahead and add some records to it so you can see them in Dreamweaver in the next few steps. Figure 24.6 shows the data in my table through the MySQL Web interface on my hosting company's site.

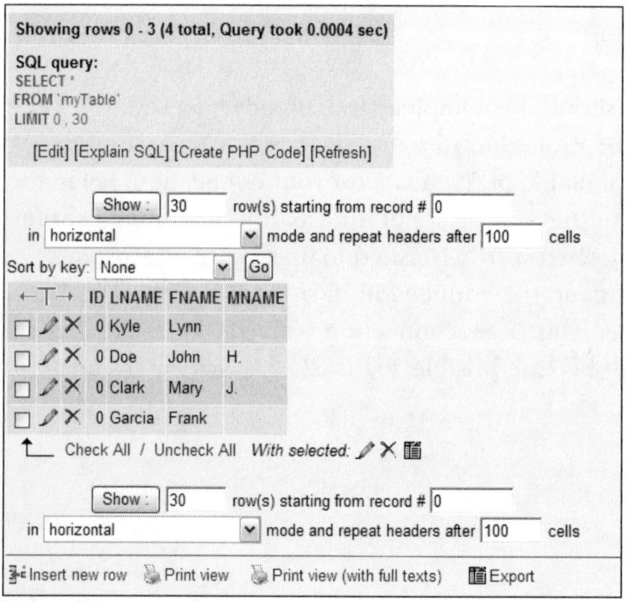
Showing rows 0 - 3 (4 total, Query took 0.0004 sec)
SQL query:
SELECT *
FROM `myTable`
LIMIT 0 , 30
[Edit] [Explain SQL] [Create PHP Code] [Refresh]
Show : 30 row(s) starting from record # 0
in horizontal mode and repeat headers after 100 cells
Sort by key: None Go
ID LNAME FNAME MNAME
0 Kyle Lynn
0 Doe John H.
0 Clark Mary J.
0 Garcia Frank
Check All / Uncheck All With selected:
Show : 30 row(s) starting from record # 0
in horizontal mode and repeat headers after 100 cells
Insert new row
Print view
Print view (with full texts)
Export

Figure 24.6. My table

Now take a look at the table in Dreamweaver. To do this, locate your table in the Databases panel. Right-click it and choose View Data from the context menu. You should see the records in your table along with the field names.

We now want to use that database connection we created in the previous section to link to our data.

1. Begin by creating a new PHP document. The steps are similar for other programming languages, so feel free to modify these instructions as needed.

2. Click in your page anywhere between the <BODY> tags. Choose Insert ⇨ Recordset. This opens the Recordset dialog box shown in Figure 24.7.

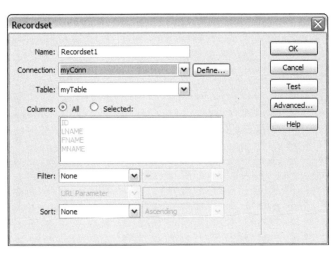

Figure 24.7. The Recordset dialog box

3. For Name, use anything you want.

4. For Connection, choose the name of your connection you created in the last section. I'm using myConn.

5. For Table, choose the table you created earlier.

6. You can select specific columns if you wish, but for this recordset I choose All columns. Filter and Sort can remain on None.

7. Click the Test button to see the contents of your table. When you are finished, click OK.

You should now see code added to your PHP page, but you won't see anything new in Design view. Take a look at the code. You should see a line similar to this one:

```
$query_Recordset1 = "SELECT * FROM myTable";
```

This is the SQL query that interacts with the database. In this case, SELECT is being used to grab all the data in your table. In the next section we'll make the data in your table appear in your page.

Figure 24.8 shows the Code view and the Bindings panel.

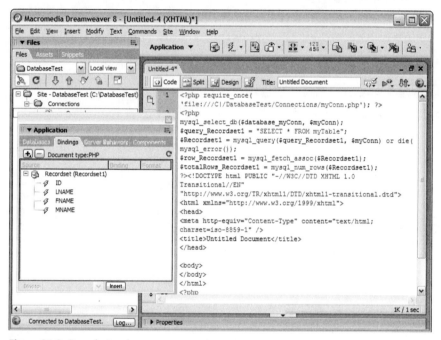

Figure 24.8. Recordset code

Displaying data

Take another look at Figure 24.8. Notice the button with the lightning icon to the right of the Show Design View button on the title bar. If you move your mouse over it, you'll see that it's the Live Data view button. Go ahead and click it so that in the next few steps you'll see your data as you work with it.

Watch Out!

Dreamweaver isn't all that careful about where it places database code. Take a look at the code of your Web page and make sure that the code you place from this point on is between the open and close <BODY> tags.

Let's display some data from our table. The simplest way to access our data is to use the commands in the Application toolbar. Figure 24.9 shows the Application toolbar, located over the top of the page. You can also get to the commands on this toolbar by choosing the menu under Insert ⇨ Application Objects.

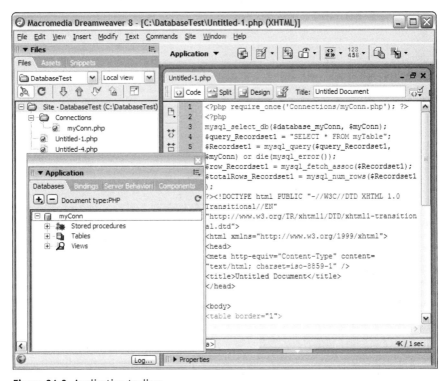

Figure 24.9. Application toolbar

In the last section, we inserted our recordset in our code. The recordset is the code that connects to the database and fetches the data we request. To actually display the data, we need to add more code. To show the entire contents of the recordset, choose Dynamic Data ⇨ Dynamic

Table from the Application toolbar or Application Objects menu. This opens the Dynamic Table dialog box.

- **Recordset** gives you a drop-down list of all recordsets in your current page.

- **Show** allows you to choose how many records you want displayed.

- **Border** defines the width of the table border.

- **Cell padding, cell spacing** define how many pixels to use for each. Click OK.

Code for a simple table is now inserted in your page. You will see something much like this:

```
<table border="1">
<tr>
<td>ID</td>
<td>LNAME</td>
<td>FNAME</td>
<td>MNAME</td>
</tr>
<?php do { ?>
<tr>
<td><?php echo $row_Recordset1['ID']; ?></td>
<td><?php echo $row_Recordset1['LNAME']; ?></td>
<td><?php echo $row_Recordset1['FNAME']; ?></td>
<td><?php echo $row_Recordset1['MNAME']; ?></td>
</tr>
<?php } while ($row_Recordset1 =
mysql_fetch_assoc($Recordset1)); ?>
</table>
```

The row_Recordset1 is an array that stores the results from the query we executed when we created the recordset. You can now take a look at your page. It may look a bit like Figure 24.10.

Creating and executing stored procedures

By stored procedure, I mean a reusable bit of database code. This code can execute standard SQL operations, such as inserting or deleting records, or altering tables.

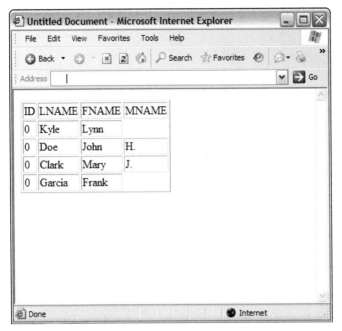

Figure 24.10. Your table

Stored procedures can be used with ColdFusion, ASP.NET, ASP, and JSP. They can't be used with MySQL and Microsoft Access databases.

All stored procedures can be accessed under the Bindings panel. Executing stored procedures differs for all four supported languages and is outside the scope of this book. To get more information for your specific environment, use the Macromedia built-in documentation.

Inserting, updating, and deleting data

Dreamweaver has created wizards to help you create Web pages to insert, update, and delete data.

Insert

Dreamweaver makes creating forms to insert data quite simple. To create a form, choose Insert ⇨ Application Objects ⇨ Insert Record ⇨ Record Insertion Form Wizard. This opens the Record Insertion Form dialog box shown in Figure 24.11.

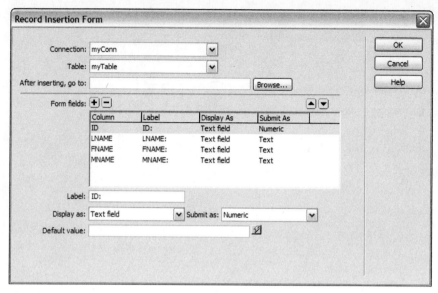

Figure 24.11. The Record Insertion Form dialog box

- **Connection** is a drop-down list of connections to the database you have created.

- **Table** contains a list of tables. This list is updated when you choose a connection.

- **After inserting, go to** is used to specify a Web page to display after the button on the Web form you are creating is clicked.

- **Form fields** list is used to specify which fields in your table you wish to include in your form. Use the plus (+) and minus (-) buttons to add and remove fields.

- **Label** applies to the currently selected form field and specifies what you want the form to say next to each text box.

- **Display as** and **Submit as** specify which data types to use for the current form field.

- **Default value** can be used to pre-fill the form field with a value.

Watch Out!

If you decide to change your form, be careful not to modify the code. Cosmetic changes in Design view will generally not change the code, but deleting or inserting fields may cause problems.

After you choose your options in this form, click OK. You can now take a look at your form. Figure 24.12 shows an example.

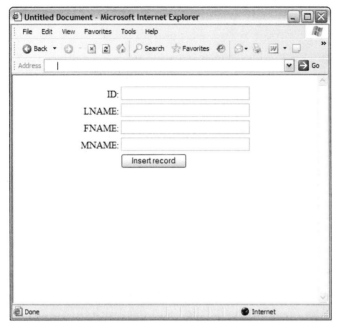

Figure 24.12. Insert form

Try inserting a record. You can then look at the contents of your table by right-clicking the table name in the Databases panel to see the data that has been added.

You can modify the layout of the form if you wish in either Code or Design view.

Update

To create an update form, choose Insert ➪ Application Objects ➪ Update Record ➪ Record Update Form Wizard. This opens the Record Update Form dialog box shown in Figure 24.13.

- **Connection** is a drop-down list of connections to the database you have created.

- **Table to update** contains a list of tables. This list is updated when you choose a connection.

- **Select record from** contains a list of recordsets. In my example, my Recordset1 contains the entire contents of the table. As a result, the record that is updated is the first one in the recordset. To modify a different record in your table, you need to change the SELECT statement in your recordset or create a new recordset.

- **Unique key column** is used to identify the record in the table. This is used in the SQL INSERT statement that Dreamweaver generates for you.

- **After updating, go to** is used to specify a Web page to display after the button on the Web form you are creating is clicked.

- **Form fields** list is used to specify which fields in your table you wish to include in your form. Use the plus (+) and minus (-) buttons to add and remove fields.

- **Label** applies to the currently selected form field and specifies what you want the form to say next to each text box.

- **Display as** and **Submit as** specify which data types to use for the current form field.

- **Text** can be used to pre-fill the form field with a value. Dreamweaver automatically pre-fills the text boxes with the values currently stored for the particular record you are updating.

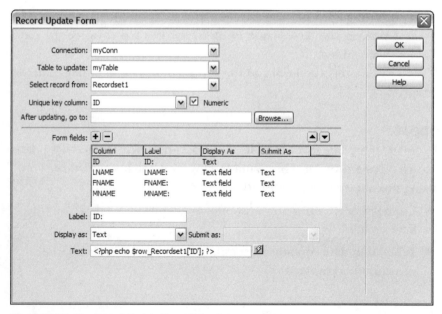

Figure 24.13. The Record Update Form dialog box

After you choose your options in this form, click OK. You can now take a look at your form. Figure 24.14 shows an example.

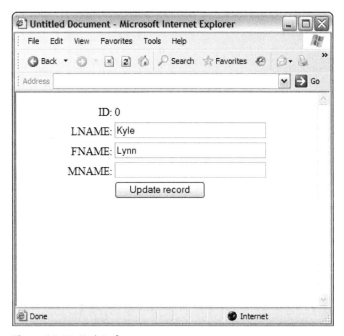

Figure 24.14. Update form

Try updating a record. You can then look at the contents of your table by right-clicking the table name in the Databases panel to see the data that has been changed.

You can modify the layout of the form if you wish in either Code or Design view.

Delete

To delete a record in your table, you need two components. First, you need to create a form with a submit button, which then calls the page with the DELETE code. This section discusses creating the DELETE code. For more information on creating forms, see Chapter 21. You may need to consult a PHP or other language reference for more information on sending variables to form result pages.

To add the delete behavior to your PHP action page, click the Delete Record button on the Application toolbar. This opens the Delete Record dialog box shown in Figure 24.15.

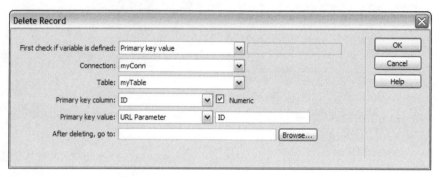

Figure 24.15. The Delete Record dialog box

- **First check if variable is defined** is used to define the primary key value. This is what the automatically generated DELETE code will use to know which record to delete from your table. It is also what you will be passing in to this code from your submittal form.

- **Connection** is a drop-down list of connections to the database you have created.

- **Table** contains a list of tables. This list is updated when you choose a connection.

- **Primary key column** is the column in your table containing record IDs. If your key is a numeric value, the Numeric check box should be checked.

- **Primary key value** specifies the type of value you are passing in to this page. It may be from a form, or from a number of different sources, including cookies and URL parameters.

- **After deleting, go to** is used to specify a Web page to display after the record is deleted.

Unlike the previous two forms, this code needs to be called and is not embedded in a Web form.

Just the facts

- A test server is used to give you an opportunity to test your site before presenting it to visitors.

- The first step in using dynamic data is connecting to a database. You need an existing database with tables, a username and password, and the name or address of your database to create a connection.

- A recordset is basically a single SQL statement performed on your database. You can create as many as you need.

- Dreamweaver can automatically create forms to insert and update records in your table through the recordset. It can also automatically write code to delete records, which can be called from a form you create.

GET THE SCOOP ON...
Controlling Flash with timelines ▪ Adding sound and
video files ▪ Inserting Java applets ▪ Modifying applet
parameters ▪ ActiveX overview

Flash and Other Media

I n previous chapters, you've learned how to insert Macromedia Flash movies in your pages, and how to work with Macromedia Dreamweaver timelines. Flash and Dreamweaver can be integrated even more closely. You can insert your Flash movies in your Web pages and control them with a timeline. Other media types, such as sound and video files, can also be added to your Dreamweaver pages.

Chapter 13 discussed in detail inserting Dreamweaver Flash objects in a Web page. Unlike the earlier chapter, the creation of this movie requires that you possess the Flash program to create the movie. If you do not have it, you will only be able to insert the Flash objects mentioned in Chapter 13 in your Web pages, or SWF files which have been created by a third party. Here we'll begin with a description of the Flash movie, and we will place it in our page. In a later section you'll see how to control this movie with a timeline.

How Dreamweaver works with Flash

The movie we will be inserting is quite simple. I have simply taken a circle, made it into a symbol, and animated it bouncing across the screen. You can use any Flash animation you wish for this exercise.

417

Here's how to insert your Flash file in a page:

1. Create a new HTML file. Unlike the example in Chapter 13, your Flash movie should go inside a layer. Choose Insert ⇨ Layout Objects ⇨ Layer.

2. Click inside your layer tags and choose Insert ⇨ Media ⇨ Flash.

3. The Select File dialog box opens, as shown in Figure 25.1. Locate the SWF file you wish to insert in your page. Mine is called bounce.swf.

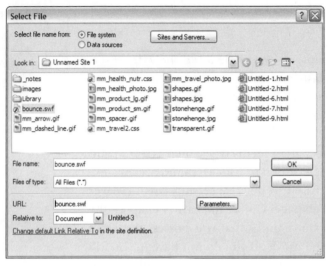

Figure 25.1. The Select File dialog box

4. Your Flash file is now inserted in your page inside a layer. Figure 25.2 shows how it looks in Design view. In Code view there is now a block of code surrounded by <OBJECT> tags. In Design view, you see a gray rectangle with the Flash logo in the middle of it.

You can preview your Flash movie by selecting it in Design view and clicking the Play button on the Properties panel.

Before we move on to controlling Flash with a Dreamweaver timeline, we should consider what makes Flash worth including, and when it is simply an annoyance to your visitor.

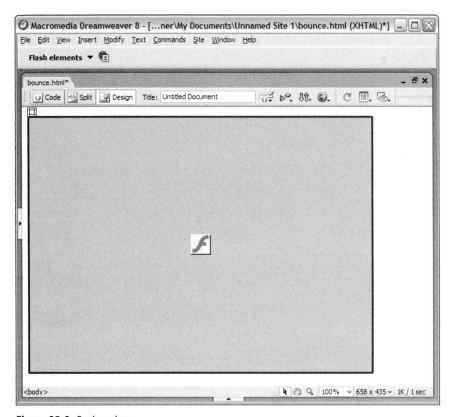

Figure 25.2. Design view

What Flash is and isn't

Consider the bouncing ball Flash movie I described in the previous section. It serves no purpose; it is simply an animation. Figure 25.3 gives you an idea of what this Flash movie looks like (you can move the book around to pretend it's bouncing).

Some Web professionals argue that any Flash on a page is a bad idea, but you'll find just as strong arguments for the judicious use of Flash. Gratuitous Flash — just to have some ball bouncing on your page — is not a good use of it. Over recent years there has been a great Flash debate. Here are some compelling arguments on Web sites that take a very negative view of Flash on the Web:

- Flash: 99% Bad (`www.useit.com/alertbox/20001029.html`)
- dack.com (`www.dack.com/web/flash_evil.html`)

- Still 99% BAD and proud of it (`http://radio.weblogs.com/0106346/stories/99pcbad.html?webword`)

Other Web sites such as the following present well-written, pro-Flash arguments and tips. They don't necessarily say any and all Flash is good, but they do emphasize well-placed and well-thought-out Flash:

- Flash 99% Good (`www.flash99good.com/`)

- moock.org (`www.moock.org`)

- Macromedia Flash Developer Center (`www.macromedia.com/devnet/flash/testing_usability.html`)

- Flash Strikes Back (`www.uie.com/articles/flash_strikes_back/`)

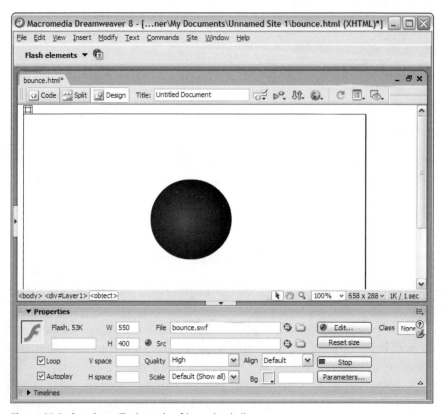

Figure 25.3. Gratuitous Flash movie of bouncing ball

Controlling Flash in your page with Dreamweaver

Now that you have taken a look at the various arguments against Flash and for Flash with a purpose, it's time to revisit the bouncing ball. As things stand, I've inserted it in my page, and it is set to loop again and again. A smarter Flash movie would be one where it bounces just once, or perhaps when a link is clicked or when you move your mouse over a hotspot. With the Dreamweaver timeline, you can control how your movie plays. Here's how:

1. Before we can control our Flash movie, we need to give it a name in the Properties panel. Select the gray square that represents your Flash movie in Design view. In the text box in the Properties Inspector under the word Flash, enter a name for your movie. I'll name mine bounceflash.

2. Open the Timelines panel. Choose Window ⇨ Timelines. This part is a little tricky: Locate the blue layer outline in Design view that surrounds your Flash movie. Click and drag the handle part of the layer into your timeline. When you're done, it will look like Figure 25.4.

3. We will now cause our movie to stop playing, no matter what, after four seconds, which is roughly the length of my movie. We need to drag the second keyframe of our timeline out to 60. This is because our Flash movie is playing at a rate of 15 frames per second, and we know it's four seconds long. That means 15×4 = 60 frames to display the entire movie.

4. Now we'll add our behavior to the keyframe at 60 on the timeline. Right-click this keyframe and choose Add Behavior, as shown in Figure 25.5.

Inside Scoop

While you can control the behavior of a Flash movie without a timeline, using one allows you to pick a specific moment in time to control the movie's behavior.

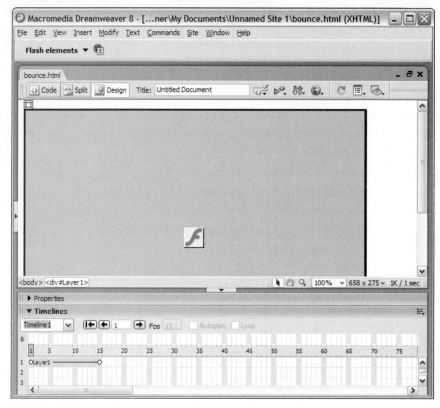

Figure 25.4. Layer dragged in timeline

5. This opens the Behavior panel. Click the plus (+) button and choose Control Shockwave or Flash.

6. The Control Shockwave or Flash dialog box opens, shown in Figure 25.6. Select Stop and the movie will stop playing at keyframe 60.

You can also rewind the movie or go to a specific frame in your movie. If you were to design a Flash movie with a number of different scenes built in, you could use this feature to play a different portion of your Flash movie when a particular section of the page is moused over, for example.

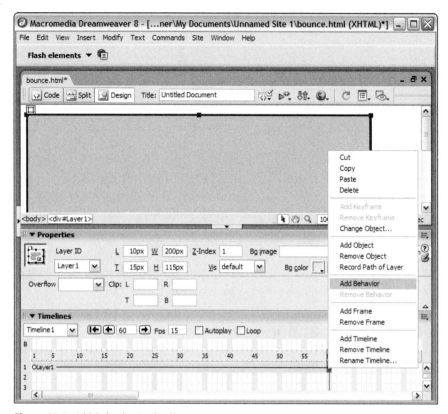

Figure 25.5. Add Behavior to timeline

Figure 25.6. The Control Shockwave or Flash dialog box

Choosing to use sound or video

By far the most complaints major Web sites get from visitors involve two things: pop-up windows and sound that automatically plays. While the site you are building for your local wedding dress shop might seem like a

Bright Idea

Before actually publishing your Web page with sound playing in it, test it. Imagine you're a visitor to your site and you have to hear the same sound play over and over for 15 minutes. If you still like it, go to another page and then come back to yours for 15 more minutes. Tired of it yet? Your visitor probably is, and may never want to come back! Better yet, have your friends try the same thing and let you know what they think, they will be more objective.

natural candidate for "Here Comes the Bride" to play when visitors arrive, most people will simply go away. Often the music can be startlingly loud, too! For every one person who loves it, ten will hate it. I strongly dislike sound in Web sites, unless it is in response to a user's request click.

The good news about video, and even about some sound files, is that Web browser plug-ins generally embed controls to allow users to stop the sounds or video. Also, you can usually specify whether the sound or video should start on page load or after a play button is clicked.

Adding sound and video

Inserting either sound or video is done the same way. Here's an example of inserting sound, in this case an mp3 file:

1. Choose Insert ⇨ Media ⇨ Plugin. The Select File dialog box opens, as shown in Figure 25.7.

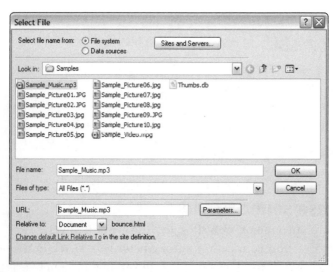

Figure 25.7. The Select File dialog box

Watch Out!

Dreamweaver doesn't automatically know the correct size for your video file; it may default to 32x32 pixels. To change this, modify it in your Code view by changing the width and height values in the <EMBED> tag.

2. You see this line of code in your HTML file:

```
<embed src="Sample_Music.mp3" width="32"
height="32"></embed>
```

This file is handled by whichever plug-in your visitor has configured to handle mp3 files.

To insert a movie, locate your movie with the Select File dialog box. The code now looks like this:

```
<embed src="Sample_Video.mpg" width="32"
height="32"></embed>
```

Using Java applets

Unless you write your own Java applets, you may not have encountered very many. There are a number of free applets on the Web that you may wish to add to a Web page. Here are a few links to sites that offer free applets:

- JavaScript Kit (www.javascriptkit.com/java/)
- Freeware Java.com (www.freewarejava.com/)
- java.sun.com (http://java.sun.com/applets/)
- Java Boutique (http://javaboutique.internet.com/)

Documentation for installing these free applets is usually quite thorough.

This example shows you how to place and customize an applet in your page:

1. Locate an applet you want to install. They are usually zipped files. This example uses the quote applet, found at http://java.sun.com/openstudio/applets/quote.html.

2. After you download the applet, unzip it. In the case of the quote applet, the downloaded zip actually contains a number of unrelated files, as well as the uncompiled source code in case you are curious

Inside Scoop

Parameters are basically name value pairs. The parameter name tells the applet what value is being changed, and the value can be any of a number of options.

about how it works. If you are following along with the example, you need all the files under the demo\quote\classes folder in the zipped file. Move the classes folder to a location under your Web site.

3. Choose Insert ⇨ Media ⇨ Applet and locate your CLASS file. For the example, select JavaQuote.class.

4. Code is automatically inserted in the page. But you may notice that the height and width are not correct, based on the documentation from the applet. You can change that in the Properties panel to a height of **125** and a width of **300.**

The example applet has a number of parameters, which are added in the next step. Here is a description of what each one does, as listed in the documentation:

bgcolor: This is the background color as a hex value.

bheight: The height of the border.

bwidth: The width of the border.

delay: How long to display each quote.

fontname: Which font to use to display the quotes.

fontsize: What font size to use to display the quotes.

link: This is the page to go to if the applet is clicked.

number: How many quotes there are.

quoteN: This is the actual quote string, along with other information, delimited by a pipe character, "|". The N indicates which quote it is, where N is a number. If you have three quotes, you'll have values for quote1, quote2, and quote3. After the quote there's a company or person's name, the text color in hex, the background color in hex, and then the time to display the quote in seconds. This sounds more confusing than it is. See the following example for more clarification.

space: The number of pixels between the quote and the company or person's name.

5. Add in the other parameters for your applet. Here are the parameters, coded as listed in the documentation that accompanied the example applet:

<param	name="bgcolor"	value="ffffff">
<param	name="bheight"	value="10">
<param	name="bwidth"	value="10">
<param	name="delay"	value="1000">
<param	name="fontname"	value="TimesRoman">
<param	name="fontsize"	value="14">
<param	name="link"	value="http://java.sun.com/events/jibe/index.html">
<param	name="number"	value="3">
<param	name="quote0"	value="In our 12 years of international application development, in 42 different languages, we have found Java the easiest to implement world spanning applications.|- MicroBurst Inc.|000000|ffffff|7">
<param	name="quote1"	value="Simplicity is key. Our customers need no special technology to enjoy our services. Because of Java, just about the entire world can come to PlayStar.|- PlayStar Corporation|000000|ffffff|7">
<param	name="quote2"	value="The ubiquity of the Internet is virtually wasted without a platform which allows applications to utilize the reach of Internet to write ubiquitous applications! That's where Java comes into the picture for us.|- NetAccent|000000|ffffff|7">
<param	name="space"	value="20">

You can either add these with the parameters button, or you can paste them in your code. Pasting them is actually much easier than using the button. Remember that they need to go inside the <APPLET> tags.

Applets generally have many parameters you can control. In the previous example, the documentation describes what each parameter is for. You can easily change the quotes and the fonts and colors and other appearance elements of the applet. Applet creators usually strive to make their code flexible.

Figure 25.8 shows the applet in a Web page.

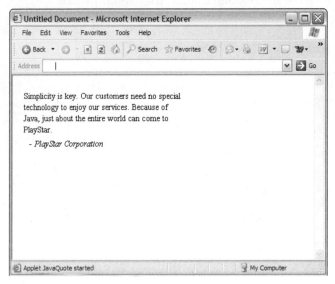

Figure 25.8. Quote applet

Adding ActiveX

ActiveX are IE- and Windows-specific bits of code that can run locally on your PC. They are not as popular as they once were, primarily due to security weaknesses and Flash and Java taking over the role they once played. You can still find them. There are a number of free ActiveX controls on the Web on these sites:

- Download.com (`www.download.com/2001-2206-0.html`)

- Activex.moonvalley.com (`www.activex.moonvalley.com`)

- Freeware Files.com (`www.freewarefiles.com/results.php?`
  `categoryid=10&subcategoryid-107&action=sort&sort=`
  `downloads`)

Watch Out!

ActiveX controls are small programs that are downloaded from Web pages and run locally on your PC. Be very careful when using them and when implementing free ones in your own Web pages. It is quite possible for malicious code to be hidden in free downloadable ActiveX controls.

- ActiveX Download.net (`www.activex-download.net/pages/Free.html`)
- Active-X.com (www.active-x.com)

Just the facts

- Dreamweaver is designed to allow you to insert code to control your Flash movies. You can add the code as behaviors, and you can add timelines to execute the code at a specific time.
- When you use Dreamweaver to insert sound files, the plug-in that it plays is determined by your visitor's browser's plug-in settings.
- Java applets can be inserted with Dreamweaver, but it may be easier to simply cut and paste the code from the applet documentation, taking care to make sure the path to the Java files is correct.
- Parameters in Java applets control the appearance and operation of the applet.
- ActiveX controls are available, but generally unpopular due to heightened security risks.

Finishing Your Site and Beyond

GET THE SCOOP ON...
Checking your site ■ Absolute and relative paths ■ Link
checking ■ Backing up your site ■ Collaboration tools

PART VI

Finishing Your Site

Y ou've built your site in Macromedia Dreamweaver.
All your pages and images have been created. You
want to put your site online and start inviting the
Web world to visit it. Before you do, there are a few last but
important steps you should take.

One of the most important preparations is to take a
close look at your text content. Check it for accuracy. Look
for and correct all typos and spelling errors. Dreamweaver
has a built in spell checker to help you. Another thing to
check for before going live is that all your links and paths
to images and files are correct. Preview your site and look
for broken images. Click every link. Dreamweaver has a
link checker that can help you detect problems.

Finally, after all of your hard work, think about how you
can protect your site. You should consider ways to backup
your content. Also, when more than one developer is working on the site, Dreamweaver's collaboration tools can help
protect the site's assets.

Checking and double-checking

Here you are, with your shiny new Web site. You've stared
at it for days, weeks, maybe even months while building it,
and it's done. Or at least you think it's done! I don't like
being the one to tell you this, but it isn't done. Chances are
there are a few pieces of lint on your new suit, maybe a bit
of shirt-tucking that still needs to happen. So before you

send out that e-mail to your mom announcing your cool new site, here is a checklist of little problems you may need to correct:

Check your spelling

There's no reason not to take this extra step with your pages. It's very simple to do.

1. Open your page in Design view.

2. Choose Text ⇨ Check Spelling, as shown in Figure 26.1.

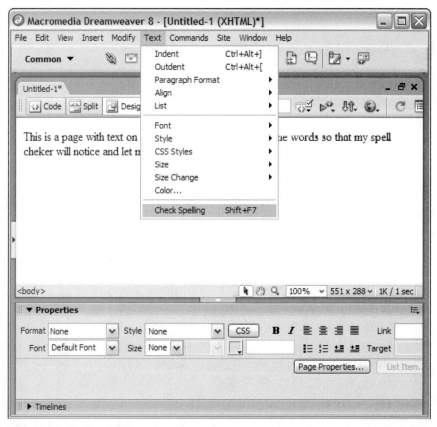

Figure 26.1. Check Spelling menu option

3. When a possible misspelled word is found, the Check Spelling dialog box opens. You are offered possible matches for the word you meant to use. Figure 26.2 shows the Check Spelling dialog box for the misspelled word "delibertly."

Inside Scoop

This dialog box gives you some useful options. You can choose to Add to Personal, which puts the word in your personal dictionary. This is useful if the spell checker keeps thinking your company name is misspelled, for example. Put words that you use again and again that are not actually misspelled in your personal dictionary to save time.

4. You can choose to add the word to your dictionary, ignore it, change it, ignore all occurrences in your page, or change all occurrences in your page.

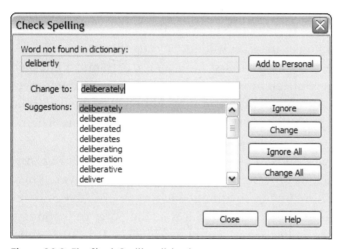

Figure 26.2. The Check Spelling dialog box

Watch for homophones

You remember what homophones are, don't you? They're those pesky words that sound alike but are spelled differently, like "their," "there," and "they're"; or an extremely common one, "its" and "it's."

Unlike spell checking, Dreamweaver can't help you find these. Since they aren't actually misspelled words, the checker has no idea that you used "hair" when you really meant "hare." Unfortunately, you are on your own. But there is something you can do to cut down on them. If you take a little time and memorize the most common ones, you can quickly scan your site for them and make certain you've used the right words. If you take just a little extra care, there's no good reason why your site can't have exactly the homophones you meant to use.

Here are a few Web sites with common homophones listed:

- `www.business-words.com/dictionary/`
- `http://owl.english.purdue.edu/handouts/grammar/g_spelhomo.html`
- `www.confusingwords.com/`
- `http://writing2.richmond.edu/writing/wweb/conford.html`

Check your grammar

It's fine for me to suggest you check your grammar, but it's not that simple. There is no grammar checker built in to Dreamweaver, and even if there were, some grammar mistakes will not be caught.

I have two suggestions for you. First, you can use a grammar checker in another program to check your writing. It's a bit of a pain, but it may help you spot serious problems in your writing. I often copy the text from my Web pages and paste them into Microsoft Word documents. Then I use the grammar checker in that program.

The second suggestion is to persuade someone who has strong writing and editing skills to proofread your site. This person is your "first reader." If this person finds something unclear, it probably will be unclear to other visitors. A second pair of eyes reading over your content can also be great for helping you rephrase sentences that are a little unclear. Make sure you thank your proofreader!

Examining your paths

As you add images and external files to your Dreamweaver pages, you need to watch the paths that are being used to refer to them. Here's an example of how you can get tripped up:

1. Say I've created a site, and now I want to add an image to a Web page. Figure 26.3 shows the Select Image Source dialog box that opens when you choose Insert ⇨ Image.

   Notice the URL is a file path, not a true URL.

Watch Out!

Using another program to check your grammar is by no means a perfect solution. While the program does often catch problems, sometimes it reports problems that do not exist. Take the suggestions with a grain of salt.

Figure 26.3. The Select Image Source dialog box

2. I select my image and click OK. Dreamweaver presents me with a warning dialog box, shown in Figure 26.4.

Figure 26.4. File path warning

3. You are given the chance for Dreamweaver to copy your image into your site. This is generally a good idea. But suppose you don't want to do this? Perhaps you are not certain that this will be the image you want, and you are just trying it out and you don't want to have to delete the new copy of the image from your site files. In my case, I click No in this warning dialog box.

4. Finally, the image shows up on my page. But when I view the code source, this is what I see:

```
<img src="file:///C|/Documents and Settings/
HP_Owner/Desktop/demo/world_map.gif" width="690"
height="408" />
```

That's not good! You never want to see "file" and hard drive names in a path for an image if you plan on publishing the page. Take a look at your pages. Make sure your files are under your site folder, and the paths to those sites make sense. Here's a way to fix my badly placed image:

1. Click the folder icon to the right of your image source (called src) in the Properties panel. Take a look at Figure 26.5 to see what I mean — the icon is just above where the words "Browse for File" appear in a yellow box.

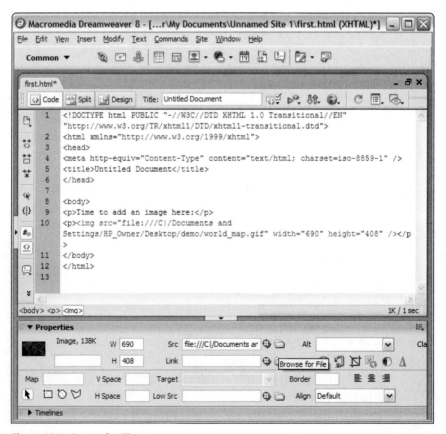

Figure 26.5. Browse for File

2. This opens the same dialog box that you saw in Figure 26.3. Re-select your image and click OK.

3. This time when the warning appears, as shown in Figure 26.4, click Yes.

4. The Copy File As dialog box opens, as shown in Figure 26.6.

In my case, I put my file in the folder called "images" that I created for my site.

Figure 26.6. The Copy File As dialog box

5. Now when I take a look at my <IMG> tag, I see the much more reasonable code:

```
<img src="images/world_map.gif" width="690"
height="408" />
```

Validating paths

When I talk about paths on Web sites, I mean both the paths to images as well as to other pages on the site. You have several options in how you create your paths on your site.

Absolute paths

When you use an absolute path, you give your image or file link the complete URL of the item. For example, in the world_map.gif image I used in the previous section, I might have used code such as this:

```
<img src="http://www.yourdomainname.com/images/
world_map.gif" width="690" height="408" />
```

A link on my Web site to another page on my site might look like this:

```
<a href ="http://www.yourdomainname.com/
about.html">About us</a>
```

The main advantage of using absolute paths is that they remain accurate even if the page with the links is moved to another directory or even to a different site entirely. Any references to images or pages outside your site always have to use absolute paths.

Site root relative paths

Site root relative paths are created based on the site root of the current server. In the world_map example, I would use the following code:

```
<img src="/images/world_map.gif" width="690"
height="408" />
```

A link on my Web site to another page on my site would look like this:

```
<a href ="/about.html">About us</a>
```

Site root relative paths start with a slash. This kind of path is usually the best way to link files in an environment where content may be moved occasionally. Links and paths will continue to work even if the document is moved within the site.

You can set the site root in your Dreamweaver settings when you create a new site or edit your current site. Dreamweaver can then automatically create links with the site root. To do this, choose Site ⇨ Manage Sites. You can select a current site and edit it, or create a new site from the Manage Sites dialog box. Select your site and choose Edit. The Site Definition dialog box opens, shown in Figure 26.7.

Inside Scoop

Site root relative paths for images and files will not work when you preview your Web pages locally. To preview your pages you need to view your pages through a Web server. If you are using a test server, you can assign a temporary site root to be changed when you go live with your site.

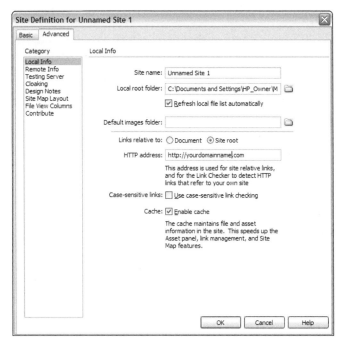

Figure 26.7. The Site Definition dialog box

Change the Links relative to option to Site root and enter the URL for the root of your site in the HTTP address box.

Document relative paths

This is the default setting Dreamweaver uses when creating paths in your site. In the examples, the code might look like this:

```
<img src="images/world_map.gif" width="690"
height="408" />
```

A link on my page to another page on my site would look like this:

```
<a href ="about.html">About us</a>
```

The links are relative to the location of the page they exist on. They are the simplest kind of link to add, but if you ever move your page, all relative links will be broken.

Figure 26.8 shows the Site Definition dialog box with the Links relative to option set to Document. This is the correct setting if you wish to use document relative paths.

Checking your links

Dreamweaver has a built-in link checker that can help you validate all the links and paths in your pages. Here's how it works:

1. Make sure the site you wish to check is open. You don't need to have any pages open.

2. Choose Site ⇨ Check Links Sitewide.

3. The Link Checker shown in Figure 26.9 opens. Any invalid links are listed.

4. You can also check links on individual pages rather than sitewide. Simply open the file you wish to check and click the green arrow on the left side of the Link Checker. Choose Check Links in Current Document.

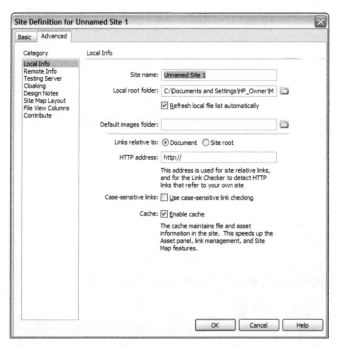

Figure 26.8. The Site Definition dialog box with HTTP Address

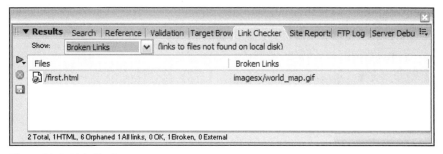

Figure 26.9. Link Checker

Changing links

If for some reason you need to move a page or an image into a different location on your site, you can change every link to it in every page quite easily. Figure out what your old link is and what your new link should be. Then choose Site ⇨ Change Link Sitewide. The Change Link Sitewide dialog box shown in Figure 26.10 opens.

Enter your old and new links and all links in all pages in your site directory will be updated with the new link.

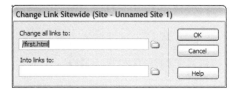

Figure 26.10. The Change Link Sitewide dialog box

Backing up pages

Once your site is completed, you should create backups of every part of it. Things happen. Files can be inadvertently deleted and hard drives can fail. It really is best to be prepared for disaster. Think of it as insurance. Nothing bad may ever happen, but if it does, you can shrug and replace your corrupted, missing, or deleted files.

If your Web hosting service has backup methods in place and a system for restoring files, you are in pretty good shape. Your company may do regular onsite backups. This is when your files are saved to a separate storage device on a periodic basis.

Possible methods they can use include:

- RAID (Redundant Array of Independent Disks)
- CD backups
- Network backups with a centralized backup system
- Backup/redundant disk drive that is backed up once a day
- Tape backups

Your company may instead do offsite backups. These can be any of the methods listed previously, but the data is sent over the Internet or network to a different physical location for safekeeping.

No matter what your Web hosting company does, you should keep your own copy of your site after every major change. This can be something as simple as burning a CD or DVD with all your data files. This method generally involves copying all the files under your site directory while maintaining the directory structure. You might also consider something more sophisticated, especially if your site is very large.

Finally, you should back up copies of artwork, such as PSD files, and any other third-party development files such as FLA files used to generate your SWF files. Fonts used in your images should also be backed up. This precaution will save you much exasperation should your development machine burst into flames!

Collaborating with other programmers and designers

Dreamweaver offers a number of features that aid collaboration between programmers and designers working on the same site. This section offers a brief overview of each. The use of these is covered in detail in previous chapters.

File Get and Put

When you work with files on your remote server and click the Put button to send the file to the remote server, you make it possible for multiple people to work on the same file at the same time. Figure 26.11 shows the File panel with the Get and Put buttons. The arrow on the Get button is green and points downward and the arrow on the Put button is blue and points upward.

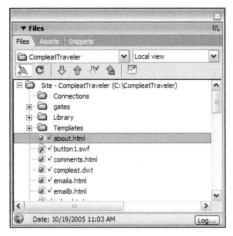

Figure 26.11. File panel

When multiple people work on the same site, working on local copies of files makes sense. Unfortunately, doing so also makes it possible for two people to work on the exact same file, and one to overwrite the other person's work. While careful communication can prevent this from happening, it's often better to use the Check In/Check Out system in conjunction with using local files.

File check in and check out

Checking files in and out allows you to not have to worry about destroying someone else's work. Just like the Put and Get buttons, the controls on the File panel allow you to easily check out files before you begin and check them in when you are done. If a file is checked out by someone, you won't be able to check it out until they check it back in.

Templates

Templates allow you to "lock" parts of a file to keep it from being edited. The regions that can be edited are designated by the template author. This prevents inadvertent changes being made to the finished parts of the file. It's also simpler for the person working on the file, because he doesn't have to remember exactly where to find that part of the page he's working on; it will be the only part of the page that allows him to edit it, and it will be the only part of the page not grayed-out in Code view. Figure 26.12 shows a template page in Code view; notice the grayed-out text.

In Design view the page looks normal, but when the mouse cursor passes over locked regions it changes to a black circle with a line through it, and nothing in those regions will be editable.

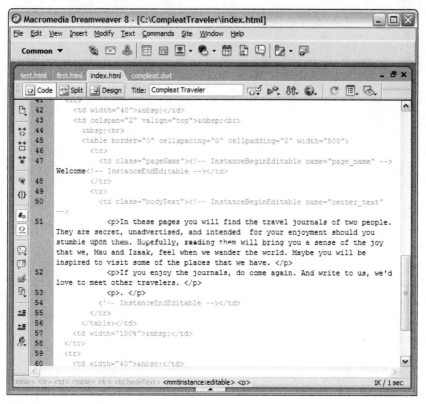

Figure 26.12. Template in Code view

Just the facts

- Dreamweaver has a built-in spell checker for your Web content.
- Watch out for homophones in your pages. Learn the common ones and check for them.
- Use a third-party grammar checker or a friend who has strong writing or editing skills to help you with your grammar and content.
- Consider which type of links to use in your site: absolute, site root relative, or document root relative.

■ You can check and change your links sitewide.

■ Make sure your site is periodically backed up, including the creative files and fonts used to create it.

■ Use File Get and Put, check in and check out, and templates when several people are working on the same site.

GET THE SCOOP ON...
Customizing Dreamweaver ■ Maintaining your site ■
Keeping your Web design current ■ Putting your
Dreamweaver skills to work ■ Dreamweaver user
communities

Going Further with Dreamweaver

By now you've mastered Macromedia Dreamweaver. Along the way, you've learned about HTML, CSS, JavaScript, and dynamic sites. Now that you know the basics, you'll want to keep learning and find ways to learn more about Dreamweaver and keep your skills current. You may even want to seek work using Dreamweaver.

You can enhance your Dreamweaver interface with the Macromedia Exchange Web site. Dreamweaver user community sites can also help you add functionality to your site and improve your skills. At the same time you are learning more about Dreamweaver, you will also be keeping your Web design and programming skills fresh.

Extending Dreamweaver

Dreamweaver is extremely customizable. In this section, I'll show you how to get started customizing Dreamweaver to better suit your individual preferences.

Setting code preferences

Dreamweaver allows you to change the default way your code appears to you and is formatted as you create it in the Dreamweaver environment. Here are a few code options you can customize.

To change your **code viewing options:**

1. Open a document in Code view in Dreamweaver.

2. Choose View ⇨ Code View Options to see the submenu shown in Figure 27.1.

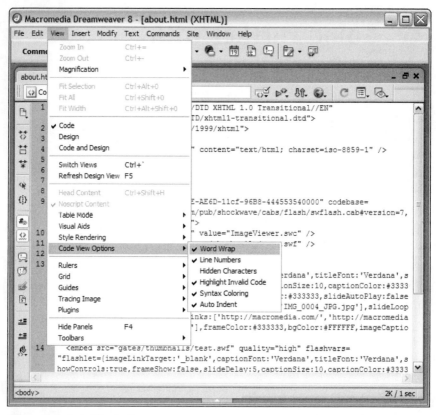

Figure 27.1. Code View Options

Check or uncheck the desired options.

Word Wrap causes lines of code longer than the code view window to wrap. This is strictly for Code view and no new lines are added to your code.

Line Numbers adds line numbers to the left column of Code view, making it easier to locate specific lines when searching your file.

Hidden Characters reveals characters normally hidden from view, such as carriage returns. This can be useful when searching for white space causing layout problems in your page.

Highlight Invalid Code reveals any code that the Dreamweaver's code checker considers invalid. This is strictly for Code view and no changes are actually made to your code.

Syntax Coloring changes the color of types of syntax in your code in Code view. You can set this using your code coloring preferences, discussed a little later in this chapter.

Auto Indent automatically indents a new line added beneath an already indented line.

Figure 27.2 shows an example of code in Code view with all options selected.

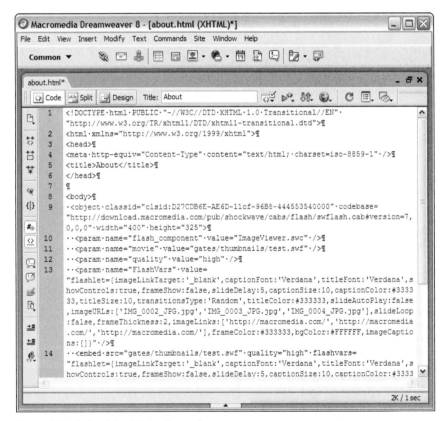

Figure 27.2. Code with all Code view options

Notice the hidden new line characters and spaces, represented by dots. Also notice the line numbers on the left. Areas where there are gaps between numbers are lines that are wrapping due to their length.

To change your code formatting options:

1. Choose Edit ⇨ Preferences.

2. The Preferences dialogbox opens. Select Code Format under Category on the left, as shown in Figure 27.3.

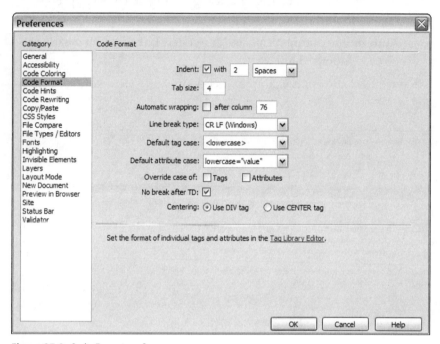

Figure 27.3. Code Format preferences

Check or uncheck the desired options.

Indent allows you to specify if your code should indent, and if so, by how many spaces or tabs.

Tab size lets you enter how many spaces wide tabs are.

Automatic wrapping specifies if your code should wrap and if so, where. Unlike the word wrap option, this does insert a real new line character in your document.

Line break type is useful if you are exporting your code to other types of machines. Unix, Mac, and Windows all differ on the standard new line characters they use. You should set this to match the type of machine your Web server runs from.

Inside Scoop

Some early browsers change the appearance of your table based on white space immediately following a <TD> tag. Make sure you test your table appearance on all applicable browsers.

Default tag case can be used to specify if Dreamweaver-produced HTML tags should be uppercase, for example <TABLE>, or lowercase, such as <table>.

Default attribute case is similar, causing attributes of tags to appear in the designated case.

Override case of Tags, Attributes check boxes can be used to force Dreamweaver to change all existing tags in your code to the specified case settings every time you open a file.

No break after TD tells Dreamweaver to immediately continue with the code on your page after a <TD> tag.

Centering specifies whether to use the newer <DIV> tag or the older, deprecated <CENTER> tag when centering content on your page.

Code rewriting options control if and how Dreamweaver modifies your code when you open a file or when adding or pasting code into a file. To change your code rewriting preferences:

1. Choose Edit ⇨ Preferences.

2. The Preferences dialog box opens. Select Code Rewriting under Category on the left, as shown in Figure 27.4.

Check or uncheck the desired options.

Rewrite code check boxes let you decide specifically what kind of code you want rewritten. Choices are HTML tags that are not closed or are nested incorrectly, form item names, and extra closing tags. You can also tell Dreamweaver to warn you when it rewrites your code.

Never rewrite code allows you to list file types you never want rewritten. This is especially useful when writing scripts with syntax that will break if standard HTML code is used.

Special characters controls automatic encoding of certain characters when they are used as attribute values.

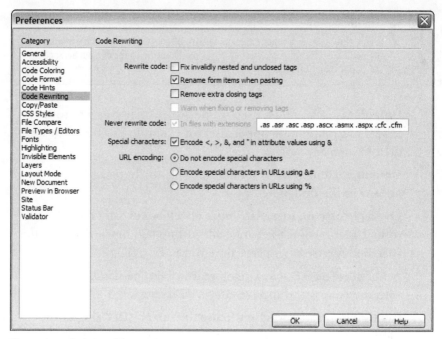

Figure 27.4. Code Rewriting preferences

> **URL encoding** controls how URL encoding takes place. This is useful if you are passing URLs to browsers that will not correctly process a URL; for example, the character ">" rather than ">".

To change your code coloring preferences:

1. Choose Edit ⇨ Preferences.

2. The Preferences dialog box opens. Select Code Coloring under Category on the left, as shown in Figure 27.5.

Code coloring controls colors and font types for syntax in your documents. This affects how your code appears in Code view but makes no changes to the actual code. From this dialog box you can choose a file type to edit. You can choose colors and fonts for various elements in your document. For example, you could make your HTML document code appear on a black background by changing the Default background color in the dialog. Dreamweaver gives you complete control over the appearance of your code while you are editing it.

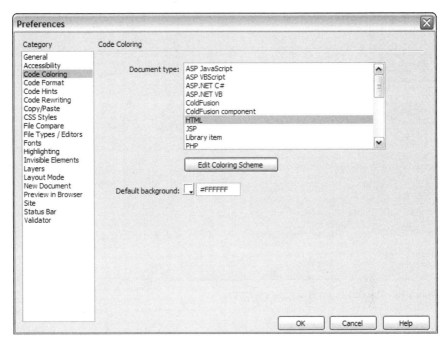

Figure 27.5. Code Coloring preferences

3. To change the coloring scheme for a particular document type, choose a type from the Document type list and click the Edit Coloring Scheme button.

4. The Edit Coloring Scheme dialog box opens, shown in Figure 27.6.

    Use this dialog box to select and color code-specific syntax items in your document. The Preview window gives you an idea what code will look like in your own Code view window if you make the specified change.

To change code hints preferences:

1. Choose Edit ⇨ Preferences.

2. The Preferences dialog box opens. Select Code Hints under Category on the left, as shown in Figure 27.7.

    A Dreamweaver code hint is a list of suggested code options that appears next to your mouse cursor as you are typing code. The suggestion closest to what you are typing is highlighted, and you can just press Enter to select it. This can save you some typing and also allows for fewer typos than if you typed the code in yourself.

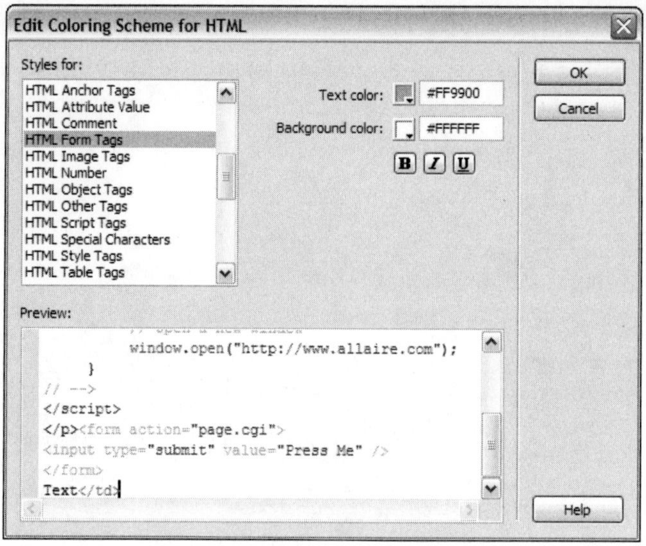

Figure 27.6. The Edit Coloring Scheme dialog box

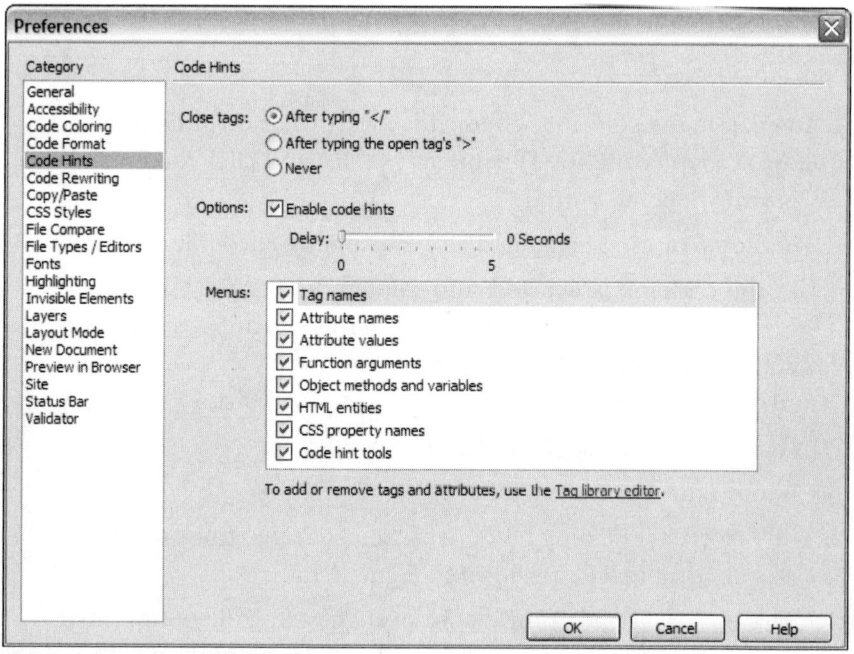

Figure 27.7. Code Hints preferences

Check or uncheck the desired options:

Close tags tells Dreamweaver when or if to automatically add the close HTML tag for the current tag you are typing.

Enable code hints check box turns code hints on or off. The Delay meter controls how quickly the pop-up menu appears.

The **Menus** list allows you to specify just what type of code hints you want to appear.

Figure 27.8 shows Code view with the code hints menu activated.

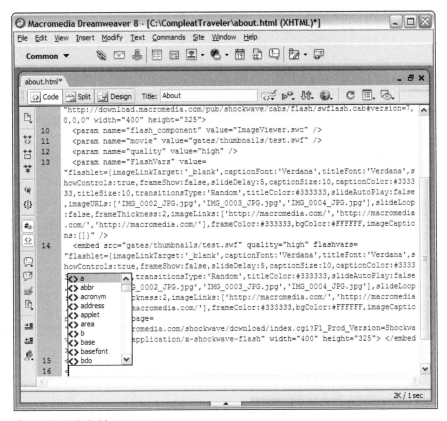

Figure 27.8. Code hints menu

Watch Out!

Documents that you have created with one set of Code view options will not display changes you make to your Code view options unless you choose Commands ⇨ Apply Source Formatting.

Customize keyboard shortcuts

Dreamweaver has a huge number of predefined keyboard shortcuts. If your personal preferences differ from these, you can use the Keyboard Shortcut Editor to change them. You can also add your own shortcuts for undefined commands. To modify or add new keyboard shortcuts:

1. Choose Edit ⇨ Keyboard Shortcuts, or Dreamweaver ⇨ Keyboard Shortcuts.

2. The Keyboard Shortcuts dialog box opens, shown in Figure 27.9.

    Current set lets you select either default shortcuts or pre-determined sets from other programs. You can also define your own set.

    Commands specifies which menu or object to list commands from. The list below the Commands menu contains all the commands it is possible to create or modify shortcuts for.

    Shortcuts lists the current shortcuts for the selected command.

    Press key shows the keys you have entered as you create or modify your selected shortcut.

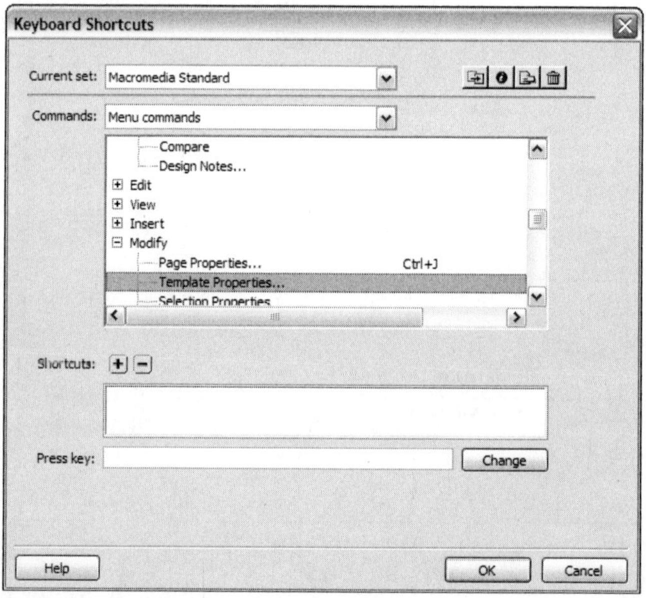

Figure 27.9. The Keyboard Shortcuts dialog box

Maintaining your site

After your site has been online for a few months, you should periodically review it. This section presents a list of tasks you should occasionally perform to keep your site working as well as possible.

Review access log

Every Web server creates a text file called an access log. Your Web master can help you locate this log and understand the information presented in it. Log files contain entries for every view of every page and image on your site every time a visitor comes to your site. Some of the specific information you can get from the log includes date and time of access, precisely which file was accessed, and the IP address of the computer of the person who visited you.

Here is an example of what an access log might look like:

```
[24/Oct/2005:11:13:01      -0400]|http://www.yourwebsite-
name.com/about.html/|acomputer.res.rr.com|GET
/about.gif    HTTP/1.1|304|304|25.160.80.180|Mozilla/4.0
(compatible;   MSIE    6.0;   Windows    NT    5.1;   SV1;
FunWebProducts; .NET CLR 1.1.4322)
[24/Oct/2005:11:13:01 -0400]|http://www.yourwebsite-
name.com/about.html/|acomputer.res.rr.com|GET
/about.html HTTP/1.1|304|304|25.160.80.180|Mozilla/4.0
(compatible; MSIE 6.0; Windows NT 5.1; SV1;
FunWebProducts; .NET CLR 1.1.4322)
[24/Oct/2005:11:22:20 -0400]| http://www.yourwebsite-
name.com | somecomputer.somehost.com |GET
/g/image_65x65_3.jpg
HTTP/1.1|304|304|192.168.1.12|Mozilla/4.0 (compatible;
MSIE 6.0; Windows NT 5.1; SV1; .NET CLR 1.1.4322)
[24/Oct/2005:11:22:20 -0400]| http://www.yourwebsite-
name.com |somecomputer.somehost.com|GET
/g/image_65x65.jpg
HTTP/1.1|304|304|192.168.1.12|Mozilla/4.0 (compatible;
MSIE 6.0; Windows NT 5.1; SV1; .NET CLR 1.1.4322)
```

Each line of the access log lists a page or file on your site that was accessed by a visitor's browser. The line includes the date and time, the visitor's IP address, and some information about which browser they are using. There are many third-party software packages that parse access logs and create charts and graphs such as the one shown in Figure 27.10.

Use the access log information to see which pages get the most hits, and where your hits are coming from, as well as what browser versions are accessing your pages. You can fine-tune your navigation to pages you wish to get more hits by paying attention to your access logs.

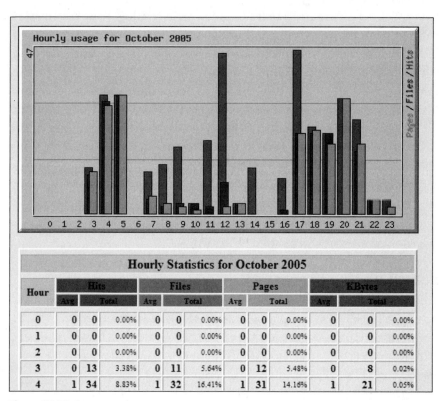

Figure 27.10. Access graph

Review error log

Like the access log, the error log is a list generated by the Web server. This list reports broken links and broken scripts on your site. You may also see a number of requests for pages or files you don't have on your site. Don't let these alarm you; often they are script processes run by would-be hackers trying to find weaknesses in your site. Here's what an error log might look like:

```
[Mon Oct 24 07:48:26 2005] [error] [client
60.200.601.80] File does not exist: /testing/index.
htmlll
```

This log entry tells you that someone tried to go to the file /testing/index.htmlll on your site, which doesn't exist. This is probably a user typo from someone typing in a URL.

Periodically view your error log to keep track of your links and scripts and ensure that they are not broken.

Check external links

The error log won't report links on your site that lead to broken pages on other sites. You should check any links on your site to other pages and make sure those pages haven't moved or still exist.

Keep your information fresh

Make sure you don't leave old, stale information on your site. If you can't frequently update your site, at least make sure your information isn't going to become obsolete. There's nothing impressive about a press release that's two years old on your front page.

Search engine placement

Take some time to search for your Web site on search engines. There are entire Web sites and books about search engine optimization (SEO), and if you need to increase traffic to your site, you should definitely research SEO strategies.

Validate with new browsers

Browsers change frequently. New browser software and new versions of current browsers come out every few months. As browser use evolves, your site should be tested for compliance with new browsers. Keep an eye on what browsers are the most likely to be used by your visitors and test your content in them.

Keeping your designs current

Web site design is an evolving process. Design fads change, and if your site still has design elements from five years ago, it may look dated.

A number of Web sites offer fresh design information and other topical advice on Web design issues. Here are some good starting places:

- A List Apart (www.alistapart.com)
- Web Page Design for Designers (www.wpdfd.com)
- Useit.com: Jakob Nielsen on Usability (www.useit.com)
- WebsiteTips.com (www.websitetips.com)
- Web Developer's Virtual Library (www.wdvl.com)
- Pixy Color Palette Generator (http://wellstyled.com/tools/)
- Zeldman - The Daily Report (www.zeldman.com)
- Moock.org (www.moock.org)

Making money with your Dreamweaver skills

By far the best way to make money with Dreamweaver is to network to discover your niche. You can often find small business owners who need a Web site built and don't necessarily have any preferences about how you create it. Build a few Web sites and build up your portfolio.

Internet job sites frequently advertise positions for Dreamweaver developers. A good strategy is to look for short-term gigs using Dreamweaver, and then work up to longer-term jobs. I've personally had reasonable success with the free Craigslist.org in finding shorter Dreamweaver gigs.

While you will often see Dreamweaver positions posted on the big sites, like Monster.com or HotJobs.com, it is often harder to find actual employment on these sites than if you spread your resume around and look at smaller, local job listings. This is subjective, but I have never gotten a response from a specific job posting I have applied to through the big sites. I have received calls from headhunters as a result of posting my resume on those sites.

If you stick to the smaller job listing sites you may not find nearly as many opportunities, but the ones you do find are generally less competitive and you are more likely to hear from the specific job posting you are interested in.

I mentioned Craigslist.org earlier, and you will find opportunities listed there. But don't overlook the power of Craiglist's resume-posting area. Employers frequently search through resumes there and don't bother posting ads at all.

Joining Dreamweaver user communities

There are quite a number of Dreamweaver user communities, and you can find a list of them in the resource links in Appendix A. User communities are great places to get help with problems you may be having using Dreamweaver. You will generally find many experts who are happy to offer advice and suggestions. You can also get the latest news about new extensions to Dreamweaver.

You may need to register with the particular Web site before you can actually become part of the specific Dreamweaver community on that site. Some communities allow you to comment on posts without being a member, others do not. Normally this is clearly stated on the site, but you may have to check out the help or FAQ pages of the particular site to determine that site's quirks. I don't know of any sites that charge for membership, but as with anything online, be cautious about giving out personal information such as credit card numbers.

Just the facts

- The Dreamweaver interface is customizable. Use the Code View preferences to control what your code looks like as you edit it.

- A number of automatic code modification options are available under the Dreamweaver preferences menu. These control things like auto completion of tags and code hints.

- Once your site is up, you should periodically review it for content, links, and browser compatibility.

- Use the access log to see where your traffic is coming from and what pages they are visiting.

- Use the error log to see what links on your site may be broken.

- You can make money with Dreamweaver by building up a portfolio of sites and creating a resume that you post on various online job sites.

- Dreamweaver user communities can provide a source of support, tricks, and news about Dreamweaver and its resources.

Appendixes

PART VII

absolute path   The entire address of an image or Web page, including the protocol (typically HTTP://). Absolute paths, must be used when you are calling material from another Web site, although this practice is generally frowned upon.

accessibility   Refers to making Web content more easily accessible to people with visual, auditory, and other disabilities.

action   A Dreamweaver term that refers to the triggering event that causes a behavior to occur. For example, if you have a JavaScript image swap, the action that triggers it might be the onMouseOver event.

alignment   Refers to the placement of text and images on the HTML page and in tables. Options include left, center, right, and justify.

alt tag   Setting the *alt=* value to a text string allows users to move their mouse over an image to see a text description of the image.

anchor   A special kind of link that allows you to link from some point in your current page to another point in your current page.

Assets panel   This panel contains a number of elements you are storing for use in your site, allowing you easy access to them for addition in your pages.

attributes   Refers to properties in HTML tags such as an image height or width.

autostretch   A column setting that causes the width of the column to change depending on the width of the browser's window. Compare to fixed width.

background color   The color of a Web page. The default is normally white.

background image   Any image used as the background of a Web page.

balanced braces   This means that every opening brace has a matching closing brace in your document.

base element   Use this to set a base URL. Every link in your page will be relative to this URL.

behavior   Pre-built JavaScript code you can attach to execute in reaction to user and browser actions.

Behaviors panel   Use this panel to add behaviors to user and browser actions.

Bindings panel   This panel is used to create and connect to database connections.

blockquote   An HTML tag that indents text, accessible by using the Indent command.

border (CSS)   CSS rules can be used to define borders and border styles, such as width and color around elements. These can be set with the CSS panel.

border (table)   Table borders are set in the HTML table tags. These can be set with the Properties panel when a table is selected.

button   Form element that performs form submission or other actions when clicked.

Cascading Style Sheets (CSS)   A set of formatting rules that can be applied to various HTML tags to control the appearance.

change link sitewide   Under the Site menu, you can select this option to change a link from one location to another for all instances in any pages of your site.

check box   Form element that indicates an option is selected when clicked.

check in/out   Using these options in the Files panel when you work on files allows you to notify others working on the same files when you are currently modifying them.

check links sitewide   This command allows you to verify that the links in your page and site are valid.

check spelling Located under the Text menu, this command checks the spelling of text content in your document.

Code view You can view and edit the source code of your documents if you open them in Code view.

color box, color picker Located on the Properties panel for many HTML elements; click to select a color for an individual element.

convert layers to tables This command, under the Modify menu, converts layer HTML code into table code. Useful if you need to support non-CSS-capable browsers.

create Web photo album Under the Commands menu, this option allows you to create an HTML-based photo album out of a directory of images without typing any code.

CSS styles panel Use this panel to control the appearance of the CSS styles you use in your site.

data source A collection of information, generally a database, but also other content sources, such as HTML forms or server objects. Use the Bindings panel to create a connection to a data source.

database A collection of information, stored in individual records in tables. Databases and other dynamic data sources form the basis of Dreamweaver's application-building code.

Databases panel This panel allows you easy access to the tools you need to connect to and view your databases. Use this panel to set up database connections, and view table structures and data in tables.

Design Notes Text files containing information about a document or file in your site. They are never displayed on a Web site, but are for your internal use to keep track of any information about a file you might find useful.

Design view You can visually edit the content of your Web page if you open it in Design view.

document-relative paths Links in a page that are created based on the location of the current document. The link contains only information that describes its location based on the location of the certain page. If the page is moved or the linked document is moved, the link is no longer correct.

editable regions   When you create a template, you can designate regions of the page that can be edited.

event   Any action detectable by JavaScript that occurs on or to a Web page. This includes actions such as onLoad and onMouseOver. When these actions are detected, they can be used to trigger behaviors.

expanded tables mode   A way to view tables in Design view to give you extra room to select individual cells and rows. Even though the table appears expanded in this mode, the code remains unchanged.

extensions   Third-party add-ons. You can use the Extension Manager, located under the Help menu, to install downloaded extensions.

external editors   Dreamweaver allows you to define file editors for specific file types. For example, you may prefer editing Perl files in Homesite. You can create associations between file types and editors in the Preferences dialog box.

external link   Any link to a file that is served from a different Web server or resides in a different domain.

Files panel   This panel lists all the files associated with a currently selected site.

fixed width   A column setting that defines a strict width. Unlike autostretch, the column remains a defined width no matter how wide the browser window is.

flash buttons   Dreamweaver has a built-in set of customizable form buttons pre-created in Macromedia Flash format.

flash text   You can add customizable strings of text created in Macromedia Flash format.

forms   HTML constructs that work with behind-the-scene scripts to gather data when filled out by visitors to your site.

frames   Browser windows within browser windows. Instead of showing visitors a single Web page at a time, using frames you can serve two or more pages at once to browsers on your site.

FTP   Short for File Transfer Protocol, it's a way of transferring data over the Internet from one computer to another. It is the primary way Dreamweaver communicates and synchronizes your files on your local machine with files on your remote Web server.

grids Lines that appear on your document in Design view. They do not actually exist in the finished page, but are visible to allow you to use them to line things up. You can modify their frequency on the page.

guides Like grids, these lines appear on your document in Design view. They do not actually exist in the finished page, but are visible to allow you to use them to line things up. Unlike grids, they are placed individually on the page.

History panel Use this panel to see and reverse the actions you have taken in Dreamweaver. You can also save groups of actions and execute them on different files.

hotspots Areas of an image that are clickable as links. Known also as image maps, they are defined in an image map code that exists in the page.

Java applets Small pre-compiled programs written in Java that can be placed in your Web page.

JavaScript Use this programming language to create responses to events and DHTML effects.

layers HTML tags that can be placed precisely on the page using CSS and can serve as containers for additional HTML code.

layout mode Using this mode in Design view allows you to precisely lay out layers on your page visually.

library items A location where you can store reusable assets for use in your Web site.

link Bits of HTML code used to create areas of text or images that, when clicked, change the page in the browser or open a new browser window with the requested page in it.

logs Access and error logs are created by Web servers. Use these to see what pages visitors go to on your site, what types of browsers they use, where they come from, and what broken links they encounter.

Property panel or inspector This panel opens under the Code or Design view workspace. It contains properties specific to the HTML element that is currently selected in the code or design and allows you to change these properties.

radio button A type of selectable object in a form page. Generally designed to occur in groups, so only one of the group of options can be selected.

rollovers Images in your page that change to different images when the mouse cursor rolls over them. Dreamweaver can automatically insert the code to accomplish this using behaviors.

root-relative paths This describes links in a page which are created based on the location of the Web site root. The link contains only information that describes its location based on the location of the site root.

rulers In Design view, you can add rulers to the top and side of your document window to help you with layout. The rulers are strictly visual elements and do not change your code.

scripts Any bits of code in your site or in separate files called by Web pages in your site. Typically scripts are written in languages such as JavaScript, VB, Perl, or PHP.

Site panel This panel displays your sites. This is a collection of HTML pages, images, code pages, plug-in files, style sheets, database connection files, and any other contents of your Web site, grouped together under a uniform site name. Use the Site menu to create and edit sites.

snippets Bits of reusable HTML code stored by Dreamweaver and easily added to your page with the snippets panel.

tables Basic HTML structures frequently used for laying out the content in Web pages.

templates Files created that are used as the basis for a set of pages. You can define areas on a template that cannot be edited and areas that can be edited.

testing server A temporary location on a Web server used as a place to test your site before you launch your site. Useful when more than one person is collaborating on a site and also when you need to keep a consistent design and want to avoid inadvertently changing final code.

text field An input element in a form that allows the user of the form to enter text.

timelines Panels that control the placement of objects on a page or behavior code in a page over time.

title   The title of a page appears on the top bar of the browser when that page is opened.

tracing image   An image that appears in Design view as a background image. It does not actually exist in the code of the page, but can be used for laying out layers and graphics to match a design created in Photoshop or other graphic editing software.

validating   JavaScript or other code that checks the data entered into a form by a user for accuracy or type consistency. Validating can also refer to using the Validate markup button to check the correctness of the HTML code in your page.

z-index   This CSS attribute of layers determines their stacking order when one is on top of the other.

zoom tool   Use this to allow you to view pages in Design view zoomed in or out.

Resource Guide

Macromedia sites

Dreamweaver.com:
www.dreamweaver.com
Exchange:
www.macromedia.com/cfusion/exchange/index
.cfm?view=sn120
Forum:
www.macromedia.com/cfusion/webforums/forum/
index.cfm?forumid=12

Help and tutorials
About.com Dreamweaver Help:
http://webdesign.about.com/cs/dreamweaver/p/
aadreamweaver.htm
AdesDesign.net:
www.adesdesign.net/php/dreamweaver.php
B-man Artworks:
www.b-man.dk/tutorials.asp
CBT Café:
www.cbtcafe.com/dreamweaver
Dreamweaver Club:
www.dreamweaverclub.com
Dreamweaver FAQ:
www.dwfaq.com

Dreamweaver Fever:

www.dreamweaverfever.com

DreamweaverSites.com:

www.dreamweaversites.com/tutorials.html

Entheos:

www.entheosweb.com/dreamweaver

Intranet Journal:

www.intranetjournal.com/articles/200002/dream_index.html

Tutorialized.com:

www.tutorialized.com/tutorials/Dreamweaver/1

Communities and forums

Dreamweaver Café:

www.dreamweavercafe.com

Forum Weaver:

www.forumweaver.com

Tek-Tips Forum:

www.tek-tips.com/threadminder.cfm?pid=248

Web language standards

HTML 3.2 Specification:

www.w3.org/pub/WWW/TR/REC-html32.html

HTML 4.0 Specification:

www.w3.org/TR/REC-html40

Cascading Style Sheets, level 1 (CSS1):

www.w3.org/pub/WWW/TR/PR-CSS1

Cascading Style Sheets, level 2 (CSS2):

www.w3.org/TR/REc-CSS2

Extensible Mark-up Language (XML) 1.0:

www.w3.org/TR/REC-xml

Document Object Model, level 1 (DOM):

www.w3.org/TR/REC-DOM-Level-1

Interviews with Experts

Macromedia Dreamweaver is software intended for use by a variety of Web professionals with significantly different goals. It can be a powerful tool, used not only by beginners but also by sophisticated Web designers and expert Web programmers. I've interviewed two Dreamweaver experts — a programmer and a designer — to get their opinions and tips about it.

Interview I: Web developer

Alanna Spence, freelance Web developer

Web site: www.angrypirate.com

Describe what you do.

User interface design and front end development for struts/tiles-based Web sites.

What is your overall opinion of Dreamweaver?

I think Dreamweaver has done a great job at empowering beginner to intermediate Web designers to be able to develop their own sites. I learned HTML without it and get frustrated at how it has tried to "hide" the complicated stuff from its users.

Tell me about a project where you or your co-workers used Dreamweaver successfully.

Many of my clients just want small, informational Web sites for their companies, and they want to be able to update the site without having to hire a Web developer to do it. I had a particular client who was having terrible problems with Web pages getting overwritten with older versions of files. Everyone in the office was working locally and using Netscape's Page Editing tool to update text. The problem was they would make updates on very old files. They would also change the navigation on only one page and since they weren't using includes, or repeatable bits of code, of any kind for common page elements such as navigation, pretty soon the whole site was a patchwork of navigation links that oftentimes didn't work. The navigation was different from page to page and was about the worst user interface you could imagine.

I set them up with a Dreamweaver template system, and for people who would be doing editing, I set up their machines so that they would not have to bother with getting their ftp connections set up. I also made them a quick user guide with about 10 simple steps to synchronizing their site with the latest server files, and with the check in/check out feature so that they wouldn't stomp on each other's files. For the most part, this solution worked great. Teaching them how to update their template files was a bit of a challenge, but nothing too painful. The solution lasted them a good couple of years, and they were finally able to update their site on a daily basis.

What do you like most about Dreamweaver?

I think it's great that anyone can have a Web site now. Dreamweaver is easy enough to learn that anyone with an ounce of computer savvy can create and run his or her own site. Dreamweaver has really revolutionized the Web in many ways. Now you have artists and creative writers designing great-looking Web sites without having to understand a markup or programming language. Without programs like Dreamweaver, they could probably not afford to hire someone to develop a site for them. The Web is still a young place, and as it matures, graphic user interface (GUI)-based Web development applications are going to be the standard; in many ways they already are. Even Java developing is moving toward integrated development environment (IDE) applications.

What do you dislike, or what features do you wish Dreamweaver had?

Dreamweaver is trying to be too many things to too many people. It's still trying to maintain its appeal to beginner-level Web designers while enticing advanced professionals. Sometimes doing just the simplest things in

Dreamweaver seems to take so much longer. I was helping a client figure out how to add images. She couldn't get Dreamweaver to add the right tags for images until she had gone and set up a site definition. This person was a freelance Web designer, still in school, and had never used Dreamweaver before. She was attempting to do some quick edits and add new images to a few pages on the client's site. Having never used Dreamweaver before, she had no idea that not having a site defined would make it so hard to add images. The image src tags were all screwy.

What do your clients, employers, or employees think of Dreamweaver?

Opinions are always mixed. Most clients are happy that Dreamweaver exists, but the nontechnical ones are intimidated by the learning curve. No matter how simple they try to make it, you still need to understand how basic HTML works, and how servers work. I think there's this attitude that you can just create a simple Web site just like that, and that it should be as simple as writing your first letter in a word processing application. There are so many other concepts to understand.

In the past, I've encountered people, usually programmers, who strongly disapprove of Web content created with Dreamweaver. Have you experienced this? How did you manage?

I've personally had to clean up Dreamweaver code for use on sites that only post squeaky-clean, super-slim, and streamlined code. Larger sites with heavy traffic are really tight about page size, and have to be. Dreamweaver doesn't produce the most streamlined code, and I find when it comes to delivering slim code, sometimes I'm just better off writing it from scratch.

What advice would you give to the new Dreamweaver user?

Take a few hours and learn about the technology. Get a basic understanding of Web servers, FTP, and HTTP. Get a basic understanding of how HTML works. Learn about image formats for the Web. You don't have to be a pro, but if you just spend some time reading about it, the pieces will start to make sense as you learn Dreamweaver. Once you start using Dreamweaver, don't be afraid of Code view. Just get used to it. Look at it and try to figure out how it's working. The more you know how the code works, the easier it's going to be to fix problems.

What tips can you give us?

You can save site definitions and give copies to co-workers or clients so they don't have to set one up. This is a lifesaver if you are working on a big project with a lot of people.

You:

1. Open the Site Definitions window by selecting Site ⇨ Manage Sites ⇨ Edit Site.

2. Highlight the site definition you want to export by clicking its name.

3. Click the Export button. You'll be asked if you want to retain the username and password, or just the server settings.

4. Save the file to somewhere convenient, like your desktop.

5. Send the file to your co-workers or clients.

Your friend or co-worker:

1. Goes to the Site Definitions window by selecting Site ⇨ Edit Site.

2. Clicks the Import button.

3. Finds the site definition file he or she was just sent and clicks the Open button.

Ta-da!

Have you ever gotten work specifically because of your Dreamweaver skill?

Yes. Some clients were working in Dreamweaver before hiring me and wanted to continue to work in it. They didn't want to waste time training anyone who didn't have Dreamweaver experience. In some situations I've worked with Web designers who handed off their designs in Dreamweaver files, and it was my job to clean them up and add proprietary code for their servers.

Interview II: Web designer

Zaldy Dingle, designer
Web site: www.zaldy.com

Describe what you do.

I am a Flash animator/designer currently working at Yahoo!. I design and animate online ads for the Yahoo! home page.

What is your overall opinion of Dreamweaver?

I absolutely love Dreamweaver! I love it because it can accommodate several types of users. Sometimes I just want to build a page really quickly and not have to mess with the HTML at all. Other times I want more control over a page, so I dig into the code and modify it to my needs.

How do you or your employees/co-workers use Dreamweaver to help with your/their jobs?

There are a number of online tools that we have built to help us streamline our work flow. We've used Dreamweaver to mock-up interfaces for these tools. We then hand off these mock-ups to our engineers, who use the HTML from the mock-ups to build out the application.

Tell me about a project where you or your co-worker used Dreamweaver successfully.

We have a Web site that outlines the specs for ads that run on the home page of Yahoo!. The site was previously just text with a very limited navigation. I was given the task of turning this text-site into a more usable and presentable Web site:

```
http://frontpage.solutions.yahoo.com/
```

I used Dreamweaver to lay out the pages and handed the pages off to our engineers.

What do you like most about Dreamweaver?

I like the fact that you can switch between a WYSIWYG interface and a more code-driven interface.

What do you dislike, or what features do you wish Dreamweaver had?

I wish Dreamweaver had a better way of working with CSS style sheets. It's currently a bit clunky and a bit of a pain to work with. The user interface they have for style sheets seems like it was added as an afterthought. Dreamweaver MX could have used some updating, and has been in Dreamweaver 8.

What do your clients, employers, or employees think of Dreamweaver?

Most designers I've talked to love Dreamweaver. It just makes creating sites easy. Most engineers I've talked to don't really like Dreamweaver.

They prefer more text-based applications such as Homesite (although I personally believe most of them dislike Dreamweaver because they're assuming things that were true five years ago are still true now).

In the past, I've encountered people, usually programmers, who strongly disapprove of Web content created with Dreamweaver. Have you experienced this? How did you manage?

Yes, I have. I gave them pages that were created in Dreamweaver and had them look over the code. After that their opinions usually change about the efficiency of Dreamweaver's code.

What advice would you give to the new Dreamweaver user?

Buy a really good Dreamweaver book!! Read the reviews from Amazon before you decide on a book. Then start a project and dive in! You can only learn by doing.

What tips can you give us?

Keep things organized! Try to avoid creating folders within folders. It will help ease the headache of maintaining assets.

If you're familiar with HTML, I find that using the Split Code and Design views are the most efficient way of working in Dreamweaver. You can make changes to the HTML code and see immediate changes in the Design view, and vice versa.

Have you ever gotten work specifically because of your Dreamweaver skills?

Not specifically from my Dreamweaver skills, but knowing how to use Dreamweaver was definitely a huge bonus.

A

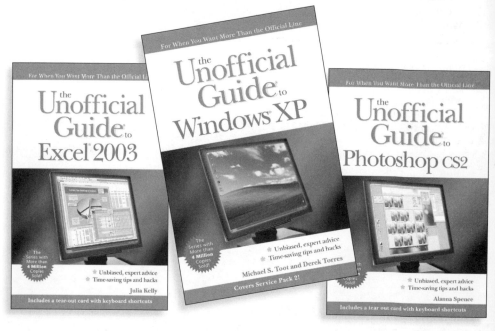